INTRODUCTION TO
ISLAMIC BANKING & FINANCE

INTRODUCTION TO
ISLAMIC BANKING & FINANCE

Mohamed Amine Hamdani

SOCIETY Publishing

www.societypublishing.com

Introduction to Islamic Banking & Finance

Mohamed Amine Hamdani

Society Publishing
4164 Lakeshore Road
Burlington, ON L7L 1A4
Canada
www.societypublishing.com
Email: orders@arclereducation.com

ISBN: 978-1-77956-352-1 (Hardcover)

ABOUT THE AUTHOR

Mohamed Amine Hamdani, PhD in Finance and Econometrics, boasts over 12 years of experience in corporate finance. He has worked with various large companies and in academia, striving to bridge theoretical frameworks with practical applications through his diverse roles. Mohamed Amine's international career has spanned North Africa, France, and Brazil, where he has honed his expertise in corporate finance and accounting. His academic journey includes a Master's degree from Ca' Foscari University of Venice and a DBA from the High Institute of Management and Planning in Algiers, Algeria. He has also participated in various research programs with the Aix-Marseille School of Economics in France, maintaining a strong connection with the latest technical updates in corporate finance.

TABLE OF CONTENTS

LIST OF FIGURES

PREFACE

The first Islamic banking experimentation was conducted in Egypt, but it didn't provide an Islamic image for fear of being viewed as an expression of Islamic passion, which was opposed by the ruling political class. In 1963, Ahmad Elnaggar directed a groundbreaking initiative that resulted in the establishment of a profit-sharing savings bank in the Egyptian town of Mit Ghamr. Up to 1967, this experiment was conducted. The ban on collecting riba, or interest or usury, is a key component of Islamic banking, which is a banking system that complies with Sharia'a, or Islamic law. Because financial risk-taking is viewed as a kind of gambling, which is prohibited in Islam, the Sharia'a forbids it as well. The notion that riba is haram is the main religious rule guiding the Islamic finance sector. This seems to exclude most facets of contemporary finance at first glance. The Qur'an forbids the production of money, although it does permit the use of money for transactions involving physical goods and profitable ventures.

Islamic banks have been in operation for a while in locations including Dubai, Bahrain, Saudi Arabia, and Malaysia. Historically, conventional bankers have seen the industry as a specialized market that caters to isolated investors. Since the GCC provides the liquidity, Southeast Asia is a hub for Islamic finance expertise and innovation. Since the industry is new and expanding quickly, careful observation is necessary to allow for the development of a strong substitute for traditional financing. Given that it tackles the challenges facing the global momentum that Islamic finance has gained, this book can be relatively relevant. The sustainability and viability have received a lot of attention as a result of the credit crunch and crisis. This book throws light on some of the aspects of Islamic banking and finance with special focus on countries where the Islamic laws are active in business. This book can help researchers in the banking sector that follows Islamic methods of financing.

INTRODUCTION

South-east Asia has not quite reached the same level of development as the Middle East in terms of the introduction and application of Islamic banking, the enormous potential of this unexplored market makes it an appealing proposition for investors, including Islamic and conventional bankers. Malaysia became the first country in Southeast Asia to create an Islamic banking industry. To establish Kuala Lumpur as a regional center for Islamic finance in South-east Asia, the government intends the share of Islamic banking assets in Malaysia's banking industry to increase. Indonesian Islamic banking is not nearly as developed as Malaysian Islamic banking. The Indonesian government enacted legislation to address the public's demand for a new banking system. This legislation implicitly permitted the establishment of Shariah-compliant banking operations as a supplement to the traditional banking system, effectively creating a dual banking system. The ban on riba was once again discussed during the decolonization process in the majority of Islamic-majority countries. A financial institution that complies with the commandments of the Qur'an and the Sunna, neither demands nor grants interest, and selects its investments based on moral standards. When Islamic financial institutions began to spring up in Geneva, Luxembourg, Dubai, and Jeddah in the early 1970s, Islamic banking began to take on a global presence. Since then, the global landscape has seen an increase in this phenomenon. Currently, there are Islamic finance organizations in more than 50 nations. Due to religious prohibitions against interest-based banking, money that had previously been kept out of the financial system is now entering it.

Chapter **1**

INTRODUCTION TO ISLAMIC BANKING

Contents

1.1. INTRODUCTION

Islam is the name of the religion that the Prophet Mohammed taught after receiving revelations from God or Allah (Abdelhak, 2016). The Qur'an is considered the most authoritative text for Muslims, the primary source of Sharia law, and evidence of Mohammed's prophecy. All Ulema or religious experts agree on this point; in fact, some claim that the Qur'an is the only source and that all other sources only explain it. Islam's organizational framework is based on pillars. Islam's stability and strength are dependent on its pillars, much like the strength and stability of any network are dependent on the pillars sustaining it. Muslims have an obligation to familiarize themselves with the characteristics of the beliefs of Islam. The 10 years that Mohammed spent in Medina before his demise in 632 A.D. established the framework for the ideal Islamic state (Hawting, 2005). A core group of devoted Muslims was formed, and the rules of the new faith were implemented in the community. The needs of the religion expanded to incorporate a number of institutions that still define Islamic religious practices today, in addition to broad moral precepts.

1.2. FOUNDATION

The Islamic five pillars are the most important of these organizations. These are the basic Islamic obligations that each mentally competent adult Muslim must fulfill. The Qur'an contains descriptions of each of the five pillars, which were already in practice when Mohammed lived (Drennan, 2012). When combined, these customs set Islamic religious practices apart from those of other faiths, even if some of them have their roots in Jewish, Christian, and other Middle Eastern religious traditions. Thus, the five pillars represent the core Islamic rituals and the fundamental tenets of the Islamic faith. Islam's piety is centered around Allah, the Almighty, All-Wisdom, All-Powerful God. The Arabic term Allah means "the God," and it is believed that this God is the one who created the universe and continues to exist until the end. Humans live in peace with the universe and acknowledge and appreciate the wisdom of creation when they follow God's instructions. So, in order to become a member of the Muslim society, one must first make their declaration of religion, or give a witness to their faith (Shahada). In the course of a regular day, a Muslim will often repeat the statement, "I bear witness that there is no God, but Allah and that Mohammed is his prophet." An individual must declare and uphold their belief in Mohammed's prophetic status and the Oneness of God (Tawhid) in order to join the Muslim society. A spoken declaration of faith must convey both real belief and true understanding of its meaning in order to be considered a valid confession of faith, which symbolizes a relationship between the speaker and God. While an individual's actions may be scrutinized by fellow Muslims, merely expressing one's beliefs is adequate proof of being a part of the Muslim community.

1.3. OBLIGATIONS

The obligation to offer the five required daily prayers is the second pillar of Islam (Salat). Every adult Muslim is required to offer five prayers, each of which must be preceded by a ritualistic body purification that occurs at various times during the day. The references found in the Qur'an also speak of standing, bowing, and prostrating when praying, as well as facing the qibla, or designated direction. Muslims were once obligated to face Jerusalem during prayer, but even during the reign of Mohammed, they were told to face the Kaaba, an old sanctuary located in Mecca (Figure 1.1).

Figure 1.1. *Mecca.*

Source: Hassan, T., Carvache-Franco, M., Carvache-Franco, W., & Carvache-Franco, O., (2022). Segmentation of religious tourism by motivations: A study of the pilgrimage to the city of Mecca. Sustainability, 14, 7861. https://doi.org/10.3390/su14137861, Creative Commons License.

The most thorough explanations of the prayer procedures are found in later Islamic traditions, which are derived from the prophet Mohammed's illustration (Ahadith) (Saad & Rabiu, 2019). These rites differ in certain details. To distinguish the Islamic rite from ancient pagan rituals of worshiping the sun when it rises or sets, the dawn, noon, and sunset prayers begin somewhat after sunrise, noon, and sunset. A prayer is composed of a series of movements known as bowings (rak'as). The worshiper recites passages from the Qur'an while standing, bowing, kneeling, and prostrating during each of these units. A muezzin, or crier, from a mosque, the Muslim house of worship, sounds the call to prayer, or adhan, five times a day, wherever there are significant Muslim populations worldwide. An imam, or prayer leader in the Sunni branch of Islam, conducts the Friday midday prayer. Compared to the regular midday prayers on other days of the week, this prayer is unique. Two sermons are given before the prayer as part of the congregational meeting's obligatory routine.

1.4. PRAYER

On other days, Muslims are free to pray wherever they choose, alone or with others. Nonetheless, they have to follow the prescribed schedule for praying, which includes facing Mecca at specific times of the day, saying the prayers in the right order, and purifying symbolically before praying. Almsgiving is the third pillar of Islam (zakat). Zakat is a religious duty that is seen as a manifestation of one's love for Allah (Bakar, 2008). It gives Muslims a way to purify their money and find salvation, and it symbolizes the need to support the less fortunate segments of society. Along with other Islamic customs, the Qur'an firmly promotes almsgiving and reminds Muslims on a daily basis of their moral duty to assist the underprivileged, widows, and orphans. It does, however, make a distinction between zakat, a required tax on Muslims' cash or produce and general, voluntary charity (Sadaqah) (Al-Bawwab, 2023). Fasting is the 4th pillar of Islam (sawm). The early emergence of fasting as a ritual practice is explained by explicit references to it in the Qur'an. During the 9th month of the 12th month Islamic lunar calendar, Ramadan, the Qur'an commands fasting.

Ramadan (Figure 1.2) is a holy month since it is believed to mark the time of the Qur'an's initial revelation. According to custom, the month begins when at least two Muslims see the new moon. Muslims are obligatory to fast from sunrise to sunset and abstain from all food, liquids, and sexual activity for the duration of the month. Women who are menstruating, travelers, and sick individuals are excused from fasting; nevertheless, they must make up for the missed days at a later time. Several traditional views hold that the fast brings both physical and spiritual discipline, reminds the wealthy of the sufferings of the poor, and, with this difficult act of prayer, cultivates a sense of solidarity and mutual care among Muslims from all socioeconomic backgrounds.

Figure 1.2. *Ramadan.*

Source: https://commons.m.wikimedia.org/wiki/File:Ramadan-Article-8.png, Creative Commons License.

The fifth pillar mandates that Muslims who are financially and physically capable do the hajj to Mecca at least once in their lifetime (Henderson, 2011). Arabs engaged in the pilgrimage practice prior to the spread of Islam, and the tradition has persisted since then. Different from other pilgrimages is the hajj. It requires the completion of a precise and multi-day series of ceremonies that must occur during Dhu al-Hijja, the 12th lunar month of the year.

The Kaaba (Figure 1.3), a cubical building, is the main focal point of all pilgrimage rites, which are performed in Mecca and the surrounding areas. Islamic tradition (Hadith) holds that the prophet Ibrahim (Abraham in the Hebrew and Christian Bibles) and his son Ismail erected the Kaaba, also known as the House of God, at God's instruction (Ishmael). Many of the ritual's components are described in detail in the Qur'an, which also depicts many of these ceremonies as recreations of the actions that Abraham and Ismail carried out while constructing the Kaaba.

The holy Black Stone, which is positioned in one corner of the Kaaba, is said to have been handed to Ibrahim by the angel Gabriel, according to a Hadith in Islam. When pilgrims go to Mecca, they undergo ceremonial purification. Both men and women put on smooth white sheets, and many shave their heads. The ban on jewelry, perfumes, and sexual activity further solidifies the equality of all Muslims before God, which is symbolized by this modest and common attire. Following this ceremonial cleaning, Muslims do several prayers and invocations, run seven times between the hills overlooking the Kaaba, and circle the Kaaba seven times.

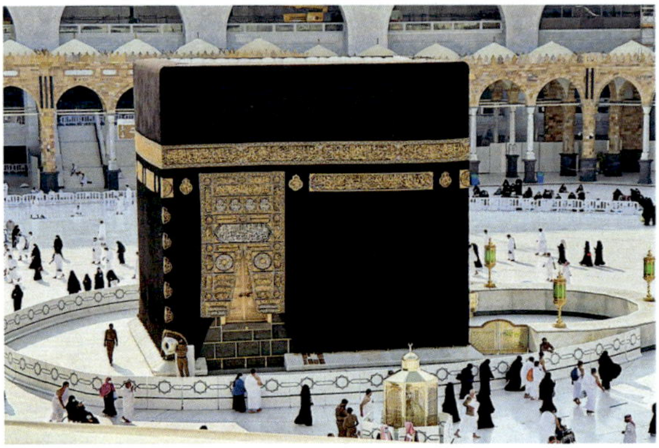

Figure 1.3. *Kaaba.*

Source: https://en.wikipedia.org/wiki/File:The_Ka%27ba,_Great_Mosque_of_Mecca,_Saudi_Arabia_(4).jpg, Creative Commons License.

1.5. PILGRIMAGE

The actual hajj begins on the seventh day and lasts for the following three days following these preliminary ceremonies. Once more, it begins with ritual purification, which is followed by prayer in the mosque of the Kaaba. The pilgrims then get together and spend the night at Mina (Figure 1.4), a hill outside of Mecca (Headley, 1924).

Figure 1.4. *Mina.*

Source: https://en.wikipedia.org/wiki/Mina,_Saudi_Arabia#/media/File:Mina_Overview.JPG, Creative Commons License.

They travel to the adjacent plain of Arafat the following morning, where they stand from midday until dusk and carry out a number of rites and prayers. After that, the pilgrims spend the night in Muzdalifa, which is midway between Arafat and Mina. The pilgrims return to Mina the following morning, throwing seven pebbles at stone pillars that represent Satan along the road. The killing of an animal completes the rite. This is a symbolic reenactment of God telling Ibrahim to sacrifice his son Ismail. After Ibrahim and Ismail complied with God's instructions, they were ready to carry out the sacrifice when God gave Ibrahim permission to kill a ram in place of their son. The majority of the animal flesh that is butchered will be given to underprivileged Muslims. The ceremonial sacrifice concludes the hajj and attendants in the sacrifice feast, 'eid al-adha.' The two main Islamic holidays that Muslims around the world commemorate are 'eid al-adha' and 'eid al-fitr,' which mark the end of Ramadan. The majority of Muslims make the trip to Medina, which is home to the Prophet's tomb, and then return to their homes. The pilgrimage ritual is known as umra if it is carried out at any time of year other than the hajj period. Umra is seen as a good deed, but it does not release the performer from their hajj obligations.

1.6. SHARIAH

The Arabic term "shariah" (Figure 1.5) refers to the correct course of action (Mohd Noor et al., 2019). This route not only leads to Allah, which is the Arabic name for God, but it is also the path that all Muslims believe Allah, the Creator, himself has shown via his Messenger, the Prophet Mohammed. Islam holds that there is only one supreme being, Allah, and that only 'He' has the authority to decree a course for humankind to follow. Muslims therefore hold that Sharia law alone may free people from servitude to powers other than Allah. Muslims are therefore required to work toward the adoption of that path and no other one. As a result, the Sharia'a places a strong emphasis on the idea that Allah is the source of law and that the Islamic community as a whole is only his trustee.

This notion is the reason for the Ummah's ability to make rules rather than having the absolute authority to create laws. The enormous, homogeneous commonwealth of people that make up the Islamic State are governed in all spiritual and temporal affairs by a common ideology, and they share a common destiny. Every member of the Muslim Ummah is required to abide by the Sharia, which gives Allah the exclusive right to sovereignty.

Every Muslim has the right to interpret Allah's law when it is required, provided they are competent and able to offer a solid judgment on Sharia'a issues. Islam is democratic in this regard. However, no Muslim official, legislative body, or religious scholar can make an independent decision in cases where a clear command of Allah or his Prophet already exists. Not even the collective Muslim population of the world has the authority to make even the smallest modification to such a command.

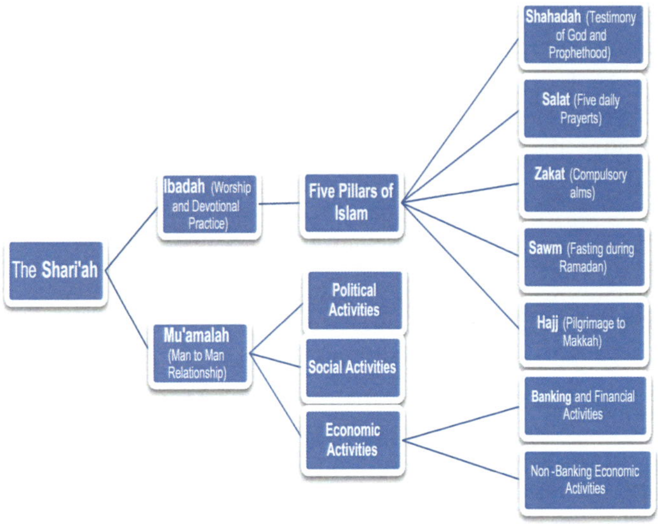

Figure 1.5. *Shariah.*

Source: Shah, S. M., Rashid, A., & Khaleequzzaman, M., (2019). Determinants of Financial Leverage in Islamic Banks. 10.1007/978-3-030-05225-6-7, Creative Commons License.

1.7. INTERPRETATION

The Council of Jurists (Ulema and Fuqaha), which is entrusted with the legislative role of interpreting laws from the Book of Allah and the Sunnah, represents the Sharia'a (Samadi, 2021). Only these persons, well-versed in the tenets of Islamic law, have the authority to enact new laws based on the demands of the moment and situation. However, the essential principle of the Islamic legal system is that laws are not passed in a discordant assembly by men who fervently support legislation for their own benefit versus men who fervently oppose it for similar reasons. Islam's regulations are considered to be in the best interests of the people collectively since they are firmly rooted in the Sharia'a. These are the product of impartial jurists, not of feuding politicians. The Qur'an and the Sunnah serve as the foundation of Sharia law, setting it apart from other legal systems. The gifts provided to the entire Ummah are the Qur'an and the Sunnah. Consequently, the administration of justice rests with the Ummah as a whole. Islamic banking has its roots in the Sharia'a, or Islamic rules, also known as Islamic Jurisprudence. Muslims believe that Islam is the religion that Allah revealed to his final prophet, Muhammad. It is a comprehensive religion that covers every aspect of a Muslim's everyday life both here on Earth and in the hereafter. Islam's teachings cover the fundamentals of Muslims' economic growth and well-being at the levels of the person, the family, the state, society, and the Ummah. The practical parts of a Muslim's daily life, or Sharia'a, are further separated into two categories: Muamalat and Ibadat. While Muamalat is concerned with the practicalities of a Muslim's ordinary everyday existence in the framework of various sorts of person-to-person connections, Ibadat deals with the realities of a Muslim's worship to Allah within the context of a man-to-Allah relationship.

The way a Muslim conducts their economic activity inside the economic system is a crucial aspect of Muamalat. The banking and financial system, which is where people conduct their banking and financial operations, is found inside the economic system. Therefore, a Muslim's banking and financial activities can be traced back through his economic activities to Muamalat, to Sharia'a, to Islam, and ultimately to Allah in the Islamic plan of life and Sharia'a framework. This is the foundation of Islamic finance and banking. The Islamic religious code is known as shariah. Islamic law encompasses all facets of life, not only rituals, because it does not distinguish between religion and everyday life. The actual codification of standard law is the outcome of the so-called science of the origins of jurisprudence and the concurrent evolution of jurisprudence proper (usul al-fiqh). During the process of formalizing Islam, a consensus was reached regarding the legitimacy of four sources: the legislative segments of the Qur'an; the Hadith that recount the Prophet's illustration; the consensus of Muslims (Ijma), which is based on a statement made by Muhammad. Ijtihad, or the application of Sharia law to circumstances not covered by prior cases or understandable by comparison with other legal systems, is another crucial idea. These foundations offer the tools necessary for the creation of normative guidelines and the assessment of society and individual behavior. The fundamental framework for all behavior is a five-tier classification system that includes required, honorable, acceptable, unacceptable, and prohibited Islamic behaviors. Over the course of Islamic history, a large number of legal schools, or Madhabs, have developed. Within Sunni Islam, four coexist today, with one or more of them dominating in certain regions: Hanafi, Shafii, Maliki (North and West Africa), and Hanbali (Saudi Arabia). The term "Jaafari" is frequently used to describe Shiite law (Dodge, 2021). These legal schools are thought to be complementing rather than antagonistic, despite differences in certain customs and practices.

1.8. BANKS

Islamic banks (Figure 1.6) and other Islamic financial organizations are required to have religious supervisory boards in order to guarantee that their financial operations comply with Sharia law. In order to ensure that Islamic principles are followed, the Sharia'a Supervisory Board (SSB; Figure 1.7), also known as the Sharia'a Supervisory Committee, reviews agreements, and transactions (Al-Zumai & Al-Wasmi, 2016).

Figure 1.6. *Islamic banks.*

Source: https://web.archive.org/web/20161024214302/http://www.panoramio.com/photo/88219686, Creative Commons License.

The SSB attests to and verifies that the banking operations adhere to halal standards (permissible). Even though the SSB is only an advisory body, the bank entrusts it with questions about the legitimacy of its operations, giving it an authoritative and respected role. Banking and financial operations are consequently governed by Sharia law on Muamalat since they are an integral part of Islamic Muamalat. Muslims consider the Sharia to be the perfect moral rule or ideal way of living.

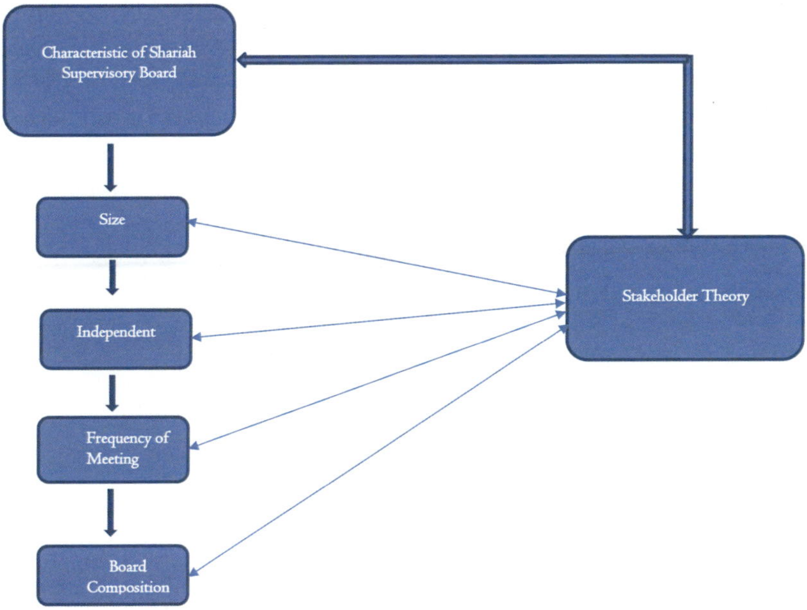

Figure 1.7. *Sharia'a supervisory board.*

Source: Islam, K. M. A., & Bhuiyan, A. B., (2019). The theoretical linkages between the Shariah Supervisory Board (SSB) and stakeholder theory in the Islamic Financial Institutes: An empirical review. International Journal of Accounting and Finance Review, 4(2), 43–49. https://doi.org/10.46281/ijafr.v4i2.436, Creative Commons License.

Compared to a typical legal system, it is far more expansive in both its scope and intent. The goal of the Sharia'a is to govern how people relate to Allah and to one another. For this reason, it is impossible to separate Islamic ethics from Sharia law. The process by which the various Qur'anic injunctions were revealed indicates that revelations occurred when moral, social, or religious necessity emerged, or when some of the Prophet's companions (the Sahaba) sought advice from the Prophet regarding any major issues that had a broad impact on Muslim lives. The primary source of Sharia law is the Qur'an. Although the number of verses containing legal injunctions has been varied by Qur'anic scholars, the approximate count is 500. These verses address a wide range of topics, including marriage, polygamy, maintenance, rights, and obligations of the parties involved, divorce and its various forms, the time following a divorce, foster care, criminal penalties, wills, inheritance, equity, fraternity, liberty, justice for all, fundamental human rights, ideal states, laws of war and peace, judicial administration, and much more.

The Prophet's Sunnah provides more clarification and practical application of the Qur'anic injunctions that are the basis of Sharia'a. The term "sunnah," which refers to the Prophet's model behavior or exemplary conduct in all that he said, did, or authorized, literally means "method, practice, or rule of life." As a result, it emerged as one of the primary sources of Shariah, second only to the Holy Qur'an in terms of authority. Islamic law heavily relies on the consensus of learned men's and jurists' opinions, or Ijma in Sharia'a terminology, in addition to the Qur'an and the Sunnah, because it offers a broad framework for advancement and reconstruction. Analogical deduction, or qiyas, is acknowledged as one of the foundational ideas of the Islamic legal system since it provides a means of meeting the ever-increasing demands of society. Such analogical reasoning is predicated on extremely rigid, rational, and methodical rules. In addition to these four sources, Istihsan, or the juristic preference or justice of a jurist as against Qiyas, is taken into account by the Sharia'a, which contributes to the flexibility and adaptability of the entire Islamic legal system. The Sharia'a system has also included the idea of al-Masalih al Mursalah, or topics that are in the public interest but are not expressly specified in it. Through Gabriel's intervention, the Qur'an was gradually revealed to humanity over a period of roughly 23 years. The Qur'an consists of 6,235 ayat (verses) and 114 suras (chapters) of varying length (Uthman, 2022). There are four ayat in the shortest sura and 286 ayat in the longest. Every chapter has its own title. The Qur'an begins with the longest suras, and as the scripture progresses, the suras get shorter. The Prophet rearranged and ultimately decided the order of the suras, as well as the order of the ayat inside each sura, in the year of his death.

1.9. QURAN

The Qur'an is made up of obvious revelation, which is the exact words of God communicated to the Prophet Mohammed by the angel Gabriel. Since the Prophet heard this revelation while awake, neither internal inspiration nor dreams played a role in the creation of the Qur'an. The Prophet was inspired by God, and he expressed the ideas in his own words. The Prophet's sayings, or Hadith, are all classified as internal revelation and are not found in the Qur'an. The consensus among the Ulema is that the entire Qur'an is mutawatir, meaning that the witness of consensus establishes the text's authenticity. Throughout the ages, it has persisted in written records and in memory.

The Qur'an (Figure 1.8) could not have been collected into a bound volume since, during the Prophet's lifetime, it was not only stored in his recollections but also in inscriptions on readily available materials such flat stones, wood, and bones. The Qur'an was first compiled by Abu Bakr, the first Caliph, shortly after the Yamamah conflict, which claimed the lives of at least 70 Qur'anic memorizers. The Prophet's scribe Zayd ibn Thabit was hired to compile the book, which he completed between AD 623 and 626 (Altine, 2023). However, a few iterations quickly became popular. Thus, in order to ensure that the text was accurate, the third Caliph, 'Uthman, once more enlisted Zayd's assistance before compiling it into a single volume. After that, every last variation was eliminated. Because of this, there is currently only one authentic text in use. Less than 10% of the more than 6,200 ayat are about law and jurisprudence; the majority of the other themes and topics are about morality and belief, the five pillars of the faith, and other topics (Gunn & Sabil, 2023). Overall, the Qur'anic call for religion supersedes the idea of economic and social justice, including its legal aspects.

Figure 1.8. *Qur'an.*

Source: http://akkasemosalman.ir/wp-content/gallery/immortal/quran-nour01.jpg, Creative Commons License.

Before the advent of Islam, the Arabs in pre-Islamic Arabia referred to the long-standing customs of their community that they had inherited from their ancestors as the Sunnah. The term "Sunnah" is used in the Qur'an to refer to a custom or code of behavior. The Qur'an, which is considered to be the word of Allah to all Muslims, is the main source of Islamic faith, as was previously mentioned. It was revealed to the Prophet exactly as it is read today; he had nothing to do with its contents. While the Qur'an provides Muslims with a fundamental code of conduct, it is silent on many other issues that require guidance for day-to-day living. Following the Prophet's use or customs in such situations was the obvious course of action (such as Sunnah). In certain cases, it was acceptable to follow old practices; nevertheless, when it came to topics specific to Islam, the early followers of the Prophet's companions and contemporaries followed their own customs. The earliest believers would presumably conduct themselves in religious affairs in accordance with the Prophet's own customs. Over time, declarations of the Sunnah of the first Muslims on a range of topics emerged. The payment and receipt of interest is considered a major transgression according to Islamic jurisprudential principles, for which the participant will face consequences in the life after death. Some Sharia'a advisory bodies have established a maximum amount of a company's revenue that can be obtained through interest and/or other banned activities, as nearly all businesses deal with interest or other prohibited activities. Investing in a company that goes over these boundaries is undesirable since these boundaries are changing and getting more complex and nuanced as a result. Businesses that could have been disqualified from participation in simpler models a few years ago might now be permitted under more recent Sharia'a models.

The company's primary operations do not contravene Sharia law. This implies that investing in the stock of businesses that offer interest-bearing financial services, such as traditional banks and insurance providers, is prohibited. Businesses engaged in other activities not permitted by Sharia law, such as the production, distribution, or provision of alcohol, pork, or other haram (forbidden) meat, as well as those engaged in gaming, nightclub activities, pornography, and other related activities, are prohibited (Bonne & Verbeke, 2008). If a corporation's primary activity is halal (allowed), like building houses, cars, or computers, but the company invests its excess cash in an interest-bearing account or takes out a loan that will pay interest, Muslim shareholders must voice their opposition to such transactions. The best way to achieve this would be to speak out against these kinds of efforts at the company's annual general meeting. If interest-bearing account income is included in the company's income, the investor cannot keep the percentage of such revenue that is included in the dividend paid to the shareholder; instead, it must be donated to charity. For instance, if interest-bearing deposits account for 5% of a company's total revenue, then 5% of the dividend must be donated to charitable organizations. Put another way, in cases where profits are distributed as dividends, a set percentage of the payout which is equal to the percentage of interest the business earns must be donated to charitable organizations. Scholars of Islam have dubbed this procedure "purification." Regarding the necessity of purification in cases where profits are obtained through capital gains, that is, when shares are bought at one price and sold at a greater price, Sharia'a scholars have differing opinions. According to some academics, the purification procedure is still required even in capital gains cases because interest payments have improved the company's performance, and the share price may indicate some degree of leverage due to interest. Some academics argue that even in cases where the activity generates a monetary gain, purification is not necessary if the share is sold.

1.10. NEGOTIATIONS

A firm's shares are only freely investable and negotiable if the company possesses nonliquid assets. These shares cannot be bought if all of a company's assets are liquid, or in the form of money that can only be bought or sold at par value. Since money cannot be exchanged other than at par under Islam, the shares in this instance merely signify money. Various modern academics have different opinions on this matter. According to some academics, the proportion of nonliquid assets should be at least 51%. On the basis of the legal precept that "the majority deserves to be treated as the totality of a thing," they contend that if such assets make up less than 50% of the total, the bulk of the assets are in liquid form and should be recognized as such. According to the opinion of other academics, a company's shares can be regarded as negotiable even if they comprise 33% of its nonliquid assets. Sharia-compliant advisors perform both consulting and supervising roles. Generally speaking, these counselors apply Sharia'a with two distinct goals in mind. First, the Sharia'a advisers check that the institutions taking part in the Islamic financial markets are operating in accordance with Sharia'a by reviewing their activities. This is comparable to a supervisory position in most ways. In the contemporary and ever-evolving realm of Islamic finance, Sharia'a consultants strive to address any queries regarding a certain transaction or product's adherence to Sharia law. When considered appropriate, they provide helpful, original, and/or different suggestions. This is essentially a consulting position. Establishing operating rules and procedures is necessary for institutions taking part in the Islamic financial markets to make sure that their operations, investments, and activities are carried out in accordance with Sharia'a criteria. It is expected of Sharia'a advisers to actively participate in and debate the Sharia'a matters that are presented to them (Karmali, 2009).

The advisors examine the goods and services to make sure they adhere to Sharia law. Sharia'a advisers in the Islamic investing sector are in charge of making sure the funds under their supervision are managed and operated in line with Sharia'a principles. This also entails having to advice and counsel investment management firms and fund managers on any issue regarding the fund's investments, trust agreement, prospectus, and other operational and administrative issues that are related to the principles of Sharia. They examine and approve relevant documents. Islamic financial market goods and services must go through a predetermined screening and endorsement procedure by Sharia advisors in order to be compliant with Sharia law. In addition to ensuring conformity with applicable Sharia'a principles and pertinent resolutions, the adviser's responsibility encompasses providing advice on all areas of Islamic securities, including documentation, structure, and investing, as well as other administrative and operational problems.

One fundamental rule that needs to be followed while examining and approving the documentation is that only the Sharia consultant is qualified to make sure that it complies with and makes sense in light of the planned Sharia transaction. They keep an eye on the institutional investments made in the Islamic financial markets. The Sharia'a adviser keeps an eye on and guarantees that the investments made by these organizations adhere to Sharia law. Here, the Sharia'a adviser is responsible for making sure the fund managers only make investments in securities that have been deemed Sharia'a compliant and approved by the Sharia board.

They discuss Sharia'a concerns that are relevant to the institutions' daily operations and offer advice based on your findings. Practitioners will encounter a variety of Sharia'a complications in the course of these institutions' daily activities, particularly in relation to the practice and execution of financial transactions. Typically, neither textbooks nor the theoretical foundations of a given transaction address these problems. Sharia'a advisors are therefore required to comprehend and address these problems. They must, for the most part, be actively involved in the practice and implementation side of things as this provides them with a deeper and more thorough awareness of the problems they are working with.

They carry out product development and research. Sharia'a advisers must create or approve novel new products that are competitive and acceptable to all stakeholders as the financial system develops in order for Islamic financial institutions to compete not only with mainstream products that are already on the market but also with those that are soon to be introduced. The most intricate financial domains that necessitate innovation that complies with Sharia law include derivatives, risk management, and hybrid financing arrangements. It is expected that Sharia'a advisers create financial solutions that are acceptable to Islam when they have a working knowledge of the fundamentals of both the Muamalat and the Fiqh (Islamic law), particularly with regard to capital and asset management concepts.

1.11. CONTRACTS

They offer Muamalat instruction and training based on Sharia'a contracts (Kamla & Rammal, 2013). To equip the vast and expanding group of Islamic finance practitioners with the skills required to oversee Islamic financing operations, they must receive a thorough education. It is important to acknowledge the dynamic nature of the Islamic financial sector as it develops and to avoid becoming complacent. In order to train as many practitioners as possible and produce successors who are well-trained before taking over from their superiors, the distribution process must be ongoing. Given that the Sharia'a advisors are knowledgeable in Muamalat, it is appropriate that they set the example for educating both these practitioners and the broader public. This is essential to applying the designated contracts in Muamalat and obtaining a true and correct grasp of Sharia'a. They offer guidance upon request and support connected parties with Sharia-compliant issues. The advisers may be consulted by associated parties of the Islamic financial market institutions, including their auditors, consultants, and legal counsel, for assistance on Sharia'a matters. The latter are supposed to offer the support required to guarantee complete adherence to Sharia law. In addition to this, they have to clarify the Sharia'a concerns, and the suggestions made for a certain course of action. The pertinent Sharia'a jurisprudential literature from reputable sources must substantiate these opinions. The Sharia'a and Fatwa supervisory board of DIB makes sure that all transactions strictly adhere to the Sharia'a principles and supervises the application of various areas of the law. The board also has the authority to reverse any practices that are determined to be in violation. Regardless of whether a decision was made by unanimous vote or by majority consensus, the board of directors is required to follow the Fatawa. Sharia board meetings take place on a regular basis or as needed.

The board oversees the Sharia'a compliance of all bank transactions through a representative, typically the general secretary, and serves as an authoritative source on Islamic principles, especially Fatawa. The board also weighs in on suggested changes to banking transactions. It examines exceptional circumstances that are not addressed by Fatawa in the bank's transactional protocols or that are brought to the attention of various divisions, branches, and occasionally even consumers. This is to guarantee Sharia compliance prior to the bank creating any new goods or putting any new policies into place. It examines Sharia compliance by analyzing contracts and agreements pertaining to the bank's transactions that are provided by the chairman of the board of directors, any branch or department within the bank, or the board itself. It verifies all banking transactions adhere to Sharia law and remedying any infractions. It examines administrative choices, problems, and things that need board approval.

It ensures compiling an annual report on the bank's conformance with Sharia law as it relates to its financial sheet. The board of directors receives an annual report from the Fatwa and Sharia'a board that includes a summary of all matters addressed to the board and the board's assessment of the bank's transactional practices.

Advisors who follow Sharia law must not be connected to any illicit banking operations (Rahman, 2013). They must not have missed payments on any loans from financial institutions, unpaid taxes, or unpaid bills in their individual or partnership capacities, or in any privately held, publicly traded, or unlisted business. Additionally, they need to be able to meet their financial responsibilities. Advisors who follow Sharia law must be truthful, free of criminal convictions, and not have engaged in any financial crimes such as fraud or forgery. They must not have had any unfavorable decisions or settlements in criminal or civil cases, especially when it comes to financial or business investments, misbehavior, fraud, the creation or administration of a corporate body, and other related issues. They cannot be associated with a company, firm, or other organization that has been denied registration or a license to engage in trade or business, nor can they have violated any of the standards and requirements of the regulatory system or the comparable standards of requirements of other regulatory authorities. They cannot have worked for or been associated with a business whose license, registration, or status has been canceled or put into liquidation. Sharia'a advisors must not have been prohibited by any religious organization or body from issuing religious judgments. They must be free from conflicts of interest; for instance, they cannot advise other financial institutions on Sharia law. Any bank, investment finance company, non-banking finance company, venture capital firm, housing finance company, leasing company, or Mudaraba company is considered a financial institution. If the SBP nominates a Sharia'a advisor to its own Sharia'a board, then there is no conflict of interest.

The traditional banking industry often perpetuates this misconception of Islamic banking. There is no room for smoke and mirrors in Islamic finance. In actuality, it concerns banking founded on Islamic ethical values, which differ greatly from traditional banking standards in many respects. As a result, the Islamic prohibition covers both a low rate of interest and excessive interest. Islamic financial systems, therefore, are committed to doing away with interest payments and receipts altogether. Islamic banks and other financial institutions are fundamentally different from their conventional counterparts because of these off-limits. Many contemporary explanations exist for why riba is seen as haram, or prohibited, but they are insignificant in comparison to the underlying religious beliefs. The Holy Qur'an and the Sunnah, which in ancient Arabia denoted ancestor precedent or tribal custom, are the two main sources of Islam.

Today, the term "Sunnah" refers to the teachings and customs of the Prophet Mohammed as they have been passed down by the guardians of true tradition. These two sources treat interest as an act of injustice and exploitation, which makes it incompatible with Islamic ideas of justice and property rights.

The fundamental query raised by this rejection of interest is what would take the place of the interest rate mechanism in an Islamic framework. Modern financial systems are based on financial intermediation. As a means of allocating resources and providing financial intermediation, profit and loss sharing (PLS) takes the place of interest (Kayed, 2012). PLS is the fundamental principle upon which Islamic financial institutions operate. Instead of charging interest, an Islamic bank takes a cut of the yield from the utilization of the money. A fixed ratio determines how much of the bank's profits are distributed to the depositors. As a result, there is a partnership between the Islamic bank and its depositors as well as between the bank and its investment clients. The bank manages the depositors' resources in a way that makes them productive. A traditional bank, on the other hand, primarily lends money while collecting interest on one side of the balance sheet and borrows money on the other. Understanding the foundations of Islamic law and the range of the instruments used are what make Islamic banking hard. The idea behind this is that the lender has to take a cut of any gains or losses the business that received the loan makes. Instead of becoming creditors, Islam urges Muslims to invest their money and form partnerships in order to split company earnings and risks. Islamic finance is predicated on the idea that capital providers and users, whether they be businesses, service providers, or small-scale traders, need to bear equal risk in commercial endeavors. In the language of banking, the risks and gains associated with funding business endeavors should be shared by the depositor, the bank, and the borrower. This contrasts with the interest-based commercial banking system, where the borrower bears entire responsibility for repaying the loan plus the agreed-upon interest whether or not his business endeavor succeeds.

1.12. RISK

The fundamental idea is that the financier is only entitled to profits in any Islamic finance agreement where risk is assumed. There has to be risk if a return is anticipated. In the event that risk, and reward are unrelated, then this financial arrangement is prohibited by Islamic law. This absence of risk associated with permitting riba is what makes interest so offensive to Muslims (Omar Farooq, 2012). The ensuing premise is that Islam promotes specific investment kinds so that the community may ultimately profit in order to guarantee that investments are made into profitable businesses. Nevertheless, Islam will not permit a loophole to remain for individuals who prefer to store money or deposit money in a bank in exchange for getting interest (riba) (Figure 1.9) on these monies without taking any risks. Therefore, investing involves risk, and not having money invested might result in loss. This is how Islam views money. Islam leaves no other option open to investors, thereby encouraging the idea of greater risks and better profits. All of this is intended to boost investments, which will stimulate the economy and motivate business owners to put in their best efforts to succeed. As previously said, one of the key characteristics of Islamic banking is that it encourages risk sharing between the fund providers, or investors, and the fund consumers. Conventional banking, on the other hand, guarantees the investor a certain interest rate. In traditional banking, the business owner assumes full risk. The owner of funds is still paid a predetermined return regardless of whether the project is profitable or unsuccessful. This form of unfair risk-sharing is prohibited in Islam. In genuine Islamic finance, the project's outcomes are fairly divided between the investor and the business owner. When it comes to profit, both split it in predetermined amounts. If there is a loss, the capital provider bears all financial loss, and the entrepreneur is penalized, at least under the Mudaraba style of Islamic finance, by not getting paid for his efforts.

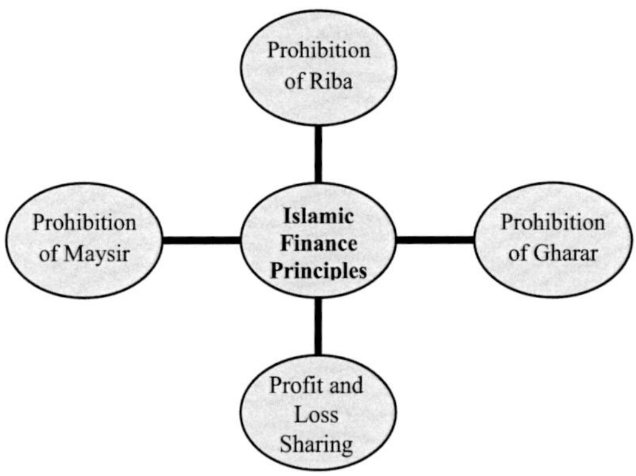

Figure 1.9. *Riba.*

Source: Komorowski, R., & Kubiszewska, K., (2016). Islamic Takaful: Has it successfully substituted conventional insurance?/Islamic Takaful: czy skutecznie zastąpił ubezpieczenia komercyjne? Prace Naukowe Uniwersytetu Ekonomicznego we Wrocławiu. 10.15611/pn.2016.415.09, Creative Commons License.

In traditional banking (Figure 1.10), a bank is primarily concerned with the timely repayment of its loans and interest. Therefore, the borrower's creditworthiness is the primary factor taken into account while making a loan.

The bank won't get paid under PLS banking until the project is profitable and successful. It follows that an Islamic bank will be more interested in the project's viability as well as the entrepreneur's business sense and managerial skills. Making money with money is not permitted in Islam. In Islam, money serves only as a means of exchange, a means of determining the worth of an item. Since it is worthless on its own, it shouldn't be permitted to produce income through fixed interest payments by being deposited in a bank or lent to another person. In a profitable endeavor, the risk and human labor, that is, initiative, become more significant than the capital invested. Money is viewed by Muslim jurists as prospective capital rather than actual capital, meaning that it only qualifies as capital when invested in businesses. As a result, funds given to a company in the form of a loan are considered debt rather than capital. It is therefore not eligible for a refund. Muslims are forbidden from hoarding money and are instead urged to spend it or invest it in profitable ventures. It is considered improper in Islam to store money.

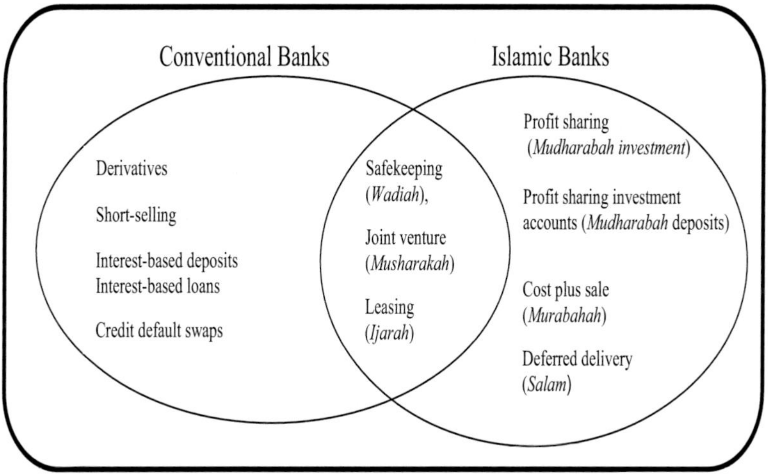

Figure 1.10. *Traditional banking.*

Source: Dridi & Hasan, (2010). The effects of the Global Crisis on Islamic and conventional banks: A comparative study. IMF Working Papers, 10(201), 1. https://doi.org/10.5089/9781455205318.001, Creative Commons License.

Money is symbolic of purchasing power in Islam, where it is believed to be the only appropriate use of money. Without first being utilized to create products and services, this purchasing power (money) cannot be used to create even more purchasing power (money). Furthermore, forbidden is gharar, or uncertainty, risk, or speculation; hence, every transaction that is made must be devoid of these components. The counter-values that are supposed to be exchanged as a result of the transactions between the contracting parties should be perfectly known to them. Unlike fixed debt in Western finance, deferral of payment is a permitted form of debt under Islamic law. Parties are also unable to predict a profit guarantee in advance. The need to shield the vulnerable from exploitation is the justification for the ban on gharar. Because forward exchange prices are based on interest rate differentials, options, and futures which are seen as extremely risky, are therefore prohibited, as are forward foreign exchange transactions.

The focus of conventional banking is secular. In the Islamic system, on the other hand, all economic actors are required to operate within the Islamic ethical framework. Islamic banks are not any different. They are therefore unable to provide funding for any business that goes against the moral principles of Islam. Islamic banks, for instance, are not permitted to provide funding for any establishments that are recognized to be detrimental to society or that are forbidden by Islam, such as nightclubs, casinos, or vineyards. The Holy Qur'an has numerous verses that support trade and commerce, and Islam holds that there should be no obstacles in the way of sincere and lawful trade and business. Muslims have an obligation to work, provide for their families, and help the less fortunate. Islam oversees industry and commerce in the same way that it influences and controls every other area of life. Muslims have a moral duty to conduct their business in a way that complies with their religious beliefs (Uddin, 2003). They ought to treat people with justice, fairness, and honesty. In Islam, there is no caveat emptor, thus vendors have a unique responsibility. Price-fixing and monopolies are forbidden. The numerous particular transactions including, for instance, and partnerships are then handled using these fundamental concepts. Islam maintains that honoring agreements and disclosing information is a religious duty. Information that is known to one side in a transaction but not to the other is known as asymmetric information. The traditional defense is that certain sellers who have firsthand knowledge of an asset's quality will refuse to accept the terms put out by a buyer who lacks expertise. The market might collapse as a result of this, or at the very least, an asset might have to be sold for less than it would be worth if all buyers and sellers had access to all available information.

In the context of equity financing, investors want insurance in order to offset the losses from supporting underperforming companies with shares of comparatively strong companies. On the other hand, the lender lacks adequate knowledge on the borrower. Insufficient information can lead to issues both before and after the transaction is completed, and this could be a big issue for Islamic profit-sharing financial arrangements. Adverse selection and moral hazard issues typically result from the availability of asymmetric knowledge.

When sellers have pertinent information about a certain feature of product quality that buyers do not (or vice versa), this is referred to as adverse selection. The word describes the issue that asymmetric information causes prior to a transaction. It happens when the people most likely to result in an unfavorable (adverse) outcome are the potential borrowers. Those with bad credit are more likely to be chosen since they actively look for loans. Financial contracts involving profit-sharing that are Islamic may have issues because of this. The result of asymmetric information after the transaction takes place is a moral hazard. Because these actions reduce the likelihood that the borrower will repay the loan, the lender bears the risk that the borrower may participate in activities that are unpleasant to the lender. In a typical debt contract, the borrower enters into a contractual arrangement with the lender to pay a specified sum of money at regular intervals. The lender gets these contractual payments and is not required to know the borrower's precise earnings when the firm experiences large profits. As long as the managers' actions do not prevent the company from meeting its loan payments on schedule, the lender is not concerned if they pursue activities that do not boost the company's profitability. The lender needs to confirm the status of the company's profits only when it is in default due to its inability to make debt payments. However, if interest payments on debt are not made, as required by Islamic financing principles, then the system is prone to moral hazard (Hussain et al., 2016).

1.13. PROFIT-SHARING

Regardless of their capital contributions, the partners are free to choose the size of their profit-sharing ratio, according to the PLS principle. Conversely, losses have to be strictly distributed with Musharaka in proportion to their capital contributions. Collateral cannot be supplied with PLS operations in the event that business risk causes the project to fail. Therefore, the Islamic bank faces financial loss should the initiative fail. As a result, asymmetric risk exists for Islamic banks. The bank may charge late payers a fee in order to enforce prompt payment of the repayment obligations and the institution's portion of the profits, if any. These fines cannot be paid to specific financial institutions; instead, they must be deposited with a charity in accordance with Sharia law. Therefore, the Islamic bank is not specifically protected in the event of a borrower default. Once more, there is an unequal danger. The lending institution should only be concerned with the profitability of the proposed project for which the loan is requested rather than the creditworthiness of the firm to which they are lending, as PLS emphasizes the distribution of both risk and profits between the lender and the borrower when a loan is made. This ought to cause the lender to make more cautious selections and necessitate closer supervision of the borrower. In the traditional banking model, depositor oversight of bank operations has been superseded by deposit insurance and bank regulation. As a result, there is no need to keep an eye on bank activity because, for small depositors, deposits made in one bank are quite comparable to deposits made in another. On the other hand, depositors are required by the interest-free, Islamic system to obtain information about the bank's safety, soundness, risk level, and profitability. Once more, asymmetric risk becomes an issue.

Interest in Islamic parlance refers to easy money. Avoiding riba in any form is one of the primary uncertainties of Muslims when it comes to financial dealings. This is true even though interest-based transactions form the cornerstone of contemporary business and finance. The Prophet predicted a day when riba would spread so widely that Muslims would find it very difficult to escape. Muslims should use extreme caution in this situation when choosing which payment methods to employ for any kind of transaction, personal or professional. Examining the textual evidence is essential to comprehending why the prohibition on interest is so fundamental to Islamic finance. The majority of Islamic scholars have highlighted that one of the main reasons is that interest is forbidden since it is unfair (zulm). Injustice to one of the parties, sometimes the borrower, sometimes the lender, occurs in an interest-based contract. The Qur'an's Sura 2: 279 makes it quite evident that taking more than the principal would be unfair (Hashmi, 2003). Since such would also be unfair, it also acknowledges the lenders or creditor's claim to the principal amount without reduction. However, the Qur'an does not explain why taking an excessive amount in the case of a loan is unfair. It presumably depends on the equality and reciprocity that are fundamental to the Islamic understanding of fairness. The Qur'an and its audience never disagreed on the unacceptable nature of injustice and unfairness.

The Qur'anic assertion that taking anything beyond the fundamental amount of fairness is incomprehensible to non-Muslims. Because a borrower may make or lose money depending on how they use a loan for their business, the riba contract is thought to be unfair to the borrower. In the event of a loss, the business owner has not been compensated for his labor or time. The borrower must also pay interest and capital to the lender in addition to this loss. Even though the company ultimately turned a loss, the financier, or lender, nevertheless receives his interest and his money back. This is the setting in which riba is considered unjust. The Qur'an makes it quite evident that people who are having trouble paying their debts should have their commitments made easier for them rather than harder. It is considered ethically reprehensible to start asking that such people be punished for their late payments, as they may truly deserve assistance. This justification which draws on the Prophet's

Farewell Address leads to the definition of riba, which is the crime committed when a person or organization that is in debt demands an increase in a debt in exchange for making a late payment. Islamic scholars contend that even though the borrower may have had difficulties, the court should prioritize the debtor's circumstances. It is maintained that demands for further damages may be justified if payment is made after the due date without excuse and there was no trouble paying. However, this is a question of judgment for a judge, and one party should not be able to impose his intended penalty on the other. For the same reason, automatic fines incorporated into contracts are unfair. It is maintained that in order for damages to be justified, they must be determined by a judge and founded on the theory of willful violation of contract. Nonpayment may arise from challenging conditions, which may not be the debtor's intention.

1.14. CREDITWORTHINESS

The borrower's creditworthiness (Figure 1.11) is the primary criterion used in an interest-based system to distribute credit (Kayed & Hassan, 2011). The productivity of the project is given more weight in an Islamic finance sharing structure, which encourages funding to flow to more fruitful ventures. In this way, bank lending is more likely to flow to high-return projects even if the borrower's creditworthiness is slightly lower, rather than low-return initiatives for borrowers with superior creditworthiness. As a result, the Islamic sharing system distributes resources more effectively. Because the return to the bank is now contingent on the project's performance, it is also thought to be more efficient. It is said that under the interest-based system, banks don't have to worry as much about project evaluation because they still get paid back on their loans regardless of the project's performance. In traditional banking as well, even in the event that the project fails, a return is guaranteed, or at least partially guaranteed, if security is offered. The idea is that interest-based systems push borrowers to continue repaying loans even when their circumstances are unsuitable for making such repayments, ultimately worsening the situation, and leading to default, even if conventional banks naturally lose money. Thus, it is suggested, interest-based banking systems may emphasize economic cycle recessions. An Islamic name for Fiqh is Murabaha (Islamic jurisprudence). In its original form, it refers to a certain type of sale that has nothing to do with financing. A transaction is referred to as a Murabaha when a vendor and buyer agree to split a profit on the sale of a certain good. The vendor discloses the true cost he paid to acquire the good and then adds a profit. This is the fundamental component of Murabaha. This profit could be based on a percentage or come as a lump sum.

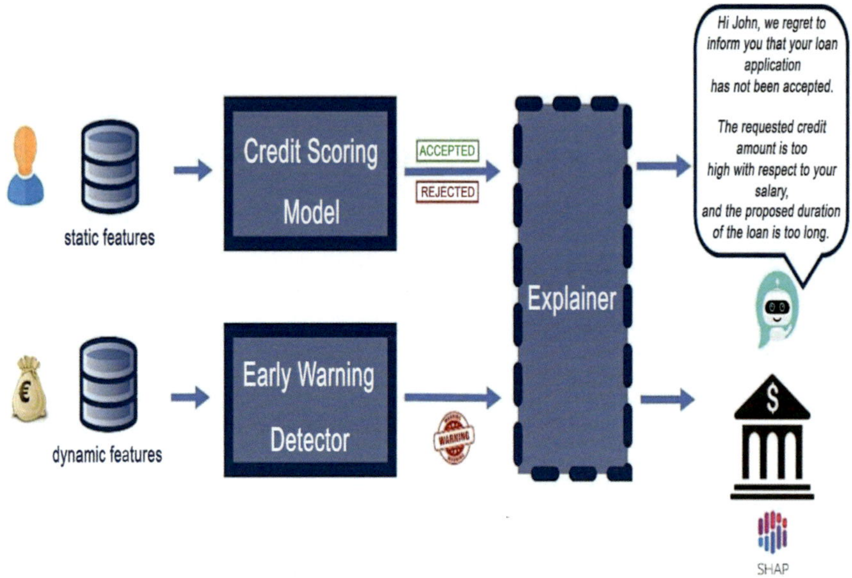

Figure 1.11. *Creditworthiness.*

Source: Cornacchia, G., Anelli, V. W., Narducci, F., Ragone, A., & Sciascio, E. D., (2023). A general architecture for a trustworthy creditworthiness-assessment platform in the financial domain. Annals of Emerging Technologies in Computing (AETiC), 7(2), Article 2. https://doi.org/10.33166/AETiC.2023.02.005, Creative Commons License.

In its original Islamic context, Murabaha refers to a simple sale. The vendor in Murabaha explicitly informs the buyer of the profit margin he plans to charge in addition to the cost, which is the only characteristic that sets it apart from other types of sales. Even though the seller is making a markup profit on his cost, if they offer a good for a lump sum price without disclosing the cost, this is not a Murabaha because the sale is not predicated on the idea of "cost-plus." The sale in this instance is known as a Musawamah. A musawama is a typical type of sale in which the buyer and seller agree on the price of the goods to be exchanged without taking into account the seller's costs or price paid. Thus, in terms of the price formula, it differs from Murabaha. In contrast to Murabaha, the seller in Musawama is not required to disclose his prices. For Musawama, all additional requirements that apply to Murabaha also apply. When a seller is unable to accurately determine the costs of the goods he is offering to sell, musawamah may be the best method of financing. To ensure that a commodity is sold for money and that the transaction is not just an exchange of money for money, it is Islamically permissible for the bank to first purchase the item with the intention of reselling it at a profit. The bank takes on certain risks in the process between the purchase and resale; for instance, a sharp decline in value could result in the client refusing to accept the items at the higher price that was agreed upon. In other words, the bank assumes liability for the good before the client receives it safely. Because of this, the services provided by an Islamic bank are thought to be very distinct from those of a regular bank, which merely lends money to the customer so they can purchase the items.

It takes a step back from traditional Western perspectives to comprehend the Islamic stance on the exchange of goods and money in regular business dealings. When it comes to trade, money and commodities are seen equally in the traditional financial system. You can exchange both. Both may be sold for whatever sum that the parties decide upon. Just as one can sell a commodity valued at one dollar for two dollars, one can sell one dollar for two dollars both now and in the future. The sole requirement is that it has to be agreed upon by both parties. That theory, however, is not supported by Islamic economics. These concepts state that because money and commodities are not the same, they should be handled differently. Islam has always regarded money and commodities differently, taking these distinctions into consideration. Money is merely a medium of exchange; it has no inherent value. As such, exchanging one unit of money for another of the same denomination can only happen at par value.

When exchanging one US dollar bank note for another, the value of the original note must equal US dollar $1,000. Due to the currency bank note's lack of inherent value and unique qualities, its price cannot be changed from US $1,000, not even during a spot transaction (recognized legally). Any excess on either side is therefore unconsidered. Thus, it is prohibited by Sharia law. This holds true for both spot exchange transactions and credit transactions involving money on both sides. In the latter case, any excess claimed will be offset only by the time value of money when money is exchanged for money in a credit transaction. Islamic law prohibits charging for the time value of money since it is considered riba. From an Islamic standpoint, there are differences in the position when dealing commodities (Naughton & Naughton, 2000). Subject to supply and demand, the owner of a commodity is free to sell it for any price he chooses because it has distinct traits and intrinsic value. With the buyer's permission, the seller may sell a good for more than the going rate as long as he doesn't engage in fraud or deception. The seller may charge the buyer the extra if the buyer consents to purchase it at that higher price. If someone is able to sell his product for more money in a cash transaction, he is equally allowed to charge more for it in a credit sale, provided that the customer agrees to pay the price voluntarily and that he does not trick or coerce him into making the purchase.

There can be no excess in transactions involving cash or credit when money is exchanged for money. However, in both cash and credit transactions, the price agreed upon by the parties when a commodity is sold for money may be more than the market price. The timing of payment may be a contributing element in determining a commodity's price, but it cannot serve as the only foundation upon which an excess claimed in return for money may be evaluated. The majority of Muslim jurists as well as all four schools of Sharia law unanimously agree with this position. All agree that it is permissible under Sharia law for a vendor to set two separate prices for cash and credit transactions, with the credit sale price being greater than the cash price. The sole requirement is that one of the two possibilities must be decided upon at the time of the actual sale in order to avoid any doubt regarding the nature of the deal. In order to ensure that the postponed price is paid promptly, the bank may require the client to provide some form of satisfactory security. It might require the customer to sign a bill of exchange or promissory note, but this needs to happen after the sale really happens. Nonetheless, the buyer is responsible for paying the amount he committed to donate in the agreement if he did so for a good cause. However, neither the seller nor the financier may include the money so recovered from the buyer in their income. The Sharia'a board will decide on a charity cause for which the vendor is required to contribute the proceeds (Joseph, 2015).

When signing the pledge, the client will be required to provide the bank with some form of security as part of the Murabaha transaction. This security, which is equal to between 5% and 10% of the deal's value, can take the shape of cash or any other liquid asset. This indicates that the client is serious because it is known as Earnest Money in Islamic banking parlance. In the case that the buyer breaks his promise to buy the items, this will be utilized to reimburse the bank. Please take note that as the sale contract has not yet been finalized, this is not a down payment. According to Sharia law, a sale cannot take place until the vendor verifies that he is in possession of the items being sold. Murabaha is utilized by numerous Gulf Cooperation Council (GCC) banks to finance the purchase of products that are subject to a mortgage, including cars (Alqahtani, 2016). The person applies to the bank for a loan to acquire an automobile. He says he will purchase it later. When the seller registers the vehicle in the bank's name, the bank sends an invoice to the seller. After submitting the necessary paperwork to the bank, the vendor gets paid. After obtaining the necessary guarantee, the bank sells the car to the buyer on a deferred payment basis, registering it in the buyer's name. The car's bank mortgage may be specified in the guaranteed condition. In a similar way, Murabaha is also used when buying buildings and property. It goes without saying that calculating a halal profit using the rate of interest is not a suitable approach. It undoubtedly gives the transaction, at least visually, the appearance of an interest-based financing. Given how strictly interest is prohibited, even this seeming similarity ought to be avoided at all costs. However, it is crucial to remember that the primary prerequisite for the legitimacy of a Murabaha is that it must be a legitimate transaction that complies with all Islamic regulations and has all required outcomes.

1.15. MURABAHA

Simply utilizing the interest rate as a guide to calculate a Murabaha transaction's profit does not make it unlawful, haram, or invalid if all the requirements are met. This is because the agreement itself does not involve interest. The sole uses for the rate of interest have been as a benchmark or an indicator. Due to the fact that there are comparatively fewer Islamic banks than conventional ones, it is crucial for Islamic banks to maintain their competitiveness and, as a result, to tailor their profit margins in line with the market. In their capacity as Mudarib, they might not be able to fulfill their goal of enhancing the reliable investments of their depositors and shareholders if they don't embrace market norms. The argument made against the LIBOR benchmarking is that it might make the transaction resemble interest-based financing because the Murabaha mark-up payments would be treated as similar to a rate of interest (Ahmed et al., 2018). The response to this issue is that the Murabaha agreement may employ any benchmark for the sole purpose of figuring out the amount of periodic mark-up, provided that all other Sharia'a requirements are met. From a Shariah perspective, the contract remains legitimate even if the conventional benchmark is used. This is because the benchmark is only used to calculate the Murabaha mark-up for the underlying asset and does not constitute interest on loan, as the bank is not lending any money. Another point that is occasionally posed is whether there is a Gharar aspect in this situation because it is uncertain how the LIBOR rate will fluctuate in the future, making the Murabaha mark-up associated with it questionable. Because all aspects in a contract must be acknowledged and accepted by the parties entering into it, gharar is prohibited by Sharia law.

The inability of the bank or financier to engage in an actual sale at the time the client requests Murabaha funding is another significant issue that has been discussed by modern Sharia scholars. This is because the necessary commodity is not yet owned by the bank. This problem calls into doubt the concept of gharar (contractual uncertainty). A potential seller cannot sell a product they do not own, and a financier cannot execute a forward sale under Sharia law. As a result, the bank must buy the goods from the provider. He can only sell it to the client once he has either constructive or physical possession of it.

The issue here for the financier is that he may find himself in a scenario where he has spent a lot of money acquiring the commodity, but the client refuses to buy it, if the client is not required to buy it after the banker has bought it from the supplier. The product can be so unique that there might not be another buyer for it on the market, and the buyer might find it extremely difficult to get rid of. The financier might incur an intolerable loss in this scenario. By asking the client to sign a commitment to buy the commodity when it is acquired by the financier, the Murabaha arrangement seeks to address this issue. This is a unilateral pledge from the customer that binds himself rather than the financier, as opposed to the bilateral contract that is typically linked with a forward sale. It can be distinguished from a bilateral forward contract because it is a one-sided promise. The criticism that a unilateral pledge generates a moral responsibility but cannot be enforced by the courts of law in accordance with Sharia law must then be considered in light of this answer. This brings up the question of whether a promise made by one party is enforceable under Sharia law. Many academics have the widespread idea that it isn't. Examining this viewpoint, therefore, in the context of the Sharia'a's principal sources is crucial. It would be evident from a careful examination of the pertinent material in the books of Islamic jurisprudence that the fuqaha, or Muslim jurists, have differing opinions on the matter. While many academics believe that keeping one's word is a noble trait and that breaking one is unacceptable, they also believe that keeping one's word is neither legally binding nor absolutely necessary.

The fact that the Murabaha payment is due at a later time is another problem with Murabaha financing. Naturally, the funder or seller wants assurance that the amount will be paid on schedule. He may request appropriate security from the client in order to accomplish this.

A mortgage (Figure 1.12), a hypothecation, or another type of lien or charge could be used as the security. When a transaction results in a liability or debt, the question of whether the security can be legitimately claimed emerges. Here, the Sharia'a norm states that no one who has not committed an obligation or debt may be asked for security. The Murabaha financing process consists of various transactions completed at various phases (Muneeza et al., 2020). The client does not accrue debt throughout the initial phases of the operation. The relationship between a creditor and a debtor doesn't exist until the financier sells him the product on credit. In a Murabaha transaction, it is proper practice for the financier to request security only after he has really sold the customer the commodity and the price has become due from him because the client now owes money. On the other hand, the client may provide security at a later stage, but only after the Murabaha price has been established. If the financier owns the security in this scenario, it will continue to be at his risk. Consequently, in the event that the commodity is destroyed prior to the client's actual purchase, he will be required to either pay the market value of the mortgaged asset and terminate the Murabaha agreement, or sell the commodity as required by the client and deduct the mortgaged asset's market value from the sale price. In a Murabaha financing, the seller may also request that the buyer or client provide a third-party guarantee.

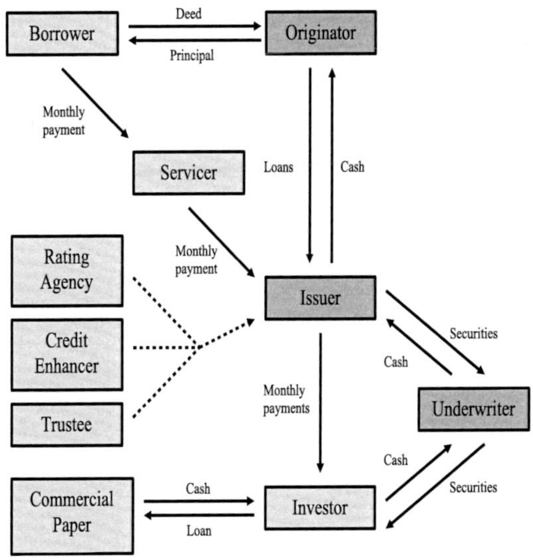

Figure 1.12. *Mortgage.*

Source: Fligstein, N., & Roehrkasse, A. F., (2016). The causes of fraud in the financial crisis of 2007 to 2009: Evidence from the mortgage-backed securities industry. American Sociological Review, 81(4), 617–643. https://doi.org/10.1177/0003122416645594, Creative Commons License.

Whatever the method of payment, Murabaha is a sale transaction with a defined sale price. Therefore, the sale price cannot be raised in the event that a client misses the payment deadline. The inability to raise the price in the event of a client default is a significant issue with Murabaha financing. When it comes to interest-based loans, the loan amount keeps rising in proportion to the length of the default period. However, once a price is set in Murabaha financing, it cannot be raised. Sometimes, dishonest clients take advantage of this Sharia-based restriction by purposefully missing the payment deadline because they know they won't be charged extra for default. Unlike traditional finance, the bulk of contemporary Sharia'a scholars reject the idea of compensation in these situations. They firmly believe that the idea of compensation is not intended to address the issue of default and does not adhere to Sharia law. It is argued in favor of imposing compensation since the Prophet forbade anybody from delaying payment of their obligations without a good reason. It is generally known that some people have purposefully taken advantage of this Sharia law restriction, fully aware that their payback obligation to an Islamic bank will remain in place even if they postpone repayment. The issue with the Murabaha contract, according to modern jurists, is that the deferral portion of the price is not explicitly valued. As a result, even though only one day has passed since the contract was entered, if a person purchases an asset at a deferred price on day one, payable in 10 years, and then files for bankruptcy on day two, they are still responsible for the full amortized purchase price.

Conventional finance would treat a delayed price independently of the time aspect, meaning that the person would only be liable for one day's interest rather than 10 years. The Fiqh Committee of the Organization for Islamic Conference (OIC) resolved that in this case, the parties may negotiate a debt reduction following bankruptcy, but they cannot agree to one before bankruptcy in accordance with an amortization plan (Ahmad et al., 2018). Due to the bilateral monopoly created by this circumstance, creditors have unfair leverage over their debtors as well as over other creditors whose obligations have shorter terms. As a result, longer-term debtors are able to get a larger claim to the bankrupt's estate than they otherwise would have. Paradoxically, in certain situations, the creditor may benefit more from the debtor's bankruptcy if there is a requirement for acceleration following bankruptcy that does not discount the debt to its current value. If a bank client under an interest-based financing arrangement is unable to make a payment by the due date for whatever reason, he may ask the bank to extend the facility for an additional term. But a Murabaha transaction cannot be postponed for more time. A Murabaha isn't a credit. It is the selling of a good whose price is postponed until a certain day. Ownership of the product is transferred to the client upon sale. The vendor is no longer the owner of it. The agreed amount, which is now owned by the buyer, is what the seller is entitled to. Therefore, it is not possible for the same parties to accomplish a second sale of the same product. It is stated that since a roll-over in a Murabaha is an agreement to charge interest only on the debt produced by the sale of the Murabaha, any roll-over in a Murabaha would only be interest.

Chapter 2

ISLAMIC FINANCE

Contents

2.1. INTRODUCTION

Islam lays forth the foundational ideas and regulations for every facet of human existence, including the financial realm (Platteau, 2008). Many concerns are known to researchers who are interested in thinking out or developing a social, economic, and financial system based on the precepts of Islam. Only in the last few decades have attempts been made to translate Islamic financial and economic principles and regulations into contemporary analytical language. Despite a large body of published research, there is still some debate over how to precisely define the many social sciences that are prefixed with the word "Islamic," such as Islamic finance. The inclination to consider discrete elements of a system without considering it as a whole is a primary contributing factor to this misconception. For instance, it's common knowledge that the phrase "Islamic finance" (Figure 2.1) refers to a framework that forbids interest. But this explanation is not only incorrect, but it also contributes to more misunderstanding. Unfortunately, a number of writers have also felt free to voice their thoughts on these topics without having a thorough understanding of Islam, its founding texts, its background, or even just a working command of Arabic, the language of Islam. Such efforts further complicate comprehension of these matters in the context of a politicized environment.

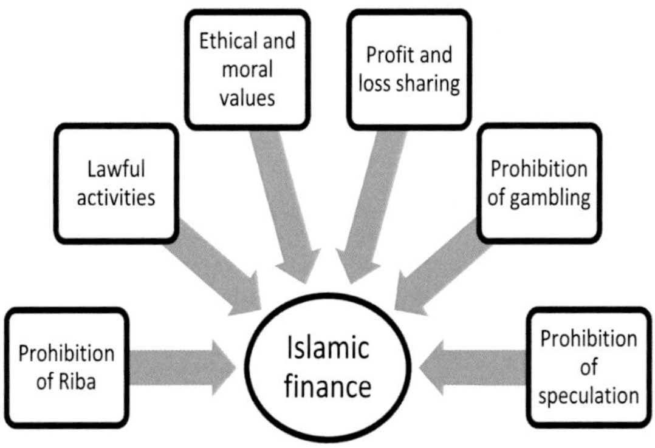

Figure 2.1. *Islamic finance.*

Source: Fayaz, A. L., & Siraj, A., (2017). Islamic finance: More expectations and less disappointment. Investment Management and Financial Innovations, 14(1), 134–141. doi: 10.21511/imfi.14(1).2017.14, Creative Commons License.

2.2. ADVANCEMENTS

Major advancements in every field of Muslim knowledge were made during the earlier era, which also saw Muslim communities experience rapid economic prosperity. History has shown how these contributions, discoveries, and the Islamic sciences' role as intermediaries truly aided in the expansion and advancement of Western economies and cultures. The published works on Islamic economics in a variety of languages attest to the discipline's revival, and this hibernation is evident when compared to the previous three decades of research and advancement in other fields. The goal of these efforts is to provide a thorough and convincing explanation of how Islam envisions structuring an economic system by addressing the fundamental questions of what, how, and for whom should be produced, who should make decisions, and how Islamic institutions might be resurrected to deal with contemporary society's issues. Islam proposes a special relationship between the Creator, humanity, and society based on Divine Law, which has an immediate impact on how different social, political, economic, and financial institution's function. Therefore, it is vital to grasp the nature of this interaction in order to understand how economic concerns are to be conducted in an Islamic system. Islam's unitary perspective, which rejects the idea of separating the sacred from the profane and maintains that all of its components must function as a whole, sets it apart from other philosophical systems. Therefore, just as it is impossible to study a portion of a circle without conceptualizing the circle itself, one cannot study a specific aspect or part of an Islamic system, its economic system, for example in isolation without also comprehending the framework that gives rise to that part or aspect.

2.3. DEBT

The idea of a debt-free and interest-free system was immediately contested by experts who argued that it would be foolish to implement such a system. They contended that if interest were prohibited, there would be an endless demand and a devoid supply of loanable funds. It would be impossible for a zero-interest economy to balance the supply/demand for loanable money. Under such a system, savings would be non-existent, which would prevent investment and growth. They argued that since there could be no liquidity management tools without a set, fixed rate of interest, there could be no monetary policy. A system like that would almost certainly result in a one-way capital flight in any nation that adopted it. Minsky and others showed in the late 1970s and early 1980s that a system like that would always be unstable due to a maturity mismatch between assets and obligations (Wray & Tymoigne, 2009). When the maturity mismatch became an issue, banks would try to manage their liabilities by raising interest rates to draw in more deposits because the nominal values of liabilities were guaranteed, but the nominal values of assets were not. There was always the chance that this process might not hold, leading to a decline in public confidence. Consequently, in order to slow the spread, such a system required debt-workout, restructuring, and lender of last resort operations.

It was evident by the early 1990s that an Islamic financial system was not only theoretically feasible but also had favorable attributes that made it the better option than a conventional debt-based system. The 1990s saw the extraordinary expansion of Islamic finance, proving the system's practical and empirical viability. The difficulties that the world financial system has been experiencing since 1997 have created an opportunity for Islamic finance to show that it is a viable alternative to the current global financial system. There are other shortcomings in the current international system, but the two most significant ones are as follows: first, a debt-based system requires an efficient lender, which the current international financial system lacks and is unlikely to develop anytime soon; and second, in order to establish a debt-based system, the current international financial system must provide structures and bankruptcy proceedings, and debt restructuring. The establishment of an international structure for restructuring debt is the subject of preliminary discussions, but there are numerous obstacles. If and when such a mechanism is developed, it will help improve risk distribution and lessen the possibility of moral hazard, but it won't solve the underlying instability of a system that is primarily dependent on debt contracts. Many of the intrinsic weaknesses of a debt-based system, including excessive leverage, a lack of market discipline, complex derivatives disconnected from actual economic transactions, and shortcomings in corporate governance, were both reaffirmed and made clear by the financial crisis. Despite the fact that Islam offers a model for how a society should be set up and how its citizens' affairs should be managed in compliance with its guidelines, the system has not been fully implemented, with the exception of a short time after its establishment. Naturally, compared to the economies of today, the economy at that time was far less complicated. The concept of interest was reduced, and commercial operations at the time followed Islamic precepts. Indeed, other major religions forbid the practice of interest, and the institution of interest was still in its infancy. Muslims have only recently been compelled to acknowledge the presence of interest in the context of the growing interest in the broader application of Islamic teachings, since interest has become an essential component of economic life.

In different ways, many Muslim communities lost contact with their historical customs, cultural heritage, and values during the colonial era. Though there is evidence of a desire to return to the Islamic tradition and resistance to the imposition of colonial ideals, these efforts were not widespread. Muslims did not start reclaiming their identities and expressing a desire to restore the principles they had lost in all facets of life, particularly the business world, until the end of the colonial era. In 1971, the Egyptian government established the Nasir Social Bank, which was the country's first interest-free institution. One of the first private initiatives was the founding of the Dubai Islamic Bank in the United Arab Emirates in 1975 (Hussain & Hassan, 2014). The Middle East's oil-rich Muslim nations saw a sharp increase in money in the 1970s, or petrodollars, which provided powerful incentives to develop Shariah-compliant investment avenues for Muslims.

Figure 2.2. *Islamic Development Bank.*

Source: https://www.britannica.com/topic/Islamic-Development-Bank, Creative Commons License.

Several of the top conventional banks as well as domestic and foreign bankers took advantage of this economic opportunity. With the dual goals of providing Shariah-compliant development finance and fostering economic development in Muslim nations, the Islamic Development Bank (IDB) (Figure 2.2) was founded in 1975 along the lines of regional development organizations. The IDB, which is headquartered in Jeddah, has been instrumental in advancing Islamic financing options and conducting insightful studies on Islamic banking, economics, and finance.

2.4. FINANCIAL SERVICES

The developing Islamic financial services sector started to grow quickly in the 1980s, and this trend persisted throughout the 1990s (Zaher & Kabir Hassan, 2001). The Islamic Republics of Iran, Pakistan, and Sudan said during that time that they intended to change their whole banking systems to comply with Shariah. Other nations, like Bahrain and Malaysia, established Islamic banking inside the confines of their pre-existing structures. Initiating study on the macroeconomic ramifications of an economy without a basis of interest is the International Monetary Fund (IMF) (Figure 2.3). Comparable studies were carried out to examine the financial stability of a profit-sharing system. Islamic banks encountered a lack of high-quality investment opportunities in the early years of the Islamic financial market.

Figure 2.3. *International Monetary Fund.*

Source: http://www.imf.org/external/np/adm/pictures/captions.htm, Creative Commons License.

This presented Western conventional banks with an opportunity to serve as middlemen, distributing Islamic banks' funds in line with the guidelines provided by the Islamic banks. By arranging for a merchant to purchase products on behalf of the Islamic bank and resale them at a markup, Western banks assisted Islamic banks in investing their capital in commerce and trade-related industries. As the Islamic financial markets grew in significance, Western banks started to provide their own Islamic products through "Islamic windows" in an effort to reach out to customers directly. Islamic windows are specialist setups within traditional financial organizations that provide their clients with items that comply with Shariah. They are not separate financial entities. Meanwhile, non-Western conventional banks began to offer Islamic windows due to the increased demand for Shariah-compliant products and the concern of losing depositors. These windows are generally intended for high-net-worth individuals who wish to engage in Islamic banking. The market had sufficiently grown by the early 1990s to draw the interest of institutions and legislators eager to launch cutting-edge goods. The Accounting and Auditing Organization for Islamic Financial Institutions (AAOIFI), a self-regulatory organization, was founded in recognition of the need for standards (Alexakis & Tsikouras, 2009). This played a crucial role in defining accounting and Shariah standards, which were subsequently accepted or acknowledged by many nations, as well as in emphasizing the unique regulatory requirements of Islamic financial organizations. But as the market grew, the regulatory and supervisory bodies, with the IMF's assistance, set up a special regulatory body called the Islamic Financial Services Board (IFSB) in the early 2000s to deal with systemic stability as well as other industry-related governance and regulatory challenges.

2.5. MARKET

In terms of establishing capital markets, more progress was made. Sukuks, or Islamic asset-backed certificates, were introduced with success in Bahrain, Malaysia, and other financial hubs. Corporations, and sovereign organizations like the Islamic Development Bank, the governments of Bahrain, Qatar, and the Islamic Republic of Pakistan were among the issuers. During the 1990s stock market boom, a number of equity funds based on stocks that comply with Shariah developed. The quantity of traditional banks providing Islamic windows increased. One of the first Western banks to open a distinct Islamic bank was Citibank in 1996 with the establishment of Citi Islamic Investment Bank (Bahrain). Today, Hong Kong and Shanghai Banking Corporation (HSBC) (Figure 2.4) has a well-established network of banks around the Muslim world.

Figure 2.4. *Hong Kong and Shanghai Banking Corporation.*

Source: https://en.wikipedia.org/wiki/HSBC_%28Hong_Kong%29#/media/File:HK_HSBC_Main_Building_2008.jpg, Creative Commons License.

Launched in 1998, HSBC Global Islamic Finance (GIF) aims to promote Islamic asset securitization, private equity, and banking in OECD nations. American Express Bank Ltd., ANZ Grindlays, BNP-Paribas, Deutsche Bank UBS, and Kleinwort Benson are among the Western banks that maintain Islamic windows. United Bank of Kuwait, Riyadh Bank, and National Commercial Bank of Saudi Arabia are the top non-Western banks with sizable Islamic windows. Globalization of Islamic finance has commenced. While Islamic transactions have always been executed and innovated in large part by Western financial centers and financial intermediaries, these activities have always taken place in the private sector and in a clandestine manner. This trend started to reverse in the early 2000s as a number of non-Muslim nations showed interest in this developing banking sector. This can be attributed to a number of things, including the surge in oil revenues that led to the accumulation of investable funds searching for lucrative investment opportunities, the growing awareness of the regulatory concerns surrounding Islamic financial intermediaries, and the desire of corporate and sovereign entities to access alternative funding sources.

In Europe, Islamic money has been around for a while. The founding of the Dar al Maal al Islami Trust in Geneva in 1981, an investment firm with holdings in multiple Islamic banks was a significant milestone (Saud, 2013). Numerous affluent customers seeking assets that adhere to Shariah transact directly with European banks, most notably UBS of Switzerland, the top supplier of such services. In July 2004, the German Federal State of Saxony-Anhalt secured €100 million (US $120 million) for a five-year sukuk sale, making it the first in Europe. While London has been involved in the industry, other parts of Europe have not yet seen a significant amount of interest in Islamic banking. The authorities and regulators in France, for instance, have been reluctant to recognize the potential of this market, despite the fact that the country's 6 million Muslims make up three times the population of the UK. A second wave of interest in Islamic finance emerged between 2005 and 2008, driven once more by the Middle East's rising oil incomes. But unlike the 1970s boom, which was restricted to the wealthy, the current expansion is the outcome of demand from a much broader range of people, including retail customers and small investors. Demand for Shariah-compliant products has suddenly increased in several nations where Islamic finance remained inactive. For instance, the National Commercial Bank, the largest bank in Saudi Arabia, has shifted its whole branch network to Shariah principles due to popular demand to adopt Islamic finance. In addition to participating in the growth of Islamic banking, Bahrain and Malaysia have worked hard to create elite financial hubs to further the cause. London is a well-liked destination for Islamic financial operations because of its historical standing, importance as a financial hub, and appeal as a time zone relative to the Middle East. The most popular Islamic financial instrument, commodity murabahah, is said to move more money through the London financial hub than any other location. There was enough demand, given the nearly 2 million Muslims living in the UK, to open the Islamic Bank of Britain in September 2004. As of the end of 2006, it had 30,000 customers depositing £83 million (US $165 million), and its assets were £120 million (US $240 million). Comparably, the goal of the European Islamic Investment Bank (EIIB), which was established in April 2006, is to advance investment banking that complies with Shariah. In order to offer Shariah-compliant banking, the European Finance House (EFH), a division of Qatar Islamic Bank, was approved a banking license in the UK in 2008.

The UK government has taken action to make its markets Islamic finance friendly, realizing the importance and promise of Islamic finance both locally and globally. For instance, it started looking into the potential for introducing a sovereign sukuk in 2007 with the goal of fostering the growth of the local Islamic financial industry and creating an international standard. These regulations were put in place to guarantee parity with traditional securities and to encourage prospective sukuk investors. The principal aims of the IIFM, situated in Bahrain, are improving collaboration across Islamic bank regulatory bodies, mitigating the liquidity issue by broadening the instrument maturity structure, and investigating the potential for sovereign asset-backed securities. The International Capital Markets Association (ICMA) and the IIFM are now collaborating on the expansion of the primary and secondary markets for Islamic bonds (sukuk) (Delle Foglie & Keshminder, 2022). The teams are collaborating to create a master agreement for murabahah commodities contracts, which are used in interbank transactions between Islamic banks and between Islamic and conventional banks, as well as a repurchase (repo) master agreement to assist central banks in managing liquidity in the sukuk market. The IIRA provides an evaluation of the risk profile of companies and instruments that can be utilized to make investment decisions in an effort to support the growth of regional financial markets. Multilateral financial institutions, a number of eminent banks, and rating agencies from several nations are the sponsors of the IIRA. The organization is comprised of a Shariah board, an independent rating committee, and a board of directors. Additionally, the IIRA offers a special service that rates how well financial institutions adhere to the good faith, both in text and spirit, requirements set forth by their Shariah committee. They also look at whether the institution has a system in place to assess its adherence to Shariah and whether the Shariah committee has the power, knowledge, and resources to carry out the assessment.

Although there isn't a formal or organized source of statistics on Islamic finance, various estimates are frequently cited by both non-commercial and commercial sources. The Islamic financial sector encompasses a multitude of entities, including capital markets, Islamic banks, Islamic windows, Islamic insurance (takaful), and other non-bank financial companies. Islamic banking, which dominates the industry, typically refers to deposit-taking commercial and investment banking, both onshore and offshore. Islamic windows are specialized windows that meet the needs of Islamic products and are offered by normal banks. Though other financial products and services have been gaining traction over the past 10 years, Islamic banking and windows have historically been the most active industry. Asset management, mutual funds, and brokerage houses are among the firms that specialize in the capital markets' usage of Islamic funds or Islamic bonds, or sukuk. The role of Islamic non-bank financial institutions is comparable to that of traditional fund management firms. These institutions are specialized and provide financial services through partnerships (Mudarabah) or leases (ijarah). A small but increasing number of institutions are involved in private equity, venture capital, and microfinance funding. For a number of reasons, uncertainties about the quality of assets held by Islamic financial institutions have increased since the economic recession. First, the market value of assets has declined as a result of Islamic banks' significant real estate investments and the drop in property values. Second, Islamic banks are more vulnerable to risk due to their propensity for sectoral and geographic concentrations. Owing to conservative measures including maintaining high levels of liquidity and sufficient equity capital, Islamic banks are predicted to weather this storm and keep expanding their deposit and asset bases.

2.6. FINANCIAL CRISIS

The financial crisis (Figure 2.5) also affected the fast-expanding Islamic capital markets. This is demonstrated by the decline in Islamic bond (sukuk) issuance in the wake of the financial crisis. Additionally, there have been a number of sukuk-related legal disputes, which have negatively impacted the market and decreased demand. But when legal disputes were resolved in a systematic manner, demand increases in the market. For instance, the IDB's 2010 sukuk was well-received by the market and had a higher demand than supply. In October 2010, a group of central banks signed an agreement aimed at creating a liquidity facility for Islamic financial institutions (Muhammad Al-Amine, 2016). The purpose of this facility is to enhance market liquidity by offering products that improve it, as well as to provide liquidity through the trading of short-term financial instruments. This is a positive development. The foundation of the Islamic economic system is a set of fixed laws that influence economic behavior and results and are independent of time and location. These laws are outlined in the principles of Shariah. There are regulations that influence economic behavior on the system's periphery, but they are flexible and can alter based on the situation. These are the outcomes of choices made by reputable authorities in an Islamic community in order to pursue policies like purposeful interventions in economic matters that will achieve their objectives. Nonetheless, these laws and activities carried out to achieve particular goals must be compliant with Shariah. The fundamental economic laws and institutions of Islamic economic systems remain the same, even though localized adoptions of these laws and institutions may differ. There cannot be discrepancies between Islamic countries regarding the system of inheritance, for instance, even though they may differ in terms of their international trade policies. We must talk about some of the main features of Islam's economic system in order to comprehend it. However, before that, a broad overview of the Islamic economy is required. It is unquestionably true that one of Islam's primary goals is to establish a robust, dynamic, and growth-oriented economy, since without it, the religion's ideals cannot be realized. Only when its laws, institutions, organizations, and methods of operation, together with the conduct of the individual and the collective, are compliant with Shariah is an economy that is both dynamic and expanding deemed healthy.

Figure 2.5. *Financial crisis.*

Source: https://en.wikipedia.org/wiki/Financial_crisis#/media/File:Schwarzer_Freitag_Wien_1873.jpg, Creative Commons License.

An economic system is a group of organizations created by society to manage the distribution of revenue and wealth that results from the creation of goods and services, the distribution of resources, and output (Rosca et al., 2017). The institutional framework of a society is defined by the set of behavioral norms that are prescribed for both individuals and collectivities within that society. These norms serve to determine the overall system that the society adheres to. Rules of behavior are upheld by mechanisms of enforcement that offer appropriate incentives for rewarding adherence to the rules and penalizing noncompliance. These mechanisms can be found in social contracts, constitutions, and legal frameworks, or they can be ingrained in social conventions, customs, habits, and cultural values. The incentive system needs to be set up so that the rules of conduct become self-enforcing, or in cases when this isn't feasible, that there are efficient channels available to ensure that the rules are applied correctly. When people have to choose between two options and take action, rules outline the behavior that will lead to the most equitable outcomes. They place limitations on what people in society can do without upsetting the social order that all members rely on to make decisions about their own behavior and to shape their expectations of the responses and actions of others. The degree of certainty in the establishment of these expectations is determined by adherence to the norms, which also serve to reinforce the social order, avoid conflict, resolve disputes, coordinate actions, and enhance collaboration. Two prerequisites must be met; one is essential, and the other is sufficient, in order to get these results. According to the former, rule compliance must be upheld, if at all feasible, by coercion. The universal enforcement of the code of behavior in every situation, regardless of the circumstances or the results, is the adequate criterion.

2.7. REGULATIONS

The rules grow more self-sustaining and self-enforcing as a society's conformity with them increases. In order to achieve this goal, the rules must be internalized by people as endogenous components of their own brains, which manifest externally when the rules are accepted as common beliefs by members of the community. Stronger coordinated group behaviors and a more stable society are directly correlated with stronger shared beliefs. The purpose of codes of conduct is to give people the tools they need to get over the challenges posed by their ignorance of specific information that is necessary to establish the general justice of the social order. Regulations outline the proper behavior in specific situations. Rules are particular tools for certain purposes. In essence, they are limitations on what each member of society is allowed to accomplish without causing disruption to the social order. Everybody depends on the social order to guide their own decisions and behaviors. Rules should therefore direct people's behavior. The rules tell them whether or not they can have something, as well as how and when they can acquire it, if their feelings and impulses tell them what they desire. Furthermore, and this is crucially important, following the rules of behavior helps people integrate into society. Rules help people cooperate with one another, resolve disagreements, and avoid confrontations. Respecting them upholds the desired social order and fosters social cohesion and integration. The way Islamic laws are enforced is that everyone is held accountable for understanding the rules for themselves and making sure others are aware of them as well. The enforcement mechanism is embedded in the most significant social duty that Muslims have making sure that everyone is aware of and abides by the conduct guidelines that Islam prescribes. Compliance will be absent or essentially poor if these regulations are not widely recognized or understood as a result of people and their collectivities avoiding their responsibilities. In that instance, imposing an Islamic economic superstructure by decree, whatever that may entail given the specifics, will not provide the intended outcome. However, it is the obligation and responsibility of all individuals, the government, and society at large to guarantee that the rules are followed and enforced once they are known and understood. The Islamic economic system is defined by the collection of these institutions, which in turn form the basis for the fundamental economic institutions found in Islam (Mirakhor, 2009).

2.8. RIGHTS

While the individual's right to property upholds man's innate desire to possess, especially when it comes to works of art, the corresponding private property obligations, as viewed through the lens of justice, are intended to effectuate community members' interdependence and to make it clear that they are unable to exist in isolation. Therefore, the idea that an individual causes no harm to other members of his group if his effort makes him better off and others do not suffer worse than they would otherwise suffer is rejected by the private property responsibilities. These duties regard private ownership to be subject to a trust, or a responsibility, in order to effect sharing, and they write the sharing principle into the delineation of interests in property. Therefore, Islam's understanding of property rights recognizes private initiative, choice, and reward; nevertheless, this acknowledgment is not permitted to undermine the sharing principle or result in the violation of community rights. An intervention by the legitimate authority to take corrective action would be considered justified if the obligation to share is shied away from or the rights of the community and society as a whole are compromised due to the expansion of society, the division of labor, or the growing complexity of markets. A collection of obligations, liabilities, and rights pertaining to an asset is referred to as property. The right of an individual to use and dispose of property, as well as the ability to bar others from using it, is regarded as private property in the western sense. This is a relatively novel understanding of property that is believed to have coincided with the development of the market economy, even in the history of western economies. The right to use and enjoy an asset was all that was granted with a grant of property rights in land and other assets prior to that time. The right to dispose of the item or bar others from using it was not included. For instance, the state did not confer the right to dispose of property along with the right to enjoy the profits from a piece of land, a corporate charter, or a monopoly. Since it was believed that the right to be granted permission to use property owned by another person was not marketable and could not be reconciled with a market economy, it is believed that the emergence of the market economy required a reform of this understanding of property. But in Islam, this right is upheld without undermining the market's function as a framework for allocating resources and transmitting impulses.

Islam acknowledges that people are endowed by divine providence with distinct and unequal skills; certain people are capable of obtaining claim to a bigger quantity of property and assets because they possess more mental and/or physical capacities. However, this merely indicates that these people have higher obligations and responsibilities than other people. Nevertheless, these people's rights to their possessions are held intact, and no one has the right to forcibly appropriate or expropriate that person's property to another after they have fulfilled their duties of sharing in the prescribed way and in the prescribed amount, provided they are not breaking any Shariah laws. This privilege is so highly valued that the development of regulations for emergency situations involving the expropriation of property for public utility projects was referred to as a legitimate infraction (Ikrah Hukmi). Even then, such measures could only be carried out following the payment of sufficient compensation to the property owner. In an economic system, people not only make decisions for themselves but also engage with other people through transactions made possible by agreements made both explicitly and implicitly within the parameters defined by the society's institutional framework. A contract is an objective, time-bound document. The responsibilities that each party is expected to carry out in order to accomplish the goals of the contract are outlined in the agreement. In Islam, the idea of a contract is fundamental to the Shariah and plays a significant role in the legal side of trade as an establishment required to meet justifiable human requirements. The divine Law is entirely contractual in nature, both in terms of its implementation and its idea. The covenant between Allah and humanity, which requires man to be obedient to his word, is the cornerstone of Shariah. A set of guidelines that make up a general theory of contracts with a clear focus on particular contracts like sales, leases, hires, and partnerships was developed over the course of Islam's legal and intellectual history using the Shariah as the foundation. Contracts are legally enforceable and have the same level of protection under Shariah as the establishment of property. The aforementioned regulations instituted the notion that, for civil and business affairs, any accord that isn't expressly forbidden by Shariah law is legitimate, legally enforceable, and subject to the treatment of all parties involved as equals by the courts.

Islam teaches man to make the most use of all the resources that Allah has created and given to him (Khan et al., 2010). Refusing to use these helpful tools is the equivalent of being unappreciative. Wealth is regarded as a crucial tool that man can use to clear the path toward achieving his ultimate goal. Wealth is referred to in Islam as good, an object of joy and satisfaction, and a means of reinforcing the society. On the other hand, forced poverty is viewed as bad and the result of disbelief. However, this specific definition of wealth is limited by the methods used to acquire, hold, and dispose of it. The emphasis placed on the idea that wealth is merely a means, not an end in and of itself, to the accomplishment of man's ultimate goal qualifies its earning. It must be acquired by good, productive, and useful labor, as that term is defined in the Shariah, which also outlines the procedures for acquiring resources in a legal manner. In addition to listing the legal ways to accumulate wealth, this list also includes the kinds of economic activities that are forbidden and can result in wealth that has been obtained illegally. The Shariah lists occupations, trades, and economic activities that are forbidden and can result in reserves obtained illegally. The Shariah outlines right and wrong behavior even inside professions. Just as reserves produced legitimately and used for a good cause are regarded as a blessing, wealth obtained or amassed illegally for its own sake is criticized as corruption and a return to the most fundamentally evil trait in human nature: greed. Islam views wealth as the community's lifeblood, which needs to be continuously in circulation; as such, owning it entails no right to hoard. The inference is that in order to enhance a community's economic well-being, wealth that has been rightfully acquired must be invested there. Wealthy people should always remember that investing their wealth is assessed not just by the financial return on investment but also by the benefits to society as a whole.

2.9. SHARIAH-BASED REGULATIONS

The Shariah regulations also apply to the nature of assets (Marzban & Asutay, 2012). The most important of these regulations is the acknowledgment of other people's rights to this money, which comes from the idea of an immutable claim to ownership. These comprise levies with predetermined amounts and those whose exact amounts are left up to the wealth owner. These taxes become payable when a person's wealth reaches above a certain threshold (nisab). The owner retains ownership of the remaining funds once these duties are fulfilled, but they must be utilized in line with Shariah laws, which prohibit waste, excess, luxury, and general financial abuse. It cannot be applied to cause harm to people, gain political power, or taint the political system. Islam views wealth as a trustee holding his fortune as a trust on behalf of Allah and the society, even if it recognizes wealth that is properly obtained, possessed, and disposed of as sacred and protected by the Shariah. Therefore, his incapacity to manage his wealth appropriately serves as the foundation for the loss of his entitlement to it. The community can view him as a Safih, a person with poor comprehension and a weak intellect, who, in addition to his personal financial and moral losses, is harming the community's interests due to his excesses, waste, and general abuse of money. Hajr is a principle that states that a person's wealth becomes the property of the community or its authorized agents, who may restrict the use of the property to what is necessary for the individual to meet his fundamental necessities. The Islamic economic paradigm's distribution/redistribution rule is one of the most significant economic institutions that operationalizes the goal of attaining social justice. The development of social justice is a fundamental mission shared by all messengers and prophets. Practically speaking, the Qur'an makes it abundantly evident that this entails building a society that is balanced and steers clear of extremes in riches and poverty, where everyone recognizes that wealth is a boon bestowed by the creator with the express intent of supporting everyone's life. According to the Islamic perspective, a large number of rich and successful people who keep concentrating all of their efforts on gaining wealth cannot exist without also producing a large number of those who are impoverished and economically deprived. Because their rights to the wealth of the powerful and wealthy are not upheld, the poor suffer from deprivation while the rich indulge in extravagant consumption.

Islam forbids the amassing of riches in order to prevent this, and it places restrictions on consumption through laws that forbid waste (Itlaf), excessive expenditure, and showy, lavish spending (Israf) (Askari et al., 2014). It then mandates that the net surplus be distributed to community members who are unable to work for a variety of reasons and whose resources could have been used to create wealth. This is after allowing for the moderate spending required to maintain a modest living standard. The Qur'an views those who possess greater ability as trustee-agents who use these resources on behalf of others who lack ability. An economy that is balanced and free from extremes of riches and poverty would be the outcome. The system of required and optional payments, including Khums (20% of income), Sadaqat, and zakat, operates to redeem the rights of the less fortunate. Following the stages of production and sale, distribution occurs when all involved parties receive their compensation for their contributions to the creation, exchange, and sale of commodities and services. In essence, these costs represent the return and redemption of other people's rights to a person's earnings and assets. A conviction in the Oneness of the creator and, by extension, the unity of all of creation and of humanity in particular is demonstrated by the redemption of these rights. It is the acknowledgement and confirmation that all people need unrestricted access to the resources that Allah has created. Human freedom is not seen as an inherent personal right in Islam, but rather as a voluntary submission to the divine will. Because of his ontological dependence on Allah, man is only able to accept gifts from the one who created him. Human rights do not precede human obligations; rather, they are the result of them. The Shariah outlines the duties that man has toward his creator, the natural world, himself, and other people. Certain liberties and rights, which are also outlined by the Shariah, are acquired when these duties are completed. The Shariah places restrictions on people's freedoms and rights with the intention of eliminating all bad outcomes from human existence. To have an Islamic identity, both the individual and the system must adhere to the duties, privileges, and restrictions outlined in the Shariah.

Individuals are entitled to some natural rights under the Shariah, including the freedom to pursue their own financial interests. Islam holds that a person's inherent rights are the same rights that Allah has bestowed upon him. Within the context of Shariah, pursuing one's economic interests is first and foremost an obligation and duty, followed by an unalienable right. The important thing to remember is that, even though a person's rights are still protected, they are no longer obligated to fulfill the commitment if they lack the capacity or ability to pursue their economic interests. The inability to fulfill one's obligation to pursue one's economic interests does not absolve one of the rights to economic advantages. In the event that someone is unable to realize their potential correctly, it still exists. On the other hand, the individual's rights are also void if they are capable yet fail to fulfill their responsibilities. Contrary to popular belief, Islam does not deny the existence of self-interest. In fact, Islam views it as the main component of its incentive-motivation system. It is also a must in every structured society for an individual to find it most advantageous to abide by the standards of behavior set forth by the system. There isn't a single Shariah norm that doesn't justify personal self-interest, so long as self-interest is understood to include both spiritual and temporal objectives. The person is asked to abide by the Shariah for his or her own material and spiritual well-being in this life as well as for their ultimate salvation and happiness in the afterlife. The Qur'an makes this plain by stating that every commandment is normally followed with the warning that doing so is for the individual's personal gain. A common practice is to list the benefits and incentives for conformity as well as the penalties for non-compliance, both now and in the afterlife. The Shariah specifies individual obligations and rights, as well as the boundaries and accountability for these rights, in the context of pursuing self-interest.

The Islamic understanding of mankind's ultimate destiny views economic existence as essentially related (Haneef & Furqani, 2009). Even in this capacity, economic matters serve merely to supply the establishments and systems required to meet the material necessities of humanity, given that humanity is permitted to exist in this world as the ultimate creation of Allah. Therefore, the economic system created in line with the core doctrines of Islam guarantees that man can enjoy his inherent freedom, rights, and responsibilities in the conduct of economic activities. The structure of the economy must be such that man is not just an instrument in the accomplishment of the states or the economy's objectives. Islam aims to lead man toward responsible economic engagement and individual action that pledges him to communal solidarity and collaboration, culminating in a vibrant and expanding economy. As a result, the individual is held responsible for the moral consequences of all of his social acts, including those pertaining to the economy, and as a result, the advancement of the society is inextricably linked to his own internal spiritual and personal development. Islam thus makes use of both competition and cooperation to structure the ideal society by bringing these two opposites into harmony and reconciling them, as well as between equally primordial and beneficial forces at all levels of social organization. From this angle, one could contend that Islam's strong emphasis on the unification of human society as a necessary result of Allah's unity is one of its most distinctive features. Accordingly, the Qur'an's view of the best course of action required for the establishment of solidarity in human society cannot be separated from the character of the Prophet. The Prophet's numerous social positions in the community reflect every aspect of his personality, which is geared toward maximizing societal harmony and integration. Furthermore, all behavioral regulations, particularly those pertaining to the economy, are intended to facilitate the integration process. In contrast, any behavior that contributes to social breakdown in any way is forbidden.

2.10. TRADITIONS

Humans can cooperate and compete for good or evil, according to the Qur'an and the Prophet's traditions, which both clearly mention the dual nature of competition and collaboration. This is what causes society to either integrate or disintegrate. Nonetheless, the foundational sources stress that cooperation and competition should be used in virtue rather than in immorality and animosity. Muslims are encouraged to compete with each other in good and moral deeds. When these forces are applied within the framework of Shariah, there is no evidence in these sources to support the suppression of one over the other. Instead, the legitimate political authority's entire regulatory and supervisory power is focused on making a constructive and equitable use of these forces. One illustration of this equilibrium is found in the Shariah regulations governing the way the market is organized and how its players behave. The Shariah regulations pertaining to economic matters establish boundaries and limits of appropriate competitive and cooperative conduct that is essential for maintaining and fostering social cohesion (Ayub, 2020). However, the individual is always the identifiable agent whose actions carry out all economic activities. Every time labor is required to produce wealth, assuming equal liberty and opportunity, the output of various individuals may fluctuate significantly in terms of both quantity and quality. Therefore, equity requires that different people receive varied rewards based on their productivity. Therefore, fairness may result in inequality, starting with the equality of liberty and opportunity of access to resources. Furthermore, the distribution of wealth at the outset and the market's structure will be reflected in the distribution of resources that result from its functioning. There is no rational basis for assuming that the market's outcome will inevitably result in an equitable distribution of wealth, even under the assumption that the market's structure and operations are both fair. Thus, it is possible, and frequently is, that fairly generated inequalities will have both short and long-term effects. Here is where the distributive processes of Islamic economic justice try to adjust the imbalances that have been produced fairly.

Islam acknowledges assertions grounded in the equality of liberty and opportunity, which are manifested in the level of resource accessibility, the degree and scope of an individual's capacity to actualize their potential for liberty and opportunity, and the entitlement to prior ownership. The various levies redeem the right of the less fortunate to share in the wealth of those who are more capable and have more opportunities to do so. The payment of these levies is not complimentary; rather, it is a contractual requirement that must be fulfilled. Beyond these required contributions, Islam also promotes charity; however, these duties take the form of giving back to others what is properly theirs. Ignoring this duty results in an unequal distribution of wealth, which Islam views as the primary cause of poverty. Islam makes it clear that neither a lack of natural resources nor an improper synchronization of the modes of production and distribution are the causes of poverty. Instead, it is the outcome of waste, excess, extravagance, and failure to pay what the less fortunate members of society are entitled to. For this reason, waste, exploitation of riches, luxury, and greed are denounced as unfair, especially when they coexist with poverty that they have the potential to reduce. Islam categorically holds that everyone has a right to a particular quality of living, and that everyone's claim must be satisfied out of fairness and justice. This is how Islam views the morality of property. Based on the idea that an owner's title to their money expires upon their death, Islamic inheritance laws alter how wealth is distributed to the following generation. Although acknowledged, a person's ability to leave their money to others is essentially limited to no more than one-third of their net worth.

The precise process for determining an heir's portion of the inheritance is laid down in the Qur'an. There is neither preferential treatment nor discrimination among the same category of heirs, yet a woman's portion is typically half that of a man's because the husband is ultimately responsible for providing for the family under Shariah law. The wife is not legally obligated to share her wealth or income with her husband, even if it comes from her own labor or inheritance. She is also not forced to contribute in any way to the family. Islam's institution of inheritance divides the wealth of each generation and redistributes it to the next in a way that ensures a large number of people receive a modest portion of such wealth, rather than it going to a single heir or a small number of heirs, in light of the nature of the family ties and mutual responsibilities urged by Islam. Economic achievements are not to be seen as ends in and of themselves because Islam views economic relationships and behavior as the means of social and spiritual unity (Zaman, 2019). Every norm of conduct pertaining to economic problems is directed towards individuals and their collectivities, symbolized by the state. It is widely believed that the state is necessary for the establishment of temporal and spiritual wealth, the spread of religion, the legitimate goals that must be achieved, and the orderly organization of social life. The state's main function is to carry out Shariah, and it gets its legitimacy by upholding its precepts. It is presumed that it has the authority to employ all available methods, within the bounds of the law, to accomplish the goals and fulfill the obligations set forth for the collectivities, including harmonizing the interests of the public and the individual.

2.11. RESPONSIBILITIES

The most important of our joint responsibilities is to make sure that justice is upheld in all spheres of society. Therefore, it is considered an essential governmental responsibility to construct a judiciary or judicial system with all the tools required to implement court decisions, accessible to all, and free of charge. Ensuring equal liberty and opportunity for access to and use of resources designated by the Shariah for individual usage is one of its other responsibilities. This includes guaranteeing that everyone has access to technology, education, and skill sets. Equitable opportunities and rights to liberty transform the creation, acquisition, and exchange of wealth into issues of equity. The state has historically been in charge of building all the infrastructure required for markets to function. At the command of the Prophet, the first market for the Muslim community (Figure 2.6) was constructed at Medina.

He stipulated that trade might occur there freely, without any fees or charges placed on the participants and designated market supervisors. Because of this, legal scholars have acknowledged that the state has an obligation to oversee the market and to regulate it only as needed. As we've seen, Islam upholds the inalienable right of individuals who are incapable to reach their full potential to enjoy the same freedoms and opportunities as those who are more fortunate.

Figure 2.6. *Muslim community.*

Source: https://en.wikipedia.org/wiki/Muslims#/media/File:Prayer_in_Cairo_1865.jpg, Creative Commons License.

Islam therefore necessitates a balance between liberal ideas in order for believers to practice it. If the mandatory taxes required by Shariah regulations are not paid, the state bears the burden of rectifying the ensuing imbalance in distribution. Second only to the preservation and promotion of faith, which is thought to be threatened by poverty, the eradication of poverty is unquestionably one of the most significant tasks assigned to the state. Islam views poverty as essentially the result of the wealthier and more capable people of society failing to carry out their assigned responsibilities. The responsibility for justice, which typically accounts for a significant amount of government spending in other systems, is thus primarily placed on the shoulders of those who can afford it. The Shariah not only specifies who is required to pay, but it also names specific recipient categories.

The Shariah has granted the state authority over the use, management, and control of a society's natural resource endowment, mineral resources, for example in order to cover the costs involved with carrying out its obligations (Saniotis, 2012). Jurists generally agree that the state has the authority to levy taxes if there is a discrepancy between the resources it can appropriate and the expenses it incurs. When and if necessary, the state may borrow money as long as it doesn't have to pay interest. The incentive-motivation structure that an economic system embodies is a crucial component of system analysis. The goal of taking this into account is to ascertain whether or not a system member will discover that adhering to the rules of behavior imposed by the system maximizes their utility. The system will function in accordance with its regulations if the response is positive. There will be exceptions to the rules if they are not incentive compatible. The foundation of Islamic religion, which holds that following its laws of conduct serves the interests of the individual both now and in the future as well as those of society at large, is where the incentive-motivation components of the Islamic system originate. These guidelines have been supplied by Islam without undermining human motivations or self-interest. In addition, the law has established channels and protocols for safeguarding the community's interests in the event that someone feels it would be more advantageous to break the law and hurt the interests of the community as a whole.

Islam's idea of barakah, which acts as a material incentive for people to follow the path of right conduct, is a key component of its incentive system. It includes every aspect of human activity, mainly among them being his economic actions. According to this concept, there will be an increasing rate of return for good conduct, which is defined as activity whose aim, and goal is to please Allah. There is more barakah when one acts in a more morally upright manner. According to this theory, if money is invested in this cause without anticipating a direct return from the beneficiary, it will grow. In actuality, the benefactor will get several rewards for such deeds. The idea motivates Muslims to go above and beyond the bare minimum required by Shariah and creates a positive association between the behavior of the system and success. The idea also holds true in reverse. In other words, acquiring, holding, or disposing of wealth in an immoral manner will deprive its possessor of their barakah. This pertains to collective conduct as well as individual behavior, and since the outcomes of barakah operations are visible, it acts as a motivator for following the law. Islam's primary goal is to use human agency to create a social structure that is morally sound, equitable, and sustainable. As a result, it is believed that the individual and the community are related. It is the duty of humanity as a whole to guarantee that each person has the chance to realize their latent potential and to remove any barriers standing in their way of achieving their ultimate objective. This shared understanding raises the issue of human unity, which results in each member's equality. The fundamental idea of Islam is that all people share the same nature. All foundations for differentiation are eliminated, with the exception of kindness, virtue, and service to Allah, and the equality of the entire human race is assumed, affirmed, and confirmed. The fundamental tenet of Islam, that all things are one and that Allah is unity and oneness is the source of the idea of humanity's unity. Based on this idea, it may be said that Islamic society is an inclusive community that includes all of humanity.

Chapter 3

RESILIENCE AND STABILITY IN ISLAMIC FINANCE

Contents

3.1. INTRODUCTION

Islamic finance is becoming more and more popular as a result of the current financial crisis. It is predicted that this industry will reach US $4,000 billion in the next five years (Chad Li, 2011). The first Sukuk defaults, however, are expected to highlight the shortcomings of Islamic finance, with the majority of investors predicted to have no more legal remedy than holders of conventional bonds because the underlying assets have not been properly transferred to them. IB&F (Islamic Banking and Finance) has demonstrated its resilience during the Asian financial crisis. These remarks brought to light the fact that, although IB&F managed to weather the Asian crisis, that crisis was limited to a specific area, therefore the organization's ability to resist future crises which would likely be more severe and affect a larger geographic area will need to be evaluated. The current financial crisis is unquestionably larger in scope and magnitude than the Asian crisis because of the processes of financial globalization and liberalization that have strengthened the interconnections between the world's financial markets.

Unlike conventional finance, Islamic finance forbids lending based on interest as mandated by Shariah. Islamic banks must take direct ownership of tangible assets and engage in trading and investment activities in addition to acting as pure lenders. This prevents unbacked credit from growing further and limits speculation. Islamic banks are unable to securitize and discharge the debt receivables that resulted from credit sale transactions, even though the majority of Shariah scholars forbid trading debt other than at par value. Even in Malaysia, where it is currently legal to securities and exchange debt receivables, the process is restricted to a single-tier transaction. Islamic banks are likewise prohibited by Shariah from acquiring securities that have credit risks related to debt. Furthermore, speculative short selling is not permitted in the Islamic financial system because Shariah forbids the sale or leasing of property that one does not own. The Shariah principles, which ensure responsibility and discipline in financial activities, necessary conditions for financial stability are essentially the source of the IB&F system's core strength. The Islamic financial system is not risk-free and can be vulnerable to financial crises for a variety of reasons, despite its solid foundation in Shariah. First, because Islamic finance and the real sector are closely related, unforeseen negative developments in the real sector could have a negative impact on Islamic banks' business operations and performance if they don't have strong and efficient risk management procedures in place. According to recent studies, risks in the real sector have been steadily falling over the past few decades, whereas risks in the financial sector have been steadily rising. This implies that compared to those that are not, financial institutions are subject to lower risks and instability. However, significant real-world economic shocks could put the Islamic banking industry at risk of systemic collapse.

Second, especially during economic growth, Islamic banks may be persuaded to adopt aggressive, speculative investment methods with higher risk and higher expected returns, all without simultaneously adhering to fundamentally solid risk management guidelines. The basic mix of aggressive lending and poor risk management, which resulted in a collapse in mutual trust between parties, was a major contributor to the current crisis. These fundamental ideas supported the requirement for strict and uniformly implemented international norms of responsible risk management as well as additional supporting infrastructure to protect the Islamic financial system's financial stability. The counterpart of Basel II in IB&F, the Islamic Financial Services Board (IFSB) has released a wide range of prudential and supervisory rules to date that address risk management, capital adequacy, corporate governance, transparency, and market discipline. The aforementioned criteria consider global prudential guidelines pertaining to the banking, investing, and securities markets while also properly addressing the unique characteristics of Islamic finance, including its associated risks and adherence to Shariah. The issue of two additional standards, one on the governance of Islamic investment funds and the other on capital adequacy standards for real estate investments and Sukuk (Figure 3.1) securitizations, was accepted by the IFSB Council in October 2008 (Radzi & Lewis, 2015). The discipline that Islam provides into Sukuk structures apparently averts situations like the current credit crisis.

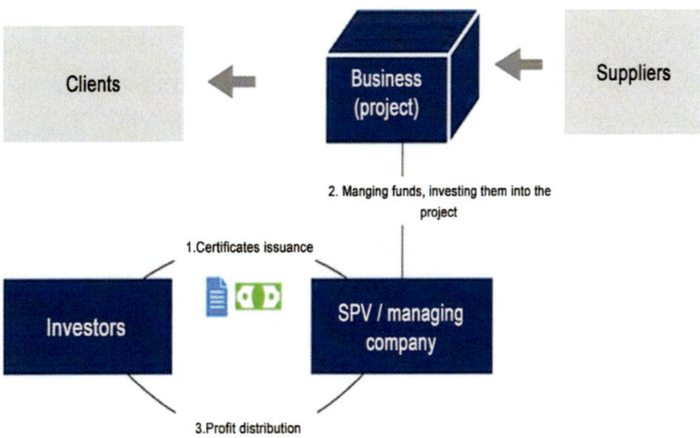

Figure 3.1. *Sukuk.*

Source: Kalimullina, M., & Hassan, M. K., (2022). Default risk as a factor preventing companies from entering the sukuk market. Risk Manag., 24, 298–326. https://doi.org/10.1057/s41283-022-00096-9, Creative Commons License.

3.2. CAPITAL

Different minimum capital adequacy standards are outlined in the capital adequacy standard for Sukuk securitizations issued by the IFSB to reflect the unique risks associated with the various Sukuk structures. The standard also addresses matters pertaining to the securitization procedure, specifically in relation to adherence to Shariah guidelines. The effective legal or beneficial transfer of ownership rights to the underlying assets, for instance, is a requirement for Islamic asset-backed securities (ABS), and it gives Sukuk investors an effective right of choice to the assets in the event of default. In contrast, bond holders in conventional financing have no ownership rights over these assets, only the right to use them as collateral. The IFSB has released a note in connection with the Capital Adequacy Standard for IB&F. This is meant to help supervisory authorities identify external rating agencies as capable of assigning risk weighting to the assets owned by the companies providing Islamic financial services (IIFS). The ECAIs should create a specific rating methodology for Shariah-compliant financing assets, as they are a unique class of assets (Hassan et al., 2019). This should help to guarantee that the rating of Islamic financial products accurately reflects the unique characteristics and risks of those instruments in a way that would better enable investors to exercise the required discipline in the market.

Shariah governance, conduct of business, the solvency of takaful operations, and corporate governance for takaful (Islamic insurance) undertakings. The IFSB is currently working on a standard on how institutions in IB&F should do business. It addresses how these institutions should handle their clients, that is, investors, policyholders, and customers. The ethical business conduct code of these establishments is based on the precepts of Shariah. Islamic institutions are required by law to uphold the standards of ethical business practices. In certain instances, such as Islamic securitization, this is also necessary for the transaction to be approved or for a contract to be binding. Indeed, questions of bad faith, dishonesty, concerns about justice, and lack of confidence are at the core of the current crisis in the traditional financial system, an ethical crisis. The strong correlation and interconnectedness between the banking, insurance, investment, and securities market sectors where vulnerability in the securities market sector had a bad effect on the banking and insurance sectors and as a result posed a threat to global financial stability is another equally significant feature of the global financial system exposed by the crisis. Essentially, the chaos highlighted the necessity for close collaboration between policymakers and financial supervisors with different mandates and jurisdictions in order to strengthen the resilience of financial institutions and markets, which cuts across national borders and even the financial sectors. Significant deficiencies in risk management have also been exposed by the current period of severe global financial distress. Fundamental shortcomings in the way financial institutions manage risk, particularly during periods of financial innovation, have also been a contributing factor in the banking and financial crises of the last 20 years.

3.3. IB & F

Given that IB&F is rapidly expanding globally with an increasing number of countries aspiring to become international Islamic financial centers, coupled with the fact that IB&F is not immune to risks, the Secretary-General of the IFSB believes that it is of the utmost importance to ensure that all the IFSB standards are promptly and properly implemented and effectively enforced in jurisdictions, where Islamic financial services are being offered. This would have the significant advantage of improving the stakeholders' comprehension of the peculiarities of Islamic financial industry and its risks, thus bolstering their capacity to properly manage these risks and achieving the intended result of financial stability in IB&F. Maintaining the foundations upon which Islamic finance has been formed becomes essential as innovation in Islamic financial products and services increases and as Islamic finance gets more intertwined with the global financial system. This will be essential to maintaining the Islamic banking system's resilience in the present, more difficult global financial situation. Embracing Shariah innovation in the creation of Islamic financial products is crucial to this (Alamad et al., 2021). To stay competitive in the globally globalized financial sector, innovation has shown to be a critical discriminator. But as the present unrest has shown, extremely complicated, unchecked innovation has the potential to become extremely destabilizing and cause significant disruptions to the financial system. Therefore, it is crucial that financial innovation follow the necessary Shariah principles and have specific Shariah goals. Shariah-based innovation would therefore support the development of Islamic financial products with unique value propositions and inherent advantages derived from the fundamental elements of Shariah.

3.4. MEASURES

Robust measures that support Shariah-based innovation in Islamic finance are essential to achieving this goal. Malaysia has implemented multiple measures. The International Shariah Research Academy for Islamic Finance (ISRA) was founded with the purpose of conducting dynamic Shariah-centric innovation applied research (Alshater et al., 2022). ISRA can offer a worldwide platform for more international collaboration and innovation-focused research. To encourage the uniform use of Islamic financial contracts, the central bank also took the effort to produce the Shariah Parameters. The goal of this project is to identify the fundamental characteristics of Islamic financial products that are drawn from important Shariah contracts. The implementation of Shariah contracts for Islamic financial products will be guided by these aspects. It is crucial to have an enabling architecture that enables the management of the risks unique to Islamic finance in order to guarantee the sustainability and resilience of Islamic finance. IB&F must have the capital requirements, solid governance, and efficient risk management necessary to adequately handle the risks associated with Islamic financial transactions. In order to provide a steady stream of income and to make sure the institutions are able to withstand the situations that arise during a crisis, it is also crucial for the institutions to distribute the risks by establishing wise asset allocation based on various Islamic contracts. To mitigate the inventory risks associated with the underlying assets and to cover any potential equity position risks incorporated into the partnership agreement, Malaysia is subject to an additional capital requirement. This is further supported by the partnership contracts' demand that board representatives be appointed to the invested firms in order to protect the Islamic financial institution's interests and enable ongoing observation and supervision. If Islamic financial institutions can show that they have the proper disclosure and governance procedures in place to guarantee an efficient risk transfer, they are also permitted to transfer risk to investors through Mudaraba, or profit-sharing and loss-bearing contracts.

In order to maintain consistent and competitive returns, Islamic banks are also allowed to set away a percentage of their income from assets financed by Mudaraba contracts (Figure 3.2) as profit equalization reserves, or PERs. A number of these specifications are derived from the worldwide standards published by IB&F. The continuous, steady growth of Islamic finance will depend on the application of IFSB standards in all relevant jurisdictions. The aforesaid methods aid in the management of risks specific to Islamic finance; but the legal, regulatory, and supervisory framework must also adapt to the industry's rapid evolution. An integrated crisis management framework must be a part of this infrastructure in order to guarantee that any new crises in the Islamic financial system would be handled quickly. Among other things, these initiatives must incorporate fundamental elements. This entails having the system and means to protect short-term liquidity, take problematic assets off of financial institutions' balance sheets, and recapitalize Islamic financial institutions. This infrastructure has been installed in Malaysia's case. To control liquidity in the financial sector, the central bank uses a variety of Islamic financial tools. An established Islamic money market bolster this. Furthermore, the lender and a comprehensive deposit insurance scheme that covers both conventional and Islamic deposits are included in Malaysia's financial safety net structure. Additionally, the Deposit Insurance Corporation has been granted enough statutory authority to guarantee a quick, efficient, and affordable resolution in order to protect the stability of the Islamic financial system. This includes, among other things, the regulatory authority and responsibility to guarantee the quick settlement of financially troubled organizations. In order to determine if Islamic financial institutions could withstand severe circumstances, the regulatory oversight also periodically tests the institutions' resilience.

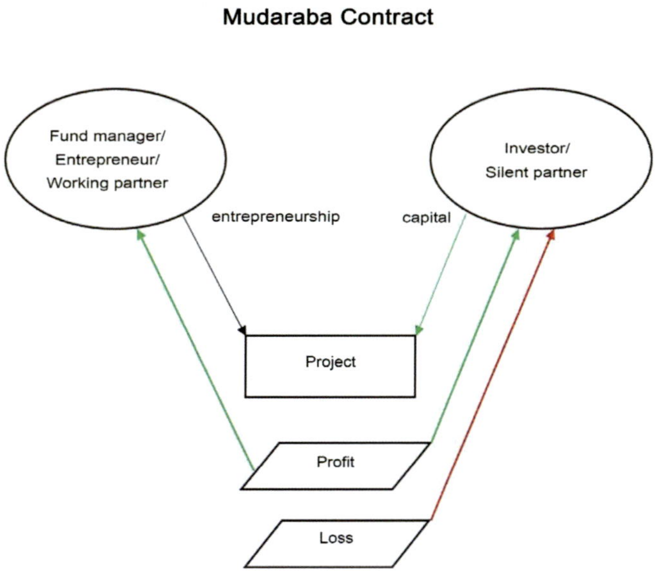

Figure 3.2. *Mudaraba contract.*

Source: https://en.wikipedia.org/wiki/Profit_and_loss_sharing#/media/File:Mudaraba.jpg, Creative Commons License.

3.5. PREVENTION

In order to prevent a catastrophe, it is essential to implement coordinated actions, such as ongoing investigations of potential weaknesses in the Islamic financial system. A prompt response, if necessary, would be made possible by the central banks' close coordination in this regard. To ensure that the necessary stakeholders realize their benefits, the infrastructure must also incorporate Shariah principles. When a significant decline occurs, the Islamic financial sector can prevent drastic measures by maintaining positive relationships with clients and other important players. The Islamic financial idea of promoting justice, fairness, and shared accountability is in line with this. Because Islamic finance places a strong emphasis on moral market behavior, its aim goes beyond simply achieving growth and financial performance. Adopting a thorough framework for consumer protection is essential to this. When Singapore introduced its first global Sukuk program, a sovereign rated Sukuk facility, in January 2009, it grabbed the lead in the Islamic banking industry (Muhammad Al-Amine, 2016). Singapore, a nation with a majority of non-Muslims, first showed interest in Islamic banking and finance in 2005. Singapore views Islamic finance as a component of financial services that could be provided by the nation, given its status as a significant global financial hub. Singapore is a country under common law. It also passes its own laws because it is a republic. Only to the degree that it does not contradict with Singapore's statutory laws does the common law apply. The rules of judicial precedent are followed when implementing the law. When the law and the facts are similar, the Singaporean courts will consider decisions rendered by the courts of other common law jurisdictions.

Under the Islamic financing arrangement based on Mudaraba, the financial institution oversees the customer's money deposits and pays the customer from the profits generated by using the money according to a predetermined schedule. The customer's effective return on the deposit is represented by the payment they received. All capital losses are borne by the client. A fee is paid to the financial institution for its management services. The arrangement is comparable to a traditional deposit where the consumer receives interest payments. For income tax purposes, the effective return that the financial institution pays the customer for using the money is treated in the same way as interest. The consumer must receive payment in accordance with the amount they deposited. Interest income from licensed Singapore banks is exempt from income tax in Singapore for both residents and non-residents. The customer's effective return from the financial institution will not be subject to taxes. As of December 31, 2008, Singapore had Double Tax Treaties with 69 nations, including Australia, Japan, and the United Kingdom. Interest is defined as revenue from debt-claims of every sort under the tax treaty, which is based on the OECD model. The effective return as defined by the tax treaty applies to the Murabaha, Mudaraba, and Ijara contracts. If an investor's effective return from a financial institution in Singapore is liable to income tax in Singapore, the maximum amount of that tax will be the treaty concessionary rate. The investor cannot conduct any business through a permanent establishment in Singapore and must be a tax resident of a nation with whom Singapore has a double tax treaty. The oil and gas industry completely dominates Brunei's economy. Therefore, Brunei has the problem of diversifying its economy, much like so many other oil economies. Brunei's high quality of living has been made possible by its substantial hydrocarbon exports.

3.6. GROWTH

Future growth will be contingent upon Brunei's ability to diversify its economy, the discovery of additional gas and oil wells, and the volatility of the oil price (Sovacool, 2010). As part of its economic diversification strategy, Brunei hopes to establish itself as a global hub for offshore finance, specifically targeting the Islamic banking and capital market sectors. In order to position Brunei as an equal partner in the globalization of financial and commercial activities, the Brunei International Financial Centre (BIFC) was founded in July 2000. Its goals include diversifying, growing, and enhancing the value-added financial services sector of the Brunei economy. The purpose of BIFC was to concentrate its growth on the small but increasing Islamic money market niche. With a vast array of international laws at its disposal, the BIFC is well-equipped to support global banking, insurance, and takaful operations as well as transactions involving mutual funds, securities, international trusts, and global business management. Within the Ministry of Finance, the BIFC is a regulatory organization tasked with overseeing licensee behavior and business operations within the financial center's boundaries.

In September 2008, the Bruneian government (Figure 3.3) introduced two new laws, the Islamic Banking Order (2008), and the Islamic Takaful Order (2008), with the support of the Sultan and Yang Di-Pertuan of Negara Brunei Darussalam. The purpose of these laws was to strengthen Brunei's position as the region's expanding center for Islamic banking and finance. There are two types of banking practiced in Brunei Darussalam: Islamic banking and mainstream banking. Brunei has aggressively promoted Islamic banking as a substitute for traditional banking during the last 15 years. The foundation of the Brunei Islamic Trust Fund, also known as Perbadanan Tabung Amanah Islam Brunei (TAIB), in September 1991 was the first step toward the development of the nation's Islamic financial system. Subsequently, the two conventional banks underwent conversions. The state-owned Development Bank of Brunei became the Islamic Development Bank of Brunei (IDBB) in July 2000, while the International Bank of Brunei became the Islamic Bank of Brunei (IBB) in January 1993. The IBB and the IDBB then combined to become the Bank Islam Brunei Darussalam in 2006 (BIBD) (Saiti, 2019). The Islamic Banking Order 2008 was recently introduced with the intention of growing the Islamic banking industry in Brunei while also enhancing competition among participants by leveling and stimulating the oversight and regulation of Islamic banking operations. With the implementation of the new Islamic Banking Order, a Shariah Advisory Body made up of three or more Muslim religious scholars is now mandatory for all Islamic banks operating in the nation. This regulation's requirement that two of the religious scholars be Bruneians is one of its intriguing features. It should be noted that the Islamic Banking Order of 2008 stipulates that local Islamic banks must have a minimum paid-up capital of B$ 100 million, or B$ 500 million for a foreign head office and B$30 million for a net head office fund.

Figure 3.3. *Bruneian government (Islamic Bank).*

Source: https://en.wikipedia.org/wiki/Bank_Islam_Brunei_Darussalam#/media/File:Bibd_HQ_in_Bandar_Seri_Begawan.jpg, Creative Commons License.

3.7. IBO

The International Banking Order (IBO) 2000 governs international banking services provided to non-residents of Brunei. Although accepting deposits is included in the traditional definition of banking, the IBO acknowledges that this is not an advanced international bank's focus. The IBO broadens its scope to reflect the developments and trends in the banking sector. Growing takaful operations in Brunei have increased competition for the traditional insurance providers, particularly since the establishment of the first shariah-compliant businesses in the 1990s. Because they primarily deal with automobile coverage, Islamic insurance and takaful operations currently account for 50% of the non-life insurance market. The traditional portion of the insurance industry is the only one governed by the Insurance Order, which was implemented in 2006. Despite not being subject to the insurance order, takaful providers have made an effort to adhere to the same rules as traditional businesses and have started using the General Insurance Association of Brunei Darussalam's recommendations. The Ministry of Finance introduced the revised Islamic Takaful Order 2008 in September of that year. The goal of the new order is to regulate the Takaful business in Brunei Darussalam and to serve other related purposes. The order is a new piece of comprehensive legislation designed to regulate the domestic Takaful business and create a fair playing field for Takaful operators and conventional insurers (Figure 3.4).

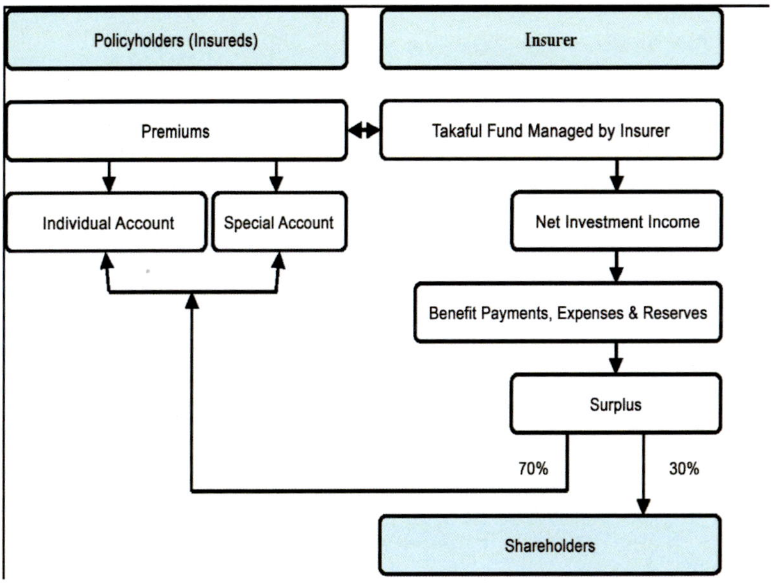

Figure 3.4. *Takaful operators.*

Source: Maysami, R.C., & Kwon, W. J., (2001). An analysis of Islamic Takaful Insurance – A Cooperative Insurance Mechanism, Creative Commons License.

An IBC, a foreign international company incorporated under the International Business Companies Order 2000 (IBCO), a company incorporated under the (domestic) Companies Act, or a company registered under Part IX of the Companies Act that holds a valid license under IITO shall conduct international insurance business, i.e., non-domestic business, conducted with non-residents, with the exception of reinsurance. Furthermore, unless he obtains a license relevant to such a company, no individual including a corporation may engage in any business as an international insurance manager, international underwriting manager, or international insurance broker. A licensee's services are restricted to those listed in the license they have been granted, and they can only be rendered to other licensees in accordance with the order. Services pertaining to domestic insurance business are prohibited, although a qualified international insurance broker is permitted to manage the reinsurance of domestic insurance business in spite of any other written laws. Now that the Islamic capital markets are beginning to pick up speed and become a thriving marketplace, Brunei is positioned to benefit, particularly in the Islamic banking and capital market sectors. Brunei has made important progress since the beginning of 2006 in its endeavor to become one of the emerging Islamic capital markets in the area. Not only is Brunei an Islamic state, but its sovereignty, political and economic stability, and most crucially, its substantial liquidity, all play significant roles in its performance as one of the region's Islamic capital markets. The country has created the necessary policies, incentives, rules, and infrastructure during the last few years to support the growth of an Islamic capital market. When Brunei created the world's first short-term investment Islamic commercial paper, the Sukuk Al-Ijara, valued at US $98.1 million in 2006, it became the first country in the world to forego traditional capital money markets, demonstrating its seriousness and effort to develop its Islamic capital market.

The country's desire to become a regional Islamic capital market is evident from this attempt alone, given the oil-rich nation has substantial liquidity and almost no debt. Currently, more than 200 funds are available through Brunei's financial institutions, with less than 10% of those funds adhering to Shariah (Maali et al., 2006). Just seven of the roughly 20 mutual funds that are registered with the MFO comply with Shariah. It is anticipated that a greater number of mutual funds, both conventional and Shariah-compliant, will be launched and registered in Brunei in 2009. Financial institutions are now encouraging and assisting in the development and construction of Shariah-compliant funds in the country. Examples of these institutions are Malaysia's CIMB and Brunei Investment Commercial Bank Capital, through its subsidiary BICB Capital. Given the rising demand for Shariah-compliant funds from both the public and private sectors, it is anticipated that the number of funds and financial institutions offering these kinds of products will increase. Under the direction of BIFC, mutual fund operations are governed by the Mutual Funds Order 2001 (MFO). An attempt is being made to guarantee that these monies are registered with and under the control of the BIFC with the implementation of the MFO. The MFO offers the legal framework for the supervision and licensing of conventional and Shariah-compliant mutual funds, as well as for individuals advertising and offering services in relation to fund-related activities in Brunei Darussalam. It permits licenses for fund operators, including fund managers and fund administrators, to operate out of and within Brunei.

3.8. MFO

The MFO regulates more than just traditional funds, in contrast to the majority of existing rules. The MFO contains significant clauses that are crucial to Brunei Darussalam's efforts to produce and promote funds that adhere to Shariah. For instance, Section 8(1) makes it clear that the authority will only issue or grant a Mutual Fund license or permits for an Islamic fund in the event that arrangements are made for the nomination of a suitable Shariah Council. The BIFC is working to strengthen the laws and is now upgrading the MFO to bring it into compliance with modern international standards. This will encourage more funds that comply with Shariah to be founded and registered in the country. The Securities Order 2001 provides the regulation and administrative activities linked to financial exchanges and investment-related activities in the nation, while the MFO offers the legal framework for fund-related activities. Intermediaries who administer, deal in, or give advice about securities, including those listed and traded on such an exchange, are subject to regulation. The definition of securities in this order is not limited; rather, it is inclusive rather than exhaustive. Stocks and shares in public or corporate entities, debt instruments like bonds and unsecured bonds, depository receipts, loan stock, bills, notes, financial instruments, and other debt instruments of governmental or non-governmental entities, whether corporate or unincorporated, are all included in the definition. Most importantly, the SO permits intermediaries to operate in and out of Brunei, offering their services to both local and foreign firms, especially as investment advisers or investment representatives, to anybody interested in providing investment-related services in Brunei.

Investment-related activities and funds have a number of advantages and incentives. For instance, with no restrictions on capital contributions, Shariah-compliant funds that have been meticulously designed under the IBCO can be made available to both domestic and foreign investors. As an alternative, funds for international investors may also be established under the ITO. Activities relating to investments and funds that are established under the IBCO and ITO are completely exempt from taxes. Despite the possibility of corporate taxation, companies formed under the domestic companies' act may be eligible for pioneer status, which exempts them from corporate taxation for a predetermined amount of time. The government of the host nation must provide strong support and guidance for market development, particularly when it comes to regulatory matters. Brunei has put in place the necessary policy measures to advance and expand its Islamic capital market. The potential for developing Brunei as a regional Islamic capital market is advantageous to the country as well as local and foreign players looking to seize the opportunities in Brunei's emerging and exciting Islamic capital market. This can be achieved by combining the various infrastructures, policies, benefits, and incentives offered by the Government of Brunei and local players, particularly financial institutions. There are still challenges that must be solved before Brunei can eventually establish a successful Islamic money market in this area. Due to its limited local market and comparatively small population, Brunei's Islamic money market may also be small. Currently, some Takaful companies offer Islamic insurance services, while other financial institutions offer Islamic banking facilities. It might not be possible to add more competitors since doing so would decrease the current firms' market share. Product innovation is happening slowly. Currently, Islamic banks in Brunei offer a range of financing and savings options, such as Mudaraba investments and Al-Wadiah savings accounts, which are founded on well-known Islamic principles. To date, Brunei has only created short-term Sukuk Al-Ijara in the capital market sector. The Brunei currency market has a lot of space to grow. One instance is the Takaful market, where Brunei's Takaful sector currently lacks family and medical Takaful products.

Because there isn't a central body that is widely recognized for Islamic banking and finance, Shariah principles vary between Islamic nations (Haqqi, 2017). For this reason, Islamic banks establish their own religious boards. With the exception of Islamic money market products, Islamic banks must obtain clearance for every new product from their local religious boards or Shariah advisors. The same financial products may be accepted by one board but rejected by another due to differences in how various schools of thought interpret Islamic principles; as a result, the same instruments may not be accepted in other nations. The absence of a system to guarantee public access to information about Islamic financial services and products, as well as the lack of qualified Islamic banking and finance professionals who can manage and analyze portfolios and create novel products in accordance with Islamic financial principles, are further concerns regarding the growth of the Islamic money market in Brunei. An efficient legal, regulatory, and supervisory framework is the distinguishing feature of a well-developed financial infrastructure, which includes the establishment of an Islamic money market in Brunei. In actuality, it is an essential and necessary part of the financial structure. The Shariah Council must be established in order to ensure that the policies governing strategic direction and the handling of financial transactions adhere to the Shariah. Only then will the Islamic financial system function as intended. An effective judicial system that can handle any matter involving Islamic banking and finance would be required to support this. The industry's expansion has been aided by a range of products and services offered by conventional and Islamic banking and finance. Throughout the past 10 or so years, academics and industry participants have effectively produced financial solutions that underpin the industry's viability. Due to the complexity of some of these products, risk analysts and accountants must be able to respond appropriately by researching the associated risks and the most effective ways to record and report the transactions in the financial statements.

Islam holds people responsible for their deeds. Individuals' actions unintentionally impact society and the community. This suggests that making a conscious effort is necessary to guarantee that a person's activities including their private commercial dealings must be lawful, equitable, and fair. Furthermore, an individual's acts must contribute to and positively impact the general welfare of society. As such, people have a genuine and implicit stewardship role in the society in which they reside. The financial reports for Islamic financial institutions have been successfully formalized and standardized due to the standards that have been developed throughout time. A profit is only legitimate when it comes with the risk of loss. It should be highlighted that this idea is not the same as a game of chance, in which there is no planned risk involved in the outcome. The chance of holding the correct cards or tossing the dice correctly would be an example of calculated risk in the context of gambling. Most notably, there is no actual output from gambling and the outcome of a win/lose position is known instantly. Because the Islamic bank works in cooperation with its customers, the success or failure of those firms has a direct impact on the bank's earnings. This is contrasted with a traditional bank, where the clients' business performance is considered incidental. Since interest profits are the foundation of conventional lending, the bank's risk is directly related to the borrower's failure to pay interest on planned dates. As a result, the bank's performance and profitability are unrelated to the performance of the investments made by its clients. Instead, when they impose penalties for late interest payments in the case of a customer default, conventional banks push their clients into more difficult financial situations. Risks to the company's finances that directly impact it are known as financial risks, and they often comprise credit, market, liquidity, and operational risks. Numerous other risks, like those pertaining to management and reputation, could also have a direct impact on the business.

3.9. ACCOUNTING

In the Enron case (Figure 3.5), the business postponed declaring its income and registering its obligations (Baker & Hayes, 2004). Accounting guidelines provide that income cannot be recognized until the transaction is finished and the buyer has received ownership. To accumulate sales that were made after the accounting period, the company did not, however, close its accounting books at the conclusion of the accounting period. This had a positive impact on sales turnover, demonstrating the management's success in hitting its sales goals. Additionally, they recorded payments later than expected and recognized revenue before services were provided. The stockholders were pleased with the increased income and profit resulting from these creative accounting tactics. In WorldCom's case, the corporation covered up $3.8 billion in expenses over a 15-month period in an attempt to significantly cut costs and record higher profit margins for the reported accounting period. The aforementioned risk may be categorized as fraud, or management risk. But this unintentionally weakens and trivializes the significance of accounting risk, which sometimes results from the gaps in accepted accounting standards.

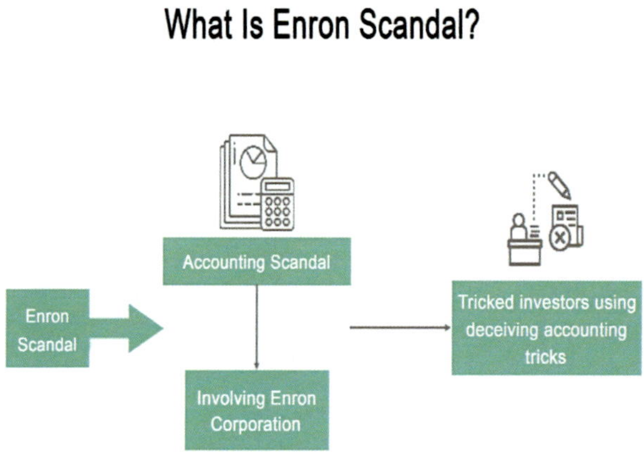

Figure 3.5. *Enron case.*

Source: https://www.wallstreetmojo.com/enron-scandal/, Creative Commons License.

Accounting issues that result from inadequate accounting disclosure or incorrect handling of accounting items are not unusual. Thus, it becomes necessary to handle accounting risk as a distinct risk factor, much like legal risk concerns. The financier and the entrepreneur will split any firm profits according to a predetermined profit ratio. In contrast, the financier bears full responsibility for any losses incurred, and the entrepreneur forfeits all time and effort invested in the business. The only exception to the norm is that the entrepreneur will be held legally liable for any losses if it is shown that he was careless or mishandled the business.

3.10. DEPOSITS

Customers deposit their excess funds in the bank according to a profit-sharing arrangement. In this instance, the bank is a Mudarib, and the client is a Rabb-Ul-Maal (Ilieva et al., 2017). Banks use the Mudaraba style of financing to entice clients to invest; as a result, the funds are recorded on the balance sheet's liabilities side. The bank positions itself as a middleman between the capital providers and the fund consumers who require the funds as a source of capital. The bank invests the money in companies that it believes will be attractive and profitable in its role as an intermediary. Either limited or unrestricted investment accounts are available for Mudaraba investment accounts. When a person has an unlimited investment account, they give the bank the freedom to decide how to use their money. These monies are typically invested alongside current account holders' deposits and the bank's own capital accounts. When opening a restricted investment account, account holders give the bank specific directions on where and how to invest their money. It is forbidden for banks to mix their own money with the restricted investment funds. The Islamic banks do not deal with granting loans to entrepreneurs in the Mudaraba style of financing. In traditional banking, banks provide the borrower with banking facilities in the form of loans and demand periodic interest payments. In Islamic banking, the bank shares in profits and losses and functions like a partner in a business enterprise. As a result, the Islamic bank receives a larger portion of the company's profits than the traditional bank does via interest. This is as a result of the Islamic bank accepting more risk and benefiting more from the entire banking transaction.

3.11. FINANCIERS

First-tier financiers and second-tier entrepreneurs are brought together by the bank. In both layers, the financier has the same risk exposures. The depositor places his money and gives over control to the bank's expertise in the first layer. Similar to this, in the second layer, the bank transfers the money to the business owner and defers to his judgment and business sense after requiring the appropriate level of caution and diligence. Because the financier has no further involvement in the use or management of the money, there is a significant level of risk. The entrepreneur alone is responsible for carrying out the fund. For this reason, the trust issue is critical. The lender needs to have faith that the Mudarib will use the money for legitimate and beneficial business ventures and then declare a genuine profit. For this transaction to be beneficial, the Islamic principles of honesty, trustworthiness, and integrity is essential. Thus, mudaraba is a financial product built on trust. Accounting bodies should enforce accounting standards that can mitigate and reduce transactional risk given the exposure to risk.

Information that influences the perilousness of a bank's investment portfolio should be available to users, regardless of whether the investment is restricted or unconstrained. Information needs to be more frequent and detailed for the benefit of both first and second-tier funders in order to make it easier to monitor the entrepreneur's actions and reduce the possibility that the money will be misused. The bank serves as a middleman. The willingness of depositors to invest their money in the bank emphasizes that the bank should not let them down in their role as Mudarib (Maali & Atmeh, 2015). Any minor setback will damage the bank's reputation as a Mudarib. The investors are unaware of what ventures or businesses they are funding, and the entrepreneurs or businesses have no idea where the initial funding came from. Banks established agreements and covenants to guarantee that clients' cash are secured, allowing for the monitoring of investments. If the money is used for a project, the bank will make sure that one of the terms and conditions includes an agreement requiring the business owner to provide regular updates on the project's status. The project site will be often visited by the account's relationship manager, who will also review reports that the business owner has issued. When funds are utilized to buy certain equity investments, like Sukuk or company shares, the fund managers will carry out performance reviews and research studies to make sure that the company is performing as planned and that any overdue dividends or returns are paid on a quarterly, half-yearly, or other agreed-upon basis. The problem still exists because the information the bank gathers is not shared with stakeholders and interested parties, despite the fact that internal auditors and employees of the bank carry out these measures conscientiously and successfully. This is due to the lack of a standardized structure that accounting authorities have recommended be used for such disclosures, as well as the lack of legislative or legal requirements for them.

Certain banks only disclose customer deposits which often account for over 60% of the bank's total liabilities in their financial reports through an appendix that refers to the financial statements' notes. It may be argued that only pertinent depositors should have access to the qualitative data for high value limited investments. However, for general depositors, fund managers and accounting relationship managers should also collect qualitative data in addition to quantitative data. All interested depositors should have access to these reports, which ought to be generated on a regular basis. Standard reporting formats for qualitative information should be established by the accounting organizations and made legally mandatory for all banks and financial institutions. In addition to serving as a deterrent, the requirement of legal disclosure of such information will make banks more careful in their investment selections. To get at a more precise estimate, the banks may potentially decide to use multiple approaches. Mortgage loans are typically utilized to calculate impairment of loss since they typically have a high loan to value ratio. The idea of accounting for declining value in a Mudaraba investment can be implemented, even if it is evident that the investment is not a loan and has no debt associated with it. Investment assets include stock market, real estate, project development, and trade of goods comprise mudaraba financing. These assets' values are subject to change in value. Therefore, if banks neglect to declare impairment losses, there will be an information imbalance that could lead to incorrect reporting in the final statements. A competitive rate of return for fund placements is a requirement for depositors and investors in order to keep account holders with the bank. Owing to the pressure on the banks to keep account holders and draw in new ones, the banks may decide to give up their claim to the full amount of their profit as Mudarib (first tier). As a result, the bank's owners bear the increased risk instead of the account holders. Thus, this might be seen as a payment made by the bank to keep its clients loyal. However, such a strategy would ultimately work against the interests of the stockholders. Therefore, the Profit Equalization Reserve or PER, was added to the bank's liabilities side of the balance sheet in order to stop this behavior. By transferring a portion of the Mudaraba income before awarding the Mudarib share, the PER account aims to return the relocated commercial risk to the account holders. The goal of this accounting trick is to raise owners' equity while maintaining a specific rate of return on investment for the holders of investment accounts.

3.12. PER

The formation of PERs for the purpose of managing account holders' funds may have unethical consequences. The bank must pay account holders the real profit amount owed to them based on the pre-agreed profit ratio in order to uphold its fiduciary duty. The account holders may gain or lose from this accounting method because the amount transferred varies from year to year based on the total amount in the PER account. For the benefit of the account holders, it is crucial to guarantee that they receive all that is owed to them, but it is equally necessary to guarantee that the bank's survival continues to be a concern. The Islamic Financial Services Board (IFSB) suggested that the pre-defined contractual requirements be followed when determining the basis for allocating funds to be transferred to PER in order to resolve this conundrum (Ashrafkashani, 2015). The directors of the Islamic financial institution should formally review these terms before the account holders approve them. A formal agreement from the account holders should also be acquired before transferring funds to the Islamic financial institution. An additional option could be for the bank to receive the transferred funds in its account and agree to pay out a smaller portion of the profit to the owners. It makes sense that the shareholders' earnings would vary depending on how well the bank performs, as they are the ones who would typically stay on as members of the financial institutions.

One of the funding methods that Islam approves of is mudaraba financing. Banks have found this financing method unappealing when it comes to the asset side of the balance sheet, despite its effective application on the liabilities side. This is because Mudaraba is a contract dependent on trust, making it susceptible to perils related to morality and other factors. Even if the bank works in a risky and unpredictable environment, it's crucial to be open and enhance the regularity and quality of information to help account holders make wise judgments. It is imperative to acknowledge that the Accounting and Auditing Organization for Islamic Financial Institutions or AAOIFI has made important contributions to the field of corporate governance through the development of accounting standards that Islamic financial institutions are required to adhere to (Mnif & Tahari, 2020). Regretfully, as AAOIFI is not a statutory authority, it is unable to enforce the Standards' implementation. As a result of their weak legal position, many banks have not followed its accounting regulations to the letter. It is appropriate that these standards be granted legal force and accorded the same standing as IAS. There is little doubt that this will enhance and standardize the financial reporting requirements among Islamic financial institutions. For any financial system to thrive, a strong legal and regulatory foundation is essential. The Malaysian government has acknowledged this and demonstrated its commitment by creating policies that are favorable to the industry, changing current regulations, and passing new legislation to support Islamic finance. In the upcoming years, Islamic finance in Malaysia is expected to achieve further breakthroughs.

3.13. MALAYSIA SITUATION

Malaysia has led the way among Muslim countries in terms of economic advancement. It has demonstrated remarkable political resolve by setting up the framework required for the growth of Islamic banking and finance (IBF). The government has also put measures into place to create an Islamic financial market that includes an Islamic money market (IMM) and an Islamic capital market (ICM) in order to further the development of a comprehensive Islamic financial system and support the IBF sector (Thani & Hussain, 2010). Recognizing the importance of a strong legal and regulatory foundation for the growth of any financial system, the government has demonstrated its commitment to advancing

Islamic finance by creating laws that are favorable to the sector, modifying current legislation, and passing new legislation. The Islamic Banking Act (IBA) of 1983 marked the beginning of the conceptualization of the framework specifically designed to support the growth of Islamic finance (Engku Ali & Oseni, 2017). The Islamic Bank Act (IBA) mandates that Islamic banks adhere to responsible banking standards and is applicable to fully operational Islamic banks. Similar to other banks, Islamic banks are subject to the same supervision and regulation by the central bank, Bank Negara Malaysia (BNM) (Figure 3.6).

Figure 3.6. *Bank Negara Malaysia.*

Source: https://en.wikipedia.org/wiki/Central_Bank_of_Malaysia#/media/File:Bank_Negara_Malaysia_(230715-0916).jpg, Creative Commons License.

To guarantee that its activities comply with Shariah, IBA mandates that an Islamic bank establish its own Shariah Advisory Council, made up of certified Shariah specialists. The Banking and Financial Institutions Act 1989 or BAFIA, which regulates traditional banks, was then amended. Section 124 of the BAFIA permits conventional banks to conduct Islamic banking and financial operations as long as they adhere to BNM policies and procedures. Now that more businesses are able to sell IBF products, BNM has established its own Shariah Advisory Council to help it keep an eye on industry norms and practices. The adoption of the Takaful Act (TA) in 1984 marked the beginning of the Islamic insurance sector. The TA permits Islamic insurance businesses to operate. The TA emphasizes that the fundamental idea of Takaful is the offering of insurance as a business model that complies with Shariah and is founded on the Islamic precepts of Al-Takaful (assurance) and Al-Mudaraba (commercial profit-sharing contract). The financial system's demand for insurance that complies with Shariah is met by the creation of Takaful business.

Chapter 4

TECHNIQUES IN ISLAMIC BANKING

Contents

4.1. INTRODUCTION

Riba/riba-free banking, often known as RF banking, is a socially conscious and faith-based financial method (Alam et al., 2019). This is a service that seeks to assist individuals of various backgrounds and faiths. It is thought that RF banking is in high demand in the West and the United States, as well as in a large number of developing countries across the globe. RF banking is a system based on renting tangible assets, such as houses, businesses, and tools and equipment, rather than money at a rate known as the interest rate. It is gradually taking the place of Islamic banking. The idea that church and state should be kept apart is deeply ingrained in American culture. It begins with the word riba, which is related to the Old Testament phrase ribit. Riba is the practice of renting money to people at a charge known as interest, thereby taking advantage of those who are in need of money to cover their fundamental needs. An ethically conscious banking brand with a strong sense of community spirit is called RF banking. The Judeo-Christian-Islamic principles that are becoming more prevalent in America are embodied in this particular type of banking (Burr, 2005). A new way of living is provided by RF banking and finance, which eliminates the need to bear the weight of constantly mounting debt from needless overuse of loans such as home equity lines of credit, and loans of all other kinds, both secured and unsecured. RF banking is meticulous about what and who it finances. For instance, RF banks don't finance companies that are involved in gambling or alcohol, like casinos or liquor stores. Additionally, it doesn't support firms that treat their workers unfairly or that disregard the environment. It is thought that RF banking would reconstruct for the world and the United States the features of the financial movement. Based on operational experience, clients from a wide range of religious backgrounds, including Hindu, Buddhist, Jewish, Christian, and Muslim, value and enjoy using the principles of RF banking.

4.2. FINANCIAL PRODUCTS

Numerous governments and municipalities in Europe engage with Islamic financial products, primarily bonds (sukuk). There are Islamic banks and/or financing corporations in many Asian countries. One of the world's most advanced and innovative Islamic banking sectors is found in Malaysia. The worst housing crisis to ever hit the United States occurred in 2007 and 2008 (Schwartz, 2012). The Great Depression's economic collapse was overshadowed by this disaster. This time, the main economies were impacted by the catastrophe. Mortgage-backed securities (MBS) were marketed as high-quality securities and sold to commercial and investment banks worldwide. Investors found that these were not AAA-rated securities after all, as the real estate market crashed, and many mortgages stopped making payments. The biggest banks in America and around the world suffered enormous losses as a result of this enormous disparity, which led to the collapse of giant banks and sharp drops in global stock markets. The financial sector suffered from a profound lack of confidence between chief investment officers and bank management as a result of these occurrences. As a result, a large number of institutions in the US and other countries had financial documents that were soon illiquid. As a result, there was a severe shortage of money, which sparked a global credit crisis. Due to this predicament, some banks have decided not to assist borrowing requirements in order to maintain short-term liquidity. Several banks around the globe awoke to find their capital completely gone or significantly diminished. A number of well-known American banks, including Lehman Brothers, were declared bankrupt. Hundreds of billions of dollars in write-offs were declared by other companies. In order to help the banks, insurance firms, and financing corporations get more capital, the governments of the United States and Europe proposed financial rescue packages totaling more than $2 trillion.

4.3. MORTGAGE

The United States government assumed control of the massive mortgage finance companies and is currently formulating strategies to save other sectors of the economy, such as the auto sector. However, many Americans lost their savings particularly the hardworking middle-class families that aspired to acquire a home, prepare for a decent retirement, or save so they could afford to send their kids and grandkids to better schools. They saved money through retirement and pension plans, the assets of which were invested in mutual funds or the stock of the bankrupt corporation. After losing their employment, some people also lost their homes. The fundamental ideas introduced by Abraham, Moses, and Jesus were revitalized by the religion of Islam as it is interpreted from the Qur'an and the tradition of Prophet Muhammad. To be a Muslim is to surrender our will to God's will by worshiping him alone and following his commands, which he gave to all of his prophets. From a conceptual standpoint, it is possible to view Islam as a continuation of the Judeo-Christian-Islamic heritage that traces its roots to Abraham, the father and patriarch of all prophets.

4.4. TEACHINGS

The teachings of Judaism, Christianity, and Islam forbade lending money and charging interest, ribit, and riba. It's also fascinating to note that many other religions and ideologies, like Buddhism and Hinduism, forbid charging interest. Muslims are taught that engaging in the culture and practice of interest, charging interest on loans, borrowing with interest, and witnessing contracts that involve interest is one of the worst sins and is divinely forbidden (haram). Borrowing money with interest, or riba, is not a conduct that is accepted in society or religion. Borrowing money and paying interest is socially embarrassing in most Muslim societies and should only be done in extreme cases. In Judaism and Christianity, it is likewise divinely forbidden to charge interest. The history of the prohibition of interest from the original teachings of Moses in the Torah (Jewish Bible) and the teachings of Jesus in the Christian Bible should be studied, learned, and considered critically in order to understand how these attitudes evolved into the laxer practices of today. Asking a follower of each religion who is an authority in the financial industry to summarize the position and original teachings of their religion regarding interest charging would be a more appropriate and credible method of researching the charging of interest in Judaism and Christianity. From there, one can discuss how these unambiguous Judeo-Christian-Islamic prohibitions against interest charging were altered and reconstructed to become the accepted practice of charging interest today.

Both the old and new testaments' fundamental teachings support the notion that charging interest on money borrowed, rent for the use of money is unfair since it entails selling something that doesn't exist, which always results in inequality and is against justice. The Islamic perspective on riba is not all that dissimilar from this. Understanding the background of the ban of interest charging in the Jewish and Christian Bibles helps to clarify riba charging and its divine prohibition (haram) in Shariah (Lewis & Kaleem, 2019). A different mindset and way of life could eventually result from this unity, which could ultimately lead to social harmony, prosperity, and peace in both local communities in the United States and throughout the world. It would also eventually improve understanding and collaboration between the leaders of the three Abrahamic faiths and the people of those faiths. Judaism, Christianity, and Islam all began with heavenly revelations that forbade the heinous act of exploiting the impoverished and destitute by charging them interest on the loans that they required to meet their fundamental necessities and survive. It is a tough choice to give up a bite (qard) of one's own money to those in need as an interest-free loan because there is no return on the investment. The Judeo-Christian-Islamic revelations view this qard as a loan to God, who guarantees a bountiful return on it both in this life and the next. Some wealthy and powerful people may reluctantly lend money to the needy and impoverished with the goal of flaunting their wealth in public or using the money as a means of controlling the poor by taking advantage of their labor or eventually seizing their homes, lands, and crops. In the past, some wealthy people donated their inferior possessions and meals to the underprivileged. They also reminded the needy and impoverished of the privileges that had been bestowed upon them by using harsh words and deeds. Such behavior is forbidden by the core precepts of Islam, Christianity, and Judaism.

Islam took Shari'ah a step further by claiming that the only recognized loan is Qard Hassan, or "a good loan," and by institutionalizing lending to the impoverished through divine decree. It is regarded by God as the one loan that is permitted in Islam. Depending on the particular circumstances and requirements of the borrowing poor and needy, the Qard Hassan can be a term loan with a time restriction with flexible and benevolent repayment terms, or, in most situations, without one. In actuality, the Qard Hassan is viewed in Shari'ah as a donation that the heavily indebted (for justifiable reasons) should return whenever they are able to. The owner's qard is seen as a loan to God. No further direct or indirect benefit such as labor, free use of the debtor's home, or receiving gifts from the borrower can be derived from a loan of this kind in Islam, as it is in the original teachings of Judaism and Christianity. This is because these are regarded as services that have a value and are therefore considered payments of implied interest. Shari'ah even advocates for the repayment to be done at the impoverished borrower's place of residence in order to spare them from having to cover the cost of transportation, which is essentially an implicit interest payment in and of itself. Judeo-Christian-Islamic laws emphasize that borrowers' dignity must be upheld by not disclosing to third parties about the loans they have received, by not attempting to exploit them, by not pressuring them to repay the loans faster, and by never even frowning in their faces. Furthermore, if the borrower is deeply in debt and unable to repay the loan, the Shariah encourages the Muslim to forgive the debt. Shari'ah also assigns the State's Department of Treasury (Bayt Ul Maal) the duty of collecting alms (Zakah) from the populace and allocating a portion of this revenue to assist those who are deeply indebted and unable to repay their loans. In Islam, almsgiving is known as the ritual of Zakah, which is the ritual of purifying one's assets by returning God's right in these assets. According to Shariah, if the debtor passes away, the lender must pardon the debt out of kindness if the debtor's family is unable to make the payment. The successors are obliged to repay the debt if they are able to do so.

4.5. AGRARIAN SYSTEMS

The agrarian systems that were common when Jesus was sent and the enslavement system of the ancient Egyptians during the time of Moses had been replaced by new global economic systems with the rise of Islam (Moon, 1987). With the growth of vast towns, cities, and villages, the world has advanced. They sought capital to help them grow their firm, finance the items, and increase their commercial activities, not because they were impoverished and in need. The fundamental teachings of the Jewish and Christian Bibles were elaborated upon by Shari'ah, as mandated by the Qur'an and the tradition of Prophet Muhammad, in order to address this need for finance and create divine regulations for financing without riba. Additionally, Prophet Muhammad managed money and conducted business. He was aware of the necessity of funding trade and commercial endeavors. In the seventh century, Islam introduced a more comprehensive set of Judeo-Christian-Islamic regulations pertaining to the funding of commerce and enterprise. The fundamental teachings of Moses and Jesus were developed in order to create a distinct and comprehensive Judeo-Christian-Islamic law (Shari'ah) pertaining to finance. A new riba-free (RF) financial system made possible by this law is suitable for fair and equitable RF banking and finance. The RF finance system views the ability to get credit as a fundamental human right and provides credit to all individuals without distinction. Bringing about peace, justice, fairness, harmony, prosperity, peace of mind, job opportunities, and mutual respect among all people of all faiths and backgrounds is a major goal of the RF Judeo-Christian-Islamic approach. This will pave the way for a wonderful future of peace and happiness for the entire world.

Loans were mainly given out for commercial purposes in the 16th century, rather than for personal use, as life grew considerably less rural and more commercial. There was a search for an acceptable vehicle for this type of business as these loans were necessary for economic success and were not what the Torah originally intended. Rabbis in Poland, and later throughout Eastern Europe, worked to develop and perfect a document known as Heter Iska. The main goal of this text is to change the lender-borrower dynamic to one of investment. The lender/investor and the borrower join forces as partners in the business, with the borrower giving the lender/investor a certain share of the realized profits. By technically redefining the loan as an investment, Jewish businesses were able to flourish without breaking the restrictions that forbid charging interest. To help assure that the lender or investor would not be exposing himself to an unacceptable level of risk and that a certain amount of return would be contractually guaranteed, the Heter Iska was revised multiple times. Even now, many still use Heter Iska. It is commonly known that Prophet Muhammad had several life experiences in addition to being God's appointed prophet. He served as a shepherd, a respected mediator in disputes, a leader in the community, and a dependable custodian of people's money through investments and trading. He learned how the world functions and how business is conducted through business, which also helped him perceive the world. When he was commissioned, there were two main currencies in use. These were the denarius, which was used by the Roman Empire and was made of gold, and the dirham, which was used by the Persian Empire and made of silver.

4.6. TRANSACTIONS

Depending on the location of the transaction, trading in multiple currencies was a crucial part of commerce. The trader's transaction concluded with the conversion of all proceeds into the local currencies of his or her clients, who had given him or her the responsibility of managing their funds and assets. Prophet Muhammad introduced a simple but ground-breaking concept that established fair pricing, the free market system, and outlawed dishonest and fraudulent practices within these markets. The multitude of currencies in use during the time of the Prophet posed a significant obstacle to the establishment of uniform exchange regulations for caravan trade. Finding a fair way to swap different items for various purposes while upholding the values of fair value pricing and fair free markets presented another difficulty. Prophet Muhammad established the guidelines for a new, ground-breaking system that would combine the teachings of Jesus and Moses into a single, riba-free system, thereby representing for the first time in history the establishment of a Judeo-Christian-Islamic system made visible by the Law (Shari'ah). Each item's price was to be compared to a standard commodity produced and/or consumed in each community. The system stipulated that goods and services had to be priced either in terms of ounces of gold or silver or in terms of a common food item in the society, like wheat, barley, dates, or salt during the Prophet's time. In addition, he declared that even in cases where repayment was made after a year and not in person, an ounce of gold borrowed must be returned to its owner in an equivalent amount. The transaction was seen as haram and classified as a riba transaction if the repayment weighed more than an ounce. But one ounce of gold can be exchanged for 10 bushels of wheat immediately or 15 bushels after a year. Under Shariah, this transaction would be acceptable and regarded as halal (Rahman et al., 2017).

People plant and grow food on farms, creating staples like rice, soybeans, wheat, corn, and barley, each of which needs a certain climate and soil preparation. Consequently, different things can be found in different places. Through free commerce, individuals not only conduct business with one another but also grow to know one another and respect one another's cultures. The soil fertility, water supplies for irrigation, the unique weather in each geographic region, and the labor of the people combined with God's gifts would result in the production of fundamental staple food goods that can serve as a benchmark commodity index. The Prophet Muhammad utilized these goods as benchmarks or indices for commerce and pricing. This idea can be compared to the printing press, which creates paper money quickly and easily, save for the political currents and analytical minds that determine, based on monetary and economic data, how much money should be printed or removed from the system. Inflation can be significantly exacerbated by printing an excessive number of banknotes without considering regional economies of production. However, the inverse is also possible. The brilliant brains of statisticians, mathematicians, monetarists, economists, and computer-based models are also essential to the system. These kinds of skills, knowledge, and abilities are valuable and might not be present in every country.

In actuality, most countries lack a substantial pool of these gifted specialists, with the exception of a few developed ones headed by the United States, Germany, and the United Kingdom. Researchers made an effort to follow the criteria by looking at the price histories of various commodities and incorporating the commodity indexation rule into our routine investment activities. Nowadays, the production and demand matrix of the typical citizen in a country is far more diverse, intricate, and unique to that country. People who wish to think in terms of wheat, for instance, wheat farmers cannot survive just on wheat because they also need to purchase farm equipment and fuel for the equipment's operation and heating. He or she will be able to finance these farming endeavors with credit. However, as we are unable to eat or drink gold, we are unable to survive on it. It is important to clarify that when we talk about the idea of commodities indexation, we are not advocating a return to the gold standard. A novel approach that employs a reference commodity, such as gold, or a basket of commodities unique to each country based on its production and demand matrix is highly advised in this case. This approach is comparable to the idea behind the inflation measuring basket and the idea put forth by James Baker III in 1987 to identify economic bubbles in local economies (Goodhart, 2001).

While the Prophet was developing this Law (Shari'ah), another problem arose with barter transactions. The difficulty lay in determining how to handle things that could be measured in multiple ways, such as palm tree dates, which were prevalent during the Prophet Muhammad's time. Palm dates (Figure 4.1) come in three sizes: large, medium, and small. They can also be measured in terms of weight or dates counted. They can be dry or fresh. Another instance involving food products is the exchange of rice for rice, but this could lead to disputes if the rice from one party is of worse quality than that from the other. When it comes to dating, it's possible that one party had bigger dates while the other had smaller, better-quality dates. In both of these situations, regardless of rice size or quality, one can only trade the same weight of rice without an increase utilizing the commodity indexation norm mandated in RF banking and finance. Grapes and dates are two more examples. Both dry dates and raisins are available, as well as fresh dates or grapes. Since dates are dates, they had to be swapped in an equal amount, meaning 100 small dates for 100 huge dates. This problem arose when Prophet Muhammad received a gift of huge, exceptionally fine dates from his Ethiopian friend Bilal. The Prophet was aware that Bilal lacked the funds to purchase these premium big dates. Bilal informed him that after setting aside his share of inferior dates for a while, he went to the market and traded them in for fewer, larger, better-quality dates. He was informed by the Prophet Muhammad that this transaction was forbidden by God and was categorized as riba (haram). When Bilal questioned what he ought to have done, the Prophet replied that he ought to have sold the tiny, inferior dates in exchange for another good or service, like gold, silver, rice, wheat, or barley, and then utilized the money received to purchase the larger, superior dates. In this manner, deceit (gharar), fabrication, and meddling with market forces would be reduced, if not completely eradicated. The proper operation of supply and demand in the market is made possible by this process, which serves to standardize and stabilize markets.

Figure 4.1. *Palm dates.*

Source: https://en.wikipedia.org/wiki/Date_palm#/media/File:Dates005.jpg, Creative Commons License.

4.7. FRAMEWORK

It establishes the framework for reasonable pricing of goods and services within an open and free market, based on actual market values. The foundation of the RF banking brand is the true measured fair market rent of real estate, companies, and services rather than the rental of money at an interest rate. For instance, think about purchasing a home. The residence should be marked to market by both the buyer seeking RF financing and the RF finance institution. The best method to achieve that is to find out how much a comparable house would rent or lease for in terms of US dollars per square foot if it were located in the same neighborhood and had comparable characteristics. When considering the purchase transaction as an investment, the rate of return on investment is determined using the mutually agreed-upon market leasing rate. The RF bank continues to finance the property if the rate of return on investment makes economic sense, that is, if it is equal to or greater than the projected return by our RF investors. Furthermore, the RF bank makes every effort to ensure that the monthly payments under the RF style of financing are on par with those provided by banks established in Riba. An extremely low return suggests that the investment would be of lower quality; the RF bank would not finance it, and the RF banker would advise the customer not to make the investment. It is crucial to remember that the terms of payment, including the sale price and the repayment period (term) agreed upon by the consumer and the RF financial institution, are final. For instance, if the customer had a valid reason to extend the agreed-upon payment term from five years to seven years, the agreed-upon sale price would remain unchanged; otherwise, the transaction would be considered riba al Jahiliyah or Riba Al Nasi'ah, which are forbidden by divine law (haram) (Shalim, 2016).

However, unless the RF finance company voluntarily decides to lower the price in order to satisfy a particular request from the customer, the agreed-upon price will remain unchanged if the customer wants to accelerate payments so that they are paid over a two-year period rather than a five-year term. This request can be turned down, which is permissible in accordance with Shariah and considered halal, or it can be granted, as is typically the case, which is also considered halal. A variety of problems are related to the Murabaha arrangement. This will cause tax events that will require the transaction to be taxed, increasing the cost of financing in many western societies. Seling to the client at a higher price by the RF finance firm can be seen as a capital gain and be liable to capital gains taxes in the US and many other countries. In this instance, the tax burden can be high. This is the reason that a rider or other contract that stipulates that the final buyer rather than the RF bank is liable for any capital gains taxes is included in a large number of cost-plus models utilized by Islamic institutions in the west. It is unjust to individuals who wish to follow their faiths to choose this option. Furthermore, it is unjust that RF Bank asserts its Islamic status while returning all risk to the client. The banking rules and regulations in the west prohibit banking institutions from acting as principals in direct transactions or from obtaining title to properties. A separate, costly offshore Special Purpose Vehicle (SPV), which purchases the property and resells it to the client, is one of the structured financial tools that many attorneys use to circumvent this rule and appear to satisfy the legal aspect of Shariah whilc possibly sacrificing the spirit of Shariah. This strategy appears to meet Shari'ah criteria while assisting the RF bank in avoiding breaking banking laws.

4.8. LENDING

In the US, any lending transaction involving an operation must disclose the interest rate in accordance with the well-known banking regulation known as regulation "Z" (Truth in Lending Act) (Mülbert, 2011). Due to the manner in which the profit element is determined and computed, cost-plus transactions remarkably resemble standard interest-based banking transactions. Typically, this profit is correlated with the market interest rate that is in effect. Shari'ah has regulations for the short and long-term leasing or renting of the right to utilize an object. According to Shariah, renting or leasing is the agreement to benefit from renting the right to utilize a thing. Here, it is crucial to emphasize that the object to be leased needs to have a usufruct. For instance, it is possible to rent the use of a car or a house without giving up ownership of the vehicle or the home. However, since an apple is fungible and disappears after consumption, renting its use would be considered violating its ownership. Because they cannot be used without being consumed, the two kinds of commodities indexation mentioned in riba Al-Fadl, food and gold or silver cannot be leased or rented. For instance, renting a cow to get its milk is not permitted. This is due to the fact that someone acts as though they own the milk when they collect it. This is problematic because the initial agreement did not concern product ownership, but rather the leasing of the product's origin.

4.9. MEDIATORS

Other money managers may likewise receive authority from the RF financial institution as a duly authorized and trusted proxy (Donald, 2005). Finding a money manager or money managers who will meet the client's defined investment objective and risk tolerance would be the responsibility of the RF bank in its capacity as a money manager (mudharib) or as an agent of the client (wakeel) according to the terms of the money management (mudaraba) contract. This type of financing is used to cover the costs associated with producing an orchard or a manufactured good in the future. The client would consent to forwarding the cost of upcoming production to the RF finance firm. At a predetermined price, the RF financial institution would agree to purchase the production of an orchard, a farm, or a manufactured good before it is produced. The producer receives payment in advance. In exchange, the producer would utilize the funds as working capital to pay salaries, buy the raw materials needed for production, and acquire the necessities of life. In this approach, by giving the producing business the money it needs, the RF financial institution would contribute to the expansion of the economy. The potential for the financing entity to hoard open markets is a crucial rule that needs to be avoided. Caravan traders who operated between Arabia and the rest of the world in the early medieval era, particularly in trade along the silk road, employed Islamic RF models. A sophisticated riba-based banking system originated and grew throughout Europe in tandem with an increase in commercial and business operations, international commerce, and money production.

Islamic law, or Shari'ah, mandates that Muslims refrain from dealing in riba. From the smallest town to the biggest city, religious authorities, and scholars throughout the Muslim Ummah are instructed that engaging in riba is a serious transgression. In order to provide credit and support business expansion, increasingly complex riba-based banking operations and trade financing tools were created in Europe as trade, commerce, and industrial development increased. This new riba-based financial system was introduced by Europeans as they started to colonize several of its former member nations and extend their trading routes into the Turkish Ottoman Empire (Figure 4.2). The majority of European businesspeople and their local representatives were the only ones whose demands were met by the riba-based banking system. Because they felt that Muslims and their leaders did not support interest-bearing banking, the Muslim business community in the area did not use it. This led to the development of a lifestyle of complete debt avoidance among the Muslim community in the area. It was carried out as informal microlending between friends and family on a local level or between businesspeople on a commercial level; it is still carried out in the 21st century. Like all developing countries, the banking demands of the Muslim world have not been fully met, particularly at the retail level. These prehistoric cultures encountered a shock when they first established contact with the outside world. They discovered that they lagged behind by at least 600 years. With the installation of an intricate and extensive global banking infrastructure, interest-bearing banking was accepted as standard practice in many of these countries. Religious leaders in the early to middle 20th century were ignored and did not have the necessary stature, so despite their repeated expressions of dissent and concern, no one took notice.

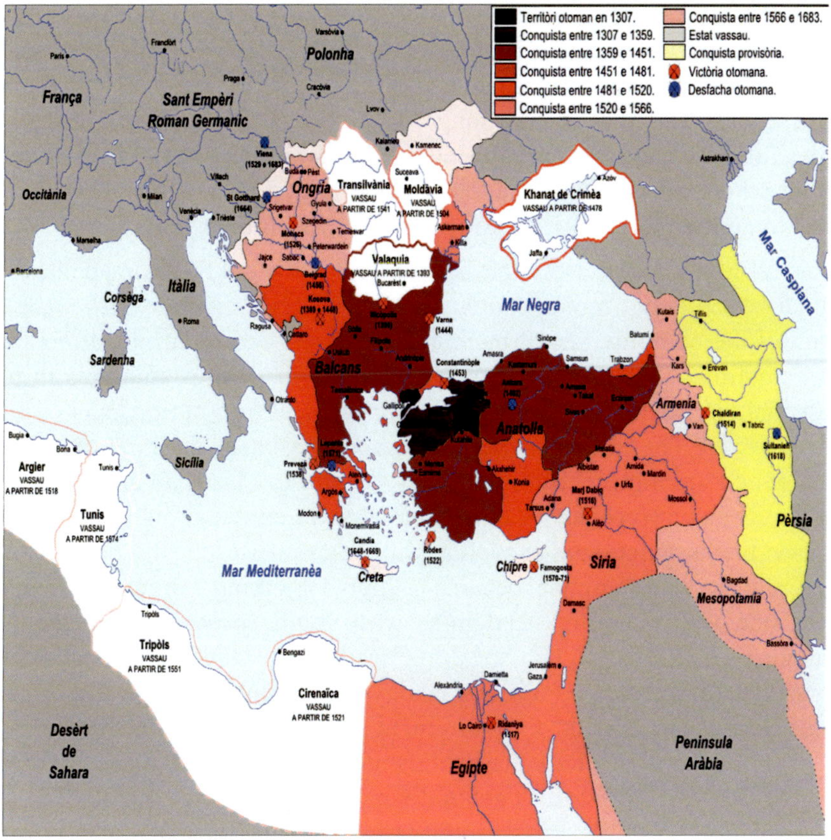

Figure 4.2. *Turkish Ottoman Empire.*

Source: https://en.wikipedia.org/wiki/Timeline_of_the_Ottoman_Empire#/media/File:Emp%C3%A8ri_Otoman_-_Expansion_territ%C3%B2riala_de_1307_a_1683.png, Creative Commons License.

4.10. OIL PRODUCING COUNTRIES

The Gulf oil-producing countries received enormous sums of money when the price of oil first spiked in 1973 (Vázquez-Fariñas, 2023). The absorptive ability of the local economies of the participating countries was the primary concern at the time. In these oil-producing nations, masses of investment and commercial bankers arrived with the goal of growing the locally operated banks and effectively connecting them to the global banking network. While many community and business leaders supported it, some were very worried by the immoral practice of riba. The late Saudi Arabian King Faisal was one of them. In 1974, he made a commitment to establish a banking system compliant with Shariah, or Islamic law. The primary issue was from the absence of a comprehensive Shariah code that addressed the complex and evolving demands of bank clients and the diverse range of products and services these banks provided, all of which were predicated on the forbidden riba. This signaled the start of a whole new area of academic study aimed at creating Shariah codes relevant to contemporary RF banking and business transactions.

The religious experts on the Shariah Board quickly realized how little they understood about money, banking, and financial matters; they were even ignorant of the complexities of banking operations and its implications for the riba community. At that time, there were only two main regulations in place: interest could not be levied, and partners to a business transaction had to split any profits or losses. The Shariah Boards received riba-based banking practitioners from Islamic banking practitioners in an attempt to close the knowledge gap. These practitioners provided a crash course-style explanation of how modern riba-based banks functioned as well as the features of each riba-based banking product and service. English became a global banking language, thus there was an increased need for academics who could speak and understand it. The majority of these English-speaking academics were from Asian Muslim countries like Bangladesh, Pakistan, Malaysia, and India, not Arabic-speaking nations. Because Arabic is a requirement for Shariah scholarship, many of these Asian academics who were proficient in English were also proficient in Arabic. At the Shariah Board level, a diverse pool of highly qualified scholars was produced through the crossbreeding of talents and a variety of cultural and educational backgrounds. There were differing views on what was and wasn't Shariah compliant, nevertheless, because of the diversity of the local cultural and educational backgrounds. Academics from the Arab Gulf, Pakistan, and India held a more rigid stance regarding the definition of what was haram (forbidden) and what was halal (permitted). Over time, countries such as Pakistan, India, Egypt, Sudan, the Arab Gulf states, Malaysia, Syria, Jordan, Lebanon, Europe, and the US produced new pioneers in the field of Islamic/Shariah-based finance law.

Regardless of the local language, applications of the Shari'ah generated a vast corpus of scholarly research by a class of academics termed fuqaha in Islamic research groups and organizations worldwide. Shari'ah encompasses the entire field of academic inquiry as well as the meticulous verification of codes, citations, and decisions. The finest efforts of the scholars and scholarly institutions involved in the research serve as the foundation for scholarly research, or the science of Fiqh. Depending on the specific circumstances, origins, culture, and intellect of each country, the opinions and directives provided by the learned academics may vary. There are state laws that are unique to each state in the United States in addition to federal laws that apply to the entire country. Because of this, opinions on Fiqh may differ or alter depending on when and where they are implemented. This is because fresh academic research may be conducted to assess the application of previous rulings in light of the necessities of the particular scenario at hand in a certain community or state. At the very least, all Muslims must carry out certain particular rites, duties, and deeds such as praying, fasting during Ramadan, giving alms, and, for those who can afford it, doing the hajj. Not doing so is categorized as divinely prohibited and disallowed (haram); also, it is regarded as a transgression of the faith since it surpasses the predetermined bounds of permissible behavior (hudood) (Mohamad, 2020).

These are only required of a Muslim as an additional effort above and beyond the minimal requirements mentioned above. Those who opt to pursue it do so with the intention of attaining excellence in their spirituality, faith, and service to God. Although completing these tasks is rewarded, failing to do so is not viewed as a transgression. All Shariah regulations stem from the idea that everything is permissible aside from what has been expressly forbidden. Since there was no mention of these activities in the corpus of scholarly Law (Fiqh) and no reference of them in the books of Law (Shariah and Fiqh), the acceptability of these behaviors is examined through a process of deduction. It is well acknowledged that pious Muslims don't do makruh. According to Shariah, certain behaviors are forbidden and are subject to the punishments outlined in the Qur'an. Worship rules, family law, inheritance law, commerce and trade transactions law, property law, civil law, criminal law, and laws and regulations covering administration, taxation, constitution, international relations, defense, peace, and war ethics, and other categories are among the branches of Fiqh, which literally translates to in-depth understanding. Following extensive investigation, discussion, and documentation, a number of academic scientific methodologies were employed to achieve a decision and results, including the consensus method (ijma). This refers to decisions or directives that have been accepted by the vast majority of Shariah's fuquahaa. When it is impossible to draw a definitive conclusion from the Qur'an and the Sunnah, consensus (ijma) is applicable. In this case, a Fatwa Board, a body that specializes in and is charged by the local government with answering questions and issuing rulings or fatwas made up of qualified, experienced, and erudite scholars (fuquahaa) will meet and decide on a workable solution to the specific issue at hand. The fuquahaa employ analogies and similarities in this method of referencing or comparing similar occurrences (qiyas) in order to interpolate and/or extrapolate the body of scholarly research and the current Shariah norms. When direct advice from the Qur'an and the Sunnah is not available, the idea of qiyas, or analogy, is used. Deduction is the method used to solve problems by comparing the current circumstance to a decision made in a case that is comparable to one that happened in the past.

Many outstanding Muslim leaders and academics (imams) dedicated their lives to the gathering, organizing, comprehension, and application of scholarly research (Fiqh) as well as the origins and methods of the law (Shari'ah) and its customs. By combining the three levels of urgencies with the five levels of goals in this two-dimensional domain, one can generate at least 15 different priority combinations. Stated differently, the faqih should thoroughly examine all 15 options and conduct a thorough situational analysis prior to issuing a decree (fatwa or opinion) (Ending Solehudin, 2018). When conflicting decisions arise, the decision from the higher block is considered to be more authoritative than the decision from the lower block. Stated differently, a rule that is deemed refined yields to a subsequent ruling that is deemed complementing, and so forth. However, it would be really helpful to think in several dimensions and create algorithms that are valuable to everyone. In the future, a new breed of intelligent, computer-savvy, and analytical scholars will contribute to this. When issuing a rule or creating a model for RF finance in a particular area of the world, it is crucial to consider this strategy, particularly in cases where Muslims make up a minority.

Globally, there has been a resurgence of religion. People from all walks of life are searching for the optimal way to live. In order to find spiritual fulfillment and answers to the numerous contemporary issues they encounter in the 21st century, people are delving deeply into their respective faiths. The believers who lack a solid education in the faith, its precepts, or Shari'ah want to lead proper lives, following the guidelines set forth by God in his writings and in Shariah. Many of the problems these puritans face call for a religious decree or decision, but the answers to those problems first appear in the public sphere as religious opinions. Since the development of effective communication channels and mass media outlets, such as hundreds of satellite TV channels, a large number of programs have addressed issues related to behavior, lifestyles, marriage, finances, business dealings, and other related topics. Due to this, there is a great need for religious authorities who are certified to give fatwas, or religious rulings. A mufti is the person who issues these fatwas. A local scholar or imam (religious leader) may issue a private fatwa; once it passes muster with academic, legal, and public scrutiny, it becomes a legally binding decree. The sole Islamic school in the Sunni Muslim area that teaches Fiqh in accordance with the five schools previously mentioned, including the Sunni and Shia schools of thought (Madh'hab), is Al-Azhar School in Cairo, Egypt, the oldest institution in the world. Students from the school graduate in a variety of fields. One area of study is Shariah and Usul Ul-Fiqh, or the foundations of Fiqh (Hassan et al., 2023). Graduates of this program gain expertise in faqih through ongoing supervised research and a history of engagement with eminent academics.

4.11. AUTHORITY

A public religious decree, or fatwa, can only be authorized by the sole final and highest authority at Al-Azhar Seminary in Egypt (Figure 4.3). The highest scholar in charge of enacting fatwas is known as the Grand Mufti. He is in charge of a group of prominent fuquahaa, or highly accomplished scholars. This committee conducts research, performs hearings, reviews the findings, and recommends fatwas. The suggestions are then submitted to the Grand Mufti and the Al-Azhar Seminary Fatwa Committee for approval. The Islamic Republic of Iran, Pakistan, Iraq, and India all follow much the same procedure. In an attempt to educate the next generation of Shariah legislators, the old scholars in Pakistan and India founded numerous universities that produce academics who hold the title of Mufti. Since many of these Indo-Pakistani graduates use the name "Mufti," it is vital to caution the reader not to be misled by it. Instead, their accomplishments in their fields after graduation must be proven. It is more appropriate to refer to them as Muftis in residence training or junior Muftis. It goes without saying that people are free to adopt the views of those they choose, but it is crucial to share with the reader the standards that ought to be applied when selecting and assessing candidates for positions as Shariah advisors in their organizations.

Sheikh Saeed bin Lutah established the first official Islamic bank in Dubai in the middle of the 1960s, but there is no documentation of a formal attempt to institutionalize the process of creating a formal body that would conduct research and create the Shariah-compliant RF banking and finance legal code. Subsequently, three prominent financial institutions were established in the middle of the 1970s in a formal and committed attempt to launch Islamic banking and finance following the abrupt spike in oil income in 1973.

These were Dar Al-Maal Al-Islami, founded in Geneva, Switzerland, by Prince Muhammad Al-Faisal, the late King Faisal's son; Bayt al Tamweel Al Kuwaiti, or Kuwait Finance House, established in Kuwait as a shareholders' Islamic finance company led by Sheikh Bazee Al Yaseen, a Kuwaiti of Iraqi descent; and Dallah Al Baraka Group, established in Jeddah, Saudi Arabia, by Sheikh Saleh Kamel, a former Department of Defense auditor who later became a significant force with vision and entrepreneurship, often at least 25 years ahead of his time.

Figure 4.3. *Al-Azhar Seminary.*

Source: https://en.wikipedia.org/wiki/Al-Azhar_University#/media/File:Cairo,_moschea_di_al-azhar,_01.JPG, Creative Commons License.

They were all faced with the task of creating a Shariah-based financial law code for the first time in modern history. They turned to Al Azhar Seminary in Cairo, Egypt, at that time, which was the greatest religious authority in the Arabic-speaking region of the Muslim world. The Grand Mufti of Egypt, Sheikh Muhammad Khater (nominated by the President of the Republic of Egypt), was put in charge of creating financial instruments and procedures that adhered to Shari'ah by Prince Al Faisal. According to Shari'ah, the goal was to assist in investing a portion of the enormous sums of "petrodollars" that came from the dividend caused by the abrupt surge in oil prices in 1973.

4.12. BOARDS

In order to reduce ambiguity and divergent views expressed by various Shariah scholars and Shariah compliance boards at various institutions, it would be beneficial to adopt the Malaysian approach, which involves the appointment, management, and oversight of a single Shariah Board within the nation's central bank. In the same manner as the central bank of the treasury department examines banks for compliance, this central bank Shariah compliance board will provide legal opinions and oversee compliance. But in this instance, adhering to the rules that conform to Shari'a as outlined in the bank's charter will be the main focus of the compliance test. Some people spend money in an attempt to feel good about themselves, maybe by showing off a pricey new watch or car to others. Because money has become such a big deal, people fight over it, feel hated for it, and, regrettably, some would even kill for it. It is incredible to see so much reverence and love for a sheet of paper that can be any color, green, red, blue, or even an astonishing assortment of hues and patterns. Only the location where it was produced and distributed may acknowledge and respect this piece of paper. Not all currencies in the world are as well-known as the main currencies, which include the British pound, the euro, the Japanese yen, and the U.S. dollar. These currencies are significant global currencies that are in high demand. The same pieces of paper will be found in the jar if money is sealed in it for two years and then opened; the only difference is that, in most circumstances, the paper will now be worth less than it did two years prior. It is also essential to realize that we are not allowed to eat or drink these pieces of paper that we refer to as money. But we may use the money to purchase food from those who grow it, enabling them to purchase necessities like clothing and medication in addition to the supplies needed to grow more of that food. All that money is a measuring tool and a vehicle of trade.

Throughout history, the creation of money has been considered an important human advancement. Small villages have benefited from the development of markets that have drawn a lot of traders and merchants, transforming them into small towns, cities, major metropolitan areas, states, and countries over time. The ability to move money around is what gives the concept of money its true value. Depending on the nation or region that issued it, it can be split into many denominations and recognized and acknowledged by people in other nations. Barter, which is the exchange of one specific commodity or service for another specified good or service, was perhaps one of the first forms of money. When one side did not desire what the other hand, or when the trading parties could not agree what something was worth in return, problems with this system occurred. In order to address that issue, commodity money was implemented. Due to their implication to regional economies, commodities such as cattle, tea, tobacco, salt, and seeds have all historically been used as currency. It was found that using commodities as money brought up new difficulties as the world advanced. It was hard to carry bags of salt and other goods. Furthermore, commodities may have a limited shelf life, beyond which they would decompose. Metal was first used as money about 5000 B.C.E. because it was easily accessible, recyclable, and abundantly available (Asare & Afriyie, 2021). Soon, coins with predetermined values were being minted in other nations. Coins were made from different metals, including gold, silver, copper, and iron. Only gold and silver retained their value; these were the two primary metals used worldwide as money. In addition to their practical purpose, gold and silver were much sought after for their worth as assets and stores of wealth. The Persian Empire utilized silver money known as dirham, while the Roman Empire used gold currency known as the denarius (dinar or drachma). From the time of the Second Caliph Omar Ibn Al-Khattab (634–644 C.E.), the official Islamic currencies of the Muslim state were the gold dinar and the silver dirham. The weight of 4.3 gm of 22-karat gold was defined as the dinar, and 3 gm of silver was defined as the dirham. The caliph established the well-known standard connection at that time, stating that seven dinars must be equal to 10 dirhams (Abu-Munshar, 2007).

Chapter 5

TRENDS IN ISLAMIC FINANCE

Contents

5.1. INTRODUCTION

It is crucial to highlight right away that Muslim civilizations do not distinguish between the sacred and the profane in their daily lives, economic activity is not seen as a separate sector in Islam. Therefore, it should not be shocking that traditional Arabic lacks a word for economics. The Arabic words Iqtisad and Ilm-Ul-Iqtisad (economics study), which relate to the understanding of finding appropriate ways to create wealth and spend it in the right ways, as well as the causes for its destruction and waste, are the closest translations of the current term economics. Al-Ghazali defines Iqtisad, the principle of moderation, in his well-known book Iyha Ulum-id-din in traditional Arabic (Marmura, 1994). Since the Islamic commercial jurisprudence places an excessive amount of emphasis on the concepts of riba, gharar (uncertainty), and halal (permissible), the word "Islamic economics" has come to be synonymous with Islamic finance and banking. But the idea of Islamic economics goes much beyond merely adhering to the unchangeable laws established by Shariah. In actuality, it does more than just research, evaluate, and comprehend economic behavior and results; it also makes an effort to operationalize the moral vision by providing answers to issues endangering human pleasure and our world. The definition of Islamic economics, in contrast to traditional economics, is not widely agreed upon.

5.2. IDEAS

Every discipline has a set of fundamental ideas. Understanding these ideas helps us make sense of the world we live in and the reasons for the ways things are the way they are. The fundamental laws of economics that inform the decisions made by producers, investors, employees, and the government are referred to as economic principles. They are viewed in mainstream economics as the only formation of the intellect, and before they are recognized as economic principles, the scientific method is employed to support the testing. Islamic economics recognizes the significance of reasoning and intellect as well. But the main source of principles (theory), with the latter (intellect) represented in the economic system, is divine guidance or revelation. Thus, the foundation of Islamic economic concepts is provided by the Qur'an and Ahadith (Hadith), while ijtihad, or human reasoning, is employed to operationalize and resolve economic issues. When it comes to production, justice means that no one should be the victim of unfair treatment by others or be able to obtain money through dishonest, illegal, or fraudulent means. All financial resources and wealth must be shared or dispersed within the community in such a way that everyone has access to the needs of life and the gap between the rich and the poor is closed in order to achieve justice in distribution. To practice justice in consumption, one must refrain from overusing resources or consuming them to the point where it violates the rights of others. Transparency, sincerity, and accountability between the two sides to the trade are necessary for justice in exchange.

5.3. INCOME

Islam has two methods for attaining socio economic justice: the interest-prohibition system and the zakat system, which redistributes income. As the third pillar of Islam, following prayer and the profession of faith (shahadah), zakat is an obligatory religious tax that represents the significance of Islam. It is imposed on all Muslims' and Islamic organizations' income. The amount exceeds the wealth requirement by 2.5%. Zakat is an act of worship that purifies wealth, improves its redistribution among society, and discourages hoarding in order to appease Allah. Fadl is a term that denotes growth or increase. Consequently, the rise that results from exchanging two identical items in an unequal manner is known as Riba Al-Fadl. This ban stems from a Hadith that describes how goods must be traded for money rather than being bartered because it is hard to find goods of the same caliber. The fact that money is used these days for exchange has made this riba less relevant. However, the idea still holds true in comparable circumstances. Riba Al-Fadl is also referred to as Riba Al-Khafi, riba ghayr al-Mubashir, or Riba Al-Buyu, which refers to interest in business (Chapra, 2008). Riba is abhorred because it goes against the principles of fairness and equity in Islam. People who have easy access to loans could be more likely to live beyond their means and spend money on unnecessary items. If a person has used their home as collateral for a loan or mortgage, they run the risk of losing it. When businesses are unable to pay back the interest on their loans due to Riba, they may be declared bankrupt, which results in the loss of jobs for the employees and productive opportunities for the community at large. High interest rates can make it difficult or even unfeasible for businesspeople to borrow money from banks, which would impede the expansion and productivity of the business sector. Riba inhibits small firms' ability to innovate since it makes them hesitant to take out loans and charges excessive interest rates for new ventures that are frequently viewed as carrying greater risk.

Governments may borrow as a result of easy access to international financial institutions, which would squeeze development resources and highlight macroeconomic issues including inflation and external imbalances. This causes some less developed nations to overuse the resources on Earth, which in turn causes the devastation of those nations' ecological systems. Some nations struggle to recover from economic downturns due to their high debt loads, which further impoverishes the entire population. Since Allah is the ultimate owner, all resources are presumably owned jointly by humans since we are all his vicegerents and have the right to use them wisely in accordance with his will. The Islamic law recognizes three distinct types of ownership: private, public, and state. Their individual purviews are, nevertheless, left up to interpretation in light of specific requirements and situations. Similar to this, Islamic teaching's guiding principles and constraints apply to the purchase, use, and disposal of property. People can acquire rights to resources and property through inheritance, their own inventive labor or effort, or by exchanging contracts with another person who has title to the property through their own efforts. The Qur'an has more than 360 verses that emphasize the value of labor. Every person will be held responsible for their deeds in this world, according to Islam. In the afterlife, their deeds will be assessed as either good or bad. Islam thus grants people the right to pursue their own interests in all spheres of human endeavor, including the economy. This indicates that Allah grants people the freedom to acquire, possess, enjoy, and use their wealth anyway they like. Nonetheless, economic liberty is restricted and restrained within the confines of Islamic ethical and spiritual principles. Islam makes a distinction between actions that are permitted (halal) and those that are not (haram). Bribery, gambling, interest, and other business malpractices are examples of unlawful means of acquiring reserves and a living. When it comes to eating, the foods that are forbidden are wine, pork, animals that are not killed in the name of Allah, and narcotics. In a similar vein, it is illegal to pay for any entertainment or services that promote drugs, lottery, or obscenity. Thus, Islam acknowledges not just personal initiative, free enterprise, and individual potential but also the role of organizations, capital, labor, and market forces in economic operations. Apart from the restrictions imposed by halal and haram, such restrictions are less usual unless they are necessary to protect the interests of society as a whole.

5.4. LAW

Islamic law imposes obligations on the state to monitor public activities and to step in to safeguard the public interest by restricting the freedom of individuals to act (Fernando, 2010). Islam places a strong emphasis on moderation in all that one does, and this has a direct bearing on the concepts of justice and balance. Finding the middle ground between different issues in a given scenario and adopting a balanced attitude will frequently result in the best course of action. This entails exercising moderation in weighing the obligations of affairs and faith. Islam expressly forbids its believers from going too far in any endeavor and from crossing lines. When it comes to production, consumption, distribution, and expenditure in the economy, the moderation concept is crucial. Islam permits people to create and amass wealth through legal means, but it also requires devotion to exercise restraint in doing so. This is particularly true if the person is preoccupied with concerns to the point where they neglect their obligations to Allah, their religion, and other people. This also holds true for expenditure and consumption. Islam prohibits being so economical that a person is unable to spend money on their own needs, let alone on charitable endeavors and deserving causes. Similar to this, Islam prohibits someone from being wasteful with their money, buying luxury for themselves and their families, and forgetting about those who are less fortunate. An essential idea in the study of economics is this one. According to economists from the west, scarcity results from a deficiency of resources to satisfy human needs. This perspective makes a distinction between absolute and relative scarcity. The second perspective, on the other hand, views scarcity as solely a matter of injustice and maldistribution rather than relative and absolute scarcity.

To put it briefly, Islam does not practice absolute scarcity. The scarcity problem may persist as a natural process owing to inadequate knowledge to utilize the resources and/or due to natural phenomena that may drive the pricing, even though the organization of the economic system can assist solve the equity problem. Therefore, in Islamic economics, limitations imposed by moral or ethical principles also apply to producers and consumers in addition to resource limits. Islamic economics is different from neoclassical economics in that it places more emphasis on values. Consequently, the rationality of a person who identifies as an economic man (homo economicus) will differ from that of a Muslim man who fears God (Homo Islamicus). The goal of a self-interested rational economic guy is to maximize profit and maximize use. On the other hand, the goal of a rational, god-fearing man will include elements of self-interest with self-sacrifice. Islam holds that life is a passing phase that ends when a person enters the afterlife, where they will either be rewarded or punished. Since the aim of a Muslim is to Attain Al-Falah, or happiness in this world and the next, economic agents in an Islamic system will therefore seek to balance rather than optimize. A Muslim person functions on different levels. Like any sane economic guy, the person's actions are motivated by his own interests at first. This is perfectly acceptable since Islam urges people to use their knowledge, ingenuity, and hard work to increase their riches.

However, on a deeper level, the same person assumes the role of an instrument or agent (vicegerent), whose decisions are influenced by his religious convictions and have far-reaching effects. For example, sacrificing self-interest for the good of the group may not seem like a good idea now, but it might pay off more in the afterlife. To put it briefly, a Muslim person balances his material and spiritual requirements in order to achieve his economic objectives. This makes them both Homo Islamicus and homo economicus. It is crucial to define the term "system" before discussing the Islamic economic system. Economic activities function inside a wide structural framework known as an economic system. An economic system is made up of various economic entities that are established by society to handle resource allocation, the production and exchange of goods and services, and the distribution of the resulting wealth and income. These entities include households, businesses, public institutions, and markets. They are established and run in accordance with a code of behavior dictated by a particular ideology or view held by society. Every economic system is different from the others. Capitalism promotes individual liberty in the quest for riches, with little to no government involvement in business matters (Box et al., 2001). The remarkable progress made by humans in science and technology has facilitated innovation and expedited industrialization, which are essential for the smooth functioning of a free market economy. In addition, markets and financial institutions made it easier for money to flow from the surplus to the deficit sector, with interest rates heavily influencing choices. Socialism and communism (Figure 5.1), in opposition to capitalism, encourage the communitarian spirit and the state's involvement in controlling the economy. The social welfare program has the drawback of decreasing people's motivation to work, even while it offers some guarantee regarding the welfare of society's most vulnerable groups. In a similar vein, limitations on private ownership could reduce output.

Figure 5.1. *Communism.*

Source: https://en.wikipedia.org/wiki/Pre-Marxist_communism#/media/File:Chiefs_of_the_Six_Nations_at_Brantford,_Canada,_explaining_their_wampum_belts_to_Horatio_Hale_September_14,_1871.jpg, Creative Commons License.

The capacities for learning, growth, and decision-making that endowed people with reliability in fulfilling their mission are embodied in this capacity. Therefore, when creating an Islamic economic system, people should consider the rules of Shariah regarding things like abstaining from forbidden (riba) activities, supporting fairness and justice in the acquisition and distribution of wealth, and encouraging innovation and entrepreneurship to deliver useful goods and services. Islamic economic systems have a unique two-dimensional utility function in which the better deeds one commits to during their lifetime, the better deeds they aspire to acquire throughout their afterlife. The advancement of the ummah, or Muslim unity, and global brotherhood is a further goal of the Islamic economic system. Everyone in a compassionate and helpful community may rely on one another's assistance when they are in need. Every Muslim community has an obligation to serve humanity by encouraging others to uphold morality and fight against injustice and evil. Additionally, communities have a duty to provide for each other's fundamental needs, which include housing, food, health care, education, and employment opportunities. Therefore, an Islamic economic system supports the institutions of zakat, charity, and other means of aiding the needy in order to create social harmony and foster brotherhood between various segments of society.

Even with the disparity in income, if everyone respects and fulfills their social function, there shouldn't be conflicts in society between the rich and the poor or between social classes. The Islamic economic system contributes to the community's moral and material advancement as well (Wajdi Dusuki, 2008). For example, the transfer of wealth through investment and expenditure multiplies the rise in the country's income. Higher incomes will result in more taxes being collected from the wealthy, allowing the government to provide social security or other benefits to the poor. This will boost the poor's purchasing power, which will raise demand for goods and services. As a result, there will be a rise in industrialization and full employment, which will enable the full use of available material and human resources and accelerate the growth of national income. In addition to fostering the spiritual and moral advancement of society, a zakat and charity system purges the human spirit of immoral principles like self-interest and greed. Islam enhances feelings of love, sacrifice, generosity, and cooperation between people by making it mandatory for a person to pay zakat and share some of his income.

5.5. ECONOMIC SYSTEM

In order to recognize any parallels and contrasts, let's now examine certain aspects of an Islamic economic system. Firstly, the Islamic economic system does not prioritize individual freedom above community rights, nor does it prioritize capitalism, which values individual liberty, over socialism, which values a communitarian spirit. Rather, it simultaneously pursues the common welfare of the group as a whole and the individual, allowing the latter to enjoy their freedom without endangering or impairing the former. The establishment of private property rights serves to satisfy people's psychological need for ownership while also limiting the demands of the public riches to create a sense of equilibrium that promotes societal growth and a sense of security and fulfillment. The Islamic economic system acknowledges that the state has a duty to intervene in certain areas of economic activity in order to prevent monopolies, exploitation, corruption, and other practices that might be detrimental to the public interest. This is in contrast to capitalism, which has minimal state intervention, and socialism, which has almost total state intervention in economic activities. Similar to this, Islamic economics holds the government responsible to its constituents and creates a distinction between private and public property. Natural resources are those that belong to society equally and include things like uncultivated land, water, oil, and minerals, oceanic resources, etc. Any citizen may utilize these resources, provided that their usage does not infringe upon the rights of other citizens, but they must be placed under the state's care and control. An Islamic economic system, like socialism, places the burden of providing social security for the unemployed and other disadvantaged members of society who require both non-financial and financial assistance to live with dignity in the state. An Islamic economic system imposes limitations on the growth of personal wealth through a variety of procedures, in contrast to capitalism, which permits people to pursue money at the highest possible level of self-interest. For example, obtaining wealth must be done so legally by making efforts and engaging in activities that are acceptable and devoid of any kind of abuse or injury to other people. The state has an obligation to prevent any potential damage that might result from an individual's accumulated wealth giving them the financial power to manipulate currency rates, bribe officials in government agencies, speculate in the stock market, or engage in any other activity that is detrimental to the community and the state.

5.6. TAX

In addition to paying taxes, a wealthy person has financial obligations such as fulfilling zakat payments and other social cohesion tasks (Mohammed et al., 2021). An Islamic economic system severely discourages unemployment, dependency, and inactivity while promoting economic activity and urging people to work in profitable and productive jobs. Although the zakat and charitable systems guarantee an equitable distribution of income, they do not support spending on the impoverished who are capable of working but would rather remain unemployed and reliant on donations. Islamic economic systems encourage the distribution of wealth among all societal segments rather than the hoarding of riches. Islamic inheritance law helps prevent injustice and family disputes as well as the concentration of wealth in a small number of hands. By distributing wealth through constructive channels, it is possible to increase the purchasing power of the impoverished. Interest is the cornerstone of capitalism, and even socialism has failed to eradicate it despite its detrimental effects on the state and society. But since the Qur'an expressly forbids it, this can be completely eliminated in an Islamic economic system. Islamic teaching defines interest as encompassing not just financial obligation but also anything associated with exploitation.

A financial system facilitates the transfer of money between lenders and borrowers in order to create capital and satisfy the short and long-term capital requirements of individuals, businesses, and governments. A financial system's institutional units, which include government agencies, businesses, and other organizations, as well as individuals, employ its services. They collaborate with one another to direct money toward the ultimate lenders and borrowers, the people who make up the financial system. Those who are prepared to lend their excess money, which results from income exceeding consumption, are known as lenders. Financial surplus owners have three options for using their excess: they may invest in tangible assets like real estate and machinery; they can just keep the money; or they can simply accumulate it. Therefore, not all owners of financial surplus are prepared to lend money, as their choice to do so may be influenced by the return they will receive, the amount of risk they are willing to accept, and the ease of liquidity, that is, the ease with which they can change an asset into cash when needed. Conversely, borrowers are people who have a financial deficit that results from either being required to take on financial obligations (debts) or from having previously accumulated financial assets. For businesses, this can mean purchasing capital equipment, while for people, it might mean purchasing consumer durables like homes or cars. The terms of the loan, including the interest rate and repayment schedule, may have an impact on the borrower's choice of borrowing. Financial systems can function on a local, national, and international scale. The financial system is connected to a collection of applied procedures at the micro level, which refers to families and businesses, in order to track the financial activities of the individual or business, including the amount and changes in revenues, expenses, assets, liabilities, and capital. Macroeconomically, a financial system is the transfer of money between lenders and borrowers via formalized financial markets and intermediaries both domestically and internationally. Globally, the financial system includes not only financial markets and intermediaries but also central banks, finance ministries, the World Bank, the International Monetary Fund (IMF), the Bank of International Settlement, and other significant organizations that engage in international lending, including hedge funds and private banks. Regional institutions like the Eurozone are also included in the financial system (Schüller & Wogart, 2017).

5.7. BONDS

In market-oriented economies such as the UK and the USA, households may hold assets in the form of bonds and shares, and market institutions are frequently well-developed. Companies use corporate equities and initial public offerings (IPOs) to raise finance. The ownership structure of corporations is frequently highly fragmented, with institutional investors holding a significant sway on the capital market's efficiency. The securities commissions, special government agencies, and rating agencies all carry out monitoring. Systems that are based on markets mostly depend on accurate information and transparent accounting.

Figure 5.2. *Waqf.*

Source: https://en.wikipedia.org/wiki/Waqf#/media/File:Waqfnameh.JPG, Creative Commons License.

In contrast, the capital markets are comparatively underdeveloped and financial institutions play a major role in financing in systems that rely on banks, such as those found in Germany and Japan. Assets owned by households are kept as claims against banks and insurance providers. Most companies are not listed, and of those that are, institutional investors have a small stake and are among the few large shareholders. Under such a framework, financial intermediaries and businesses have a long-term partnership built on information sharing. These kinds of interactions reduce borrowing costs and information asymmetry. Banks oversee investment initiatives and monitor the financial sector, taking appropriate action as needed. They might opt to engage in the Islamic bond or stock markets to take part in the Islamic capital market in the direct financial market. There is less liquidity in the securities traded in those marketplaces. Financial intermediaries, such as Islamic commercial and merchant banks, Islamic financial services companies, takaful operators (Islamic insurance companies), unit trusts companies, Islamic cooperatives, Islamic microfinance institutions, and other institutions like waqf (endowment) (Figure 5.2) and zakat (alms and charity) (Figure 5.3), are available to those who lack the time or expertise to handle investments or funding activities on their own.

Figure 5.3. *Zakat.*

Source: https://en.wikipedia.org/wiki/Zakat#/media/File:Slot_at_the_Zaouia_Moulay_Idriss_II_1.jpg, Creative Commons License.

Since Shariah is the foundation of the Islamic financial system, Shariah must also inform the system's risk sharing, liquidity, and information disclosure services. In order to reduce risks, investors require a wider range of products to choose from. To meet this need, Islamic financial institutions must innovate their products. It is important to remember that Islam forbids risk-avoidance behavior and encourages risk aversion. Risk aversion in Islam is defined as the willingness to take more calculated risks in the hope of obtaining larger benefits. This legal dictum emphasizes that taking risks is the only way to achieve profit. Such behavior is the exact opposite of riba, which permits capital to increase without the chance of decline and does not involve taking any risks in order to extract surplus from a debt. It is forbidden for investors to avoid risk because they anticipate a set return and capital protection, both of which are equivalent to riba. Early human communities traded goods for one another without regard to value equivalency, a practice known as barter. There was also no money in these societies. Subsequently, some commodities took on the function of money since their usefulness made them more desirable. Commodity money, such as salt, wheat, barley, cattle, and even shells, has been utilized as a means of transaction. Coins consisting of gold, silver, and nickel were used as a foundation for keeping wealth and as a medium of exchange after precious metals were discovered, displacing commodity money. Initially, this metallic currency had a full body, meaning that its metallic value matched its face value. Subsequently, manufactured coins for smaller amounts and paper notes for greater denominations were used in place of the entire metallic currency as tender money, meaning that no one could refuse to accept it and it could be used to settle debts.

5.8. CURRENCY

Initially, the gold standard notes were made legal currency and could be exchanged for predetermined, fixed amounts of gold. Nearly all countries had embraced the gold standard by the turn of the 20th century, backing their legal tender notes with set quantities of gold. Nevertheless, the Bretton Woods Agreement established the US dollar as the default worldwide reserve currency following World War II, and only the USD was convertible into gold (Bordo, 2014). A portion of the reason the USD was taken off the gold standard in 1971 was the USA's incapacity to have sufficient gold reserves. Consequently, the other nations gave up on the gold standard as well. Therefore, there is no intrinsic worth to the paper money that is currently in use, nor is there any assurance that it can be turned into a valuable item (gold). Rather, its value is derived only from government decrees (fiat), and it is issued as legal money by the central bank of the relevant country. It is essential to the economy since it allows for the settlement of many transactions without the need for paper money. A check is an order for money to be transferred from the payer's bank account to the payee's bank; there may be a fee for this service from both banks. It's a type of credit with fixed expenses that don't depend on the check amount. These days, using check guarantee cards is rare and electronic payments are more convenient. Float describes checks that are being cleared. The payer's account remains credited until the check is cleared by the clearinghouse system. Float, therefore, is a short-term, interest-free loan to the payer. A bill of exchange is a formal written agreement that requires one party to give another party a certain amount of money at a specified time or upon request. International trade is the main application for this. Three parties are involved in it, usually transferred by endorsements: the drawee, who pays the amount stipulated in the bill of exchange; the payee, who is the recipient of that amount; and the drawer, who is the person requiring the drawee to pay the payee. Since there is no interest associated with bills of exchange, they are essentially postdated checks. A payment made on a payer's behalf that the issuing bank guarantees is known as a bank draft. The payee gets credit for that amount the same day he deposits the draft in his bank.

The World Wide Web's establishment in 1991 and the advancement of computer technology have made it possible to create systems for electronic money transactions (e-money). Both decentralized and centralized e-money are possible. In the former scenario, several sources exert influence over the money supply, whereas in the later scenario, a single central authority controls the money supply. Debit and credit cards that allow for the electronic exchange of money and payments at the point of sale in place of paper money are examples of centralized e-money. When a debit card is used at the point of sale, the money is immediately transferred from the current account to the merchant's account. In the UK, standard debit cards are those issued by banks such as Barclays and Santander. As long as a minimum payment is made each month, credit card charges can either be paid in whole or have financing extended up to the credit limit provided by the card issuer. MasterCard and Visa are the two networks that are most often utilized. On the other hand, a charge card, like the ones that American Express offers, needs to be fully paid off each month. In addition to plastic cards (credit, debit, and charge cards), mobile digital wallets, or e-wallets, are another form of centralized e-money.

5.9. PAYMENT TRANSFER SYSTEMS

E-wallets (Figure 5.4) are essentially contactless payment transfer systems that make payments easier by giving the payee greater confidence without requiring them to release their electronic wallet during the transaction. Cryptocurrencies, which are essentially digital or virtual currencies intended to be used as a means of exchange, are one type of decentralized electronic money. Because it promises to have less transaction fees than conventional online payment methods, virtual currency is becoming more and more popular. Prices for cryptocurrencies are solely determined by supply and demand. The cryptocurrency, Bitcoin, was created in 2009 and was created (Satoshi Nakamoto) (Bradbury, 2013). It evolved into the virtual currencies' gold standard. There are more than 800 different cryptocurrencies. When money is utilized as a unit of account, it serves as a common denominator for comparing the relative values of different goods and services. In barter, every good's price must be recorded in relation to every other good, whereas in money, every good's price is recorded in terms of money. A price process cannot exist without a monetary measure of value, and without a pricing process, specialized production and structured marketing might not be feasible. All types of economic planning also require money as a unit of measurement. Consumers compare the value of different purchases in monetary terms.

Figure 5.4. *E-wallets.*

Source: https://upload.wikimedia.org/wikipedia/en/3/36/Apple_Wallet_screenshot.png, Creative Commons License.

Producers schedule their production outputs and earnings in terms of money and compare the values of potential acquisitions. Therefore, maintaining a steady value of money over an extended period of time is essential. One type of financial asset that can be kept as riches is money (income saved and not consumed). Money is special in that it can be used as a medium of exchange quickly and easily, but other assets like shares, bonds, and real estate may also be used as goods of value. Money is the most liquid store of value by definition. The ability of money to hold onto its value, however, determines how valuable it is as a store of value. All goods experience a general increase in price during inflation. The value of money will be halved if all prices double. On the other hand, in instances of hyperinflation, where monthly inflation rates surpass 50%, customers have been known to completely give up using cash and turn to bartering. Since money is the most liquid resource available, it is widely regarded as a commodity. The ability to purchase nearly any good, wherever, is conferred by having money. This special characteristic sets money apart from all other commodities. Preference for money hence equates to preference for liquidity. Payments that are made at a later date for transactions that occurred in the present are referred to as deferred payments. As the benchmark for postponed or delayed payments, money greatly simplifies borrowing and lending activities because it often retains a steady value over time. As a result, money supports the operations of financial intermediaries like banks, investment trusts, and stock exchanges as well as the development of capital markets. Simply put, money is the thread that binds the ideals of today with those of tomorrow.

5.10. MONEY SUPPLIERS

Money serves as both a means of transferring resources efficiently and as a symbol of prosperity. Rather than becoming creditors, Islam urges Muslims to invest their money and form partnerships in order to share business risks and gains. As a result, ownership, use, and earning of money are the three main facets of the Islamic understanding of money. The Prophet gave his approval for money to aid as a store of value and a medium of exchange in Islam. Barter trading is not recommended for Muslims since it can result in unfairness and exploitation. Riba Al-Fadl is the result of transactions involving similar commodities exchanged in unequal quantities or the possession of a product that was not transferred right away (Daly & Frikha, 2016). Muslims are also encouraged to use money to buy and sell goods, demonstrating that money is accepted as a form of payment. The Prophet affirms the significance of money as a store of wealth by imposing zakat, or alms, on any wealth that has the potential to increase in value. Zakat is levied on financial assets, which implies that money is a significant productive agent with the capacity to increase in value. Nonetheless, Islam forbids using money as a commodity or for lending. Islam prohibits the use of money as a commodity since, on its own, it has no intrinsic value and cannot be sold or rented out to create surplus value. However, commodities with inherent worth, like gold (dinar; Figure 5.5) and silver (dirham; Figure 5.6), can still be used as commodity money and still grant their owners the right to profit from the usufruct of their assets.

Figure 5.5. *Dinar.*

Source: https://en.wikipedia.org/wiki/Kuwaiti_dinar#/media/File:1_Kuwaiti_dinar_in_2014_Obverse.jpg, Creative Commons License.

Figure 5.6. *Dirham.*

Source: https://en.wikipedia.org/wiki/United_Arab_Emirates_dirham#/media/File:UAE5polymer.jpg, Creative Commons License.

Islam also prohibits lending money with the intention of profiting from it, since this would be the same as making money off of money, or riba. According to Islam, the only ways to make money are through legitimate commerce and investment, in which all participants share the risks and rewards. Since money has no opportunity cost on its own, it is only considered capital when joined with other elements of production. Therefore, lenders are unable to grant loans and demand payment in exchange for taking no risk while giving up the funds during the credit period. Reward opportunities are limited to investors who share the risks, become partners in commerce, and provide funds.

Money is acknowledged as a factor of production in both Islam and the capitalist system; nevertheless, the latter views money as capital that should get rewards regardless of the outcome of the economic activity. The idea of money has entwined itself with the interest-based institution, giving rise to the current interest-based banking system. Because credit cards are essentially a short-term loan facility that charges a high interest rate due to high loan default risk, overheads, and the cost of financing the loans, the question of whether they are permissible (halal) has drawn attention in the past. Only approximately 40% of credit card customers pay up their short-term loans before the issuer assesses interest using their cards as payment methods. These days, all clients who would rather use a credit card based on Shariah principles accept Islamic credit cards. Customers using an Islamic credit card enjoy all the advantages of a traditional credit card, with the added assurance that all payments and repayments adhere to the strict guidelines of Shariah. The bank offers a credit card that is free from interest and penalties by using the delayed payment sale principles. The bank will process the transaction on behalf of the credit card holder and concurrently sell the products back to the customer as they are bought using this credit card. This credit must be paid in installments within a specified time period over a deferred term. The status and use of cryptocurrency is the most recent contentious topic in the Muslim world. Scholars of Shariah disagree about whether it is permissible. Muslim nations including Malaysia, Indonesia, Saudi Arabia, and the United Arab Emirates are welcoming the use of blockchain technology and digital currencies to develop breakthroughs in Islamic banking. In fact, market regulations pertaining to this kind of money are presently being developed.

5.11. CENTRAL BANK

The central bank can buy bonds, bills, or other notes issued by the government to promote economic growth when it wishes to expand the amount of money in circulation and lower the cost of borrowing, or interest rate. The central bank can absorb funds by selling government bonds on the open market, which will lower inflation and shrink the economy. The interest rate will then increase, discouraging borrowing as a result. Therefore, the central bank can manage inflation, the money supply, and prices through open market operations, which include buying and selling government securities to increase or decrease the amount of money in the banking system. In its capacity as the government's banker, the central bank manages the government's bank account and handles a variety of banking tasks on its behalf, including taking in payments, sending them out, managing public debt, floating public loans, and providing short-term loans to the government in hard times. The central bank, acting as a government agency, makes sure that general exchange regulation is implemented. In terms of its function as the government's advisor, it offers advice on all financial and economic issues. Because it handles all trading of government bonds and other securities, the central bank is commonly referred to as the government's bank. However, its operations would be autonomous of political decisions. The central bank holds gold and foreign currencies in order to print reserve notes and cover any imbalances in the country's balance of payments. As a result, it takes on the role of guardian for the country's foreign exchange or foreign currency reserves. In certain countries, it is in charge of overseeing exchange control and other state-imposed limitations in addition to maintaining the exchange rate that the government sets. In certain nations, it also manipulates the foreign exchange markets at the government's request to affect the value of the local currency.

At times, central banks might need to intervene to stop depositors from making large withdrawals in order to save the economy and keep financial institutions from collapsing. Therefore, in times of stress and hardship, the central bank takes on the duty of satisfying all legitimate demands made by commercial banks by serving as the lender of last resort. In times of crisis, this often entails providing member banks with cash to strengthen the position of their cash reserves by the rediscounting of first-class bills. To enhance their cash reserves as quickly as feasible, member banks can also take advantage of advances on central bank-approved short-term securities. A commercial bank can rely on the central bank to lend them extra money if it lacks the liquidity to meet the demands of its clients, that is, if it does not have enough reserves to meet the needs of its own customers. In this case, the bank will be charged at the current discount rate set by the central bank. Business cycles are the irregular periodic rise and downward trend of the total production of the economy. Recession and inflation are the terms used to describe a prolonged or persistent downturn and upward trend in the business cycle, respectively. While inflation denotes a sharp increase in the money supply, recession indicates a sharp drop in the pace of money growth. Every member of society will be impacted in one way or another by both circumstances, not just the economy and its participants. Additionally, central banks are involved in regulating the general operations of banks as well as overseeing their activities in various parts of the world. They also assist banks in setting up a variety of transactions with particular activity and customers. The majority of these activities occur inside the interest-based structure, which is forbidden by Islamic law (Ghafar & Tohirin, 2010).

Since the emergence of Islamic finance, the central banks' collaboration with Islamic banks has been essential to the expansion and development of these institutions. The type of relationship they have varies from nation to nation, mostly due to the legislative structure that governs Islamic banks' position in various nations. The Islamic Financial Services Board or IFSB was created by the central banks of several nations with a majority of Muslims to support the growth and advancement of a financial services sector that complies with Shariah and is distinguished by caution and transparency by adopting global standards that are in line with Islamic banking practices and principles. In countries that have two banking systems, laws specific to Islamic banks have been passed in addition to those governing regular banks. Initiatives have been made in different nations to create and implement laws that permit the establishment of Islamic banks in compliance with particular rules and regulations. Central banks are thought to be in a strong position to offer the crucial support to compete with traditional banks, regardless of the jurisdiction. They can support the function Islamic banks provide in a nation's socio-economic sector by creating special funds and imposing limitations on ownership, licensing, and the opening of new branches. Unfortunately, the premise for these loans is interest accumulation, which is prohibited in Islamic finance. Central banks can supply Islamic banks with liquidity in the form of partnership or joint venture capital, based on profit and risk sharing, in order to meet the requirements of Shariah. They would split any gains made from the Islamic bank's investment of the money that the central banks had advanced.

5.12. CLEARING HOUSE

In its capacity as a clearing house, the central bank can be of great assistance to Islamic banks by offering services pertaining to letters of credit and guarantees, as well as facilities for the settlement of checks and other payments, in exchange for a fee (El-Gamal, 1999). In order to utilize the clearing system, Islamic banks must first create a current account with the central bank. They also need to meet the requirements for a limited time, interest-free overdraft facility in order to offset any deficits that may arise during the settlement process. Furthermore, the central bank establishes a particular interest-free fund plan that Islamic banks can use during the deficit on a profit-sharing basis. In its capacity as the watchdog over monetary policy, the central bank guarantees stability in economic growth by enforcing strict regulations that limit the amount of money in the market and mandate that Islamic banks keep a specific amount of liquidity on their books. Because Islamic deals have a different structure, the central banks have developed a model based on common data gathered from Islamic banks to help them and their representatives follow the guidelines of Islamic banking practices. The central bank has now set lower liquidity ratios for Islamic banks in comparison to their conventional counterparts due to a greater grasp of the unique nature of their activities. Central banks must take into account several forms of control in addition to liquidity management, such as mandatory cash reserve requirements, deposit insurance programs, credit ceilings, profit-sharing for Islamic banks, bank inspections, profit-equalization funds, and monetary assets. Owing to the distinctive features of Islamic banks, the central bank must first approve the Islamic bank's statute before allowing it to function. This will make it easier for the central bank to monitor the Islamic bank's operations and look into its procedures. The central banks must create a unique set of norms and regulations for inspection purposes in order to protect the interests of investors in Islamic banks and evaluate their investment programs.

The payment of interest on cash reserves is an additional factor that central banks need to take into account. The ratio of reserves required from Islamic banks by the central banks may be lowered because Islamic banks are not permissible to deal with interest. When it comes to credit ceilings, the central banks ought to give Islamic banks extra consideration. Rather than imposing the minimum interest rates that are required of commercial banks on savings and time deposits, Islamic banks should use a weighted system to distribute profits to their depositors. Financial intermediaries are the next part of the financial system. These are the organizations that transfer money from those who have excess to those who need it but don't have enough of it. By converting a pool of short-term cash into a few sizable loans over longer terms for the borrower, financial intermediaries assist in creating assets for lenders and liabilities for borrowers. By charging the borrower a higher interest rate and giving the lender a portion of the interest, the middleman profits. Financial intermediaries are advantageous to society at large as well as lenders and borrowers. By alleviating household liquidity limitations, lowering transaction costs related to lending and borrowing, spreading risks over time, and lessening the issue of asymmetric knowledge, they contribute to increased economic efficiency.

5.13. BANKING

Banking (deposit taking) and non-banking (non-deposit taking) institutions make up financial intermediaries. Institutions that accept deposits include commercial banks and savings banks, whose primary funding source is deposits from individuals, corporations, and governmental bodies; in the case of credit unions, the source is deposits made by credit union members. When it comes to how the money is used, credit unions use it to lend money to other credit union members, whereas commercial banks and savings institutions use it to buy corporate and government assets and make loans to individuals and businesses. Institutions that do not accept deposits can be further divided into investment intermediaries, which include brokerage houses, mutual fund companies, insurance companies, pension fund companies, and contractual savings institutions. Islamic commercial banks act as indirect middlemen by purchasing money through the provision of a range of Shariah-compliant deposit products, including investment accounts, Mudarabah-based savings accounts, and current accounts (Wadiah and Qard-Hassan) (Haji Mohammad, 2015). They then offer a range of Islamic debt and equity financing options for the sale of the funds.

In addition, Islamic financial intermediaries help with the supply and demand of intangible and contingent assets and liabilities such collateral, guarantees, financial services, and custodial services. They also provide brokerage between lenders and borrowers. Financial markets are systems that make it easier to purchase and sell currencies, commodities, financial instruments, and other fungible goods. Transactions in these markets can take place in any physical location. The nature of the assets and transactions in financial markets can be categorized according to a number of factors, including the type of transaction (direct or indirect), the size of the transaction (retail and wholesale markets), the style and complexity of the transaction, and the duration or term to maturity. Money markets facilitate the brief deployment of excess money and the temporary scarcity of funds by dealing with short-term financial assets, often lasting less than a year. In comparison to securities, they are more liquid and more extensively traded. The interbank market is one particular type of money market that enables banks with surplus liquidity to lend money to other banks that are short on funds, on an unsecured basis. The financial system operates better when there is an efficient interbank market because it makes it easier for the central bank to inject or remove liquidity from the system. It permits banks to transfer their respective excesses and liquidity shortages among themselves without inadvertently raising interest rates. Conversely, capital markets deal with longer-term debt and equity capital. Governments, corporations, organizations, banks, and other financial institutions are among the players in the capital markets, as are individual and institutional investors. While capital consumers aim to raise funds at the lowest possible cost, capital suppliers anticipate receiving the highest return on their investment at the lowest risk. Primary and secondary markets are subcategories of capital markets.

5.14. COMMODITIES

Hard commodities are those natural resources, like gold, oil, and tin, which need to be mined or extracted. Conversely, agricultural and livestock products including coffee, wheat, corn, sheep, and cattle are considered soft commodities. Currency trading is the focus of foreign exchange or currency markets, also referred to as Forex or FX. Commercial banks, securities dealers, hedge funds, big international corporations, institutional investors, and central banks are the primary players. For the aim of funding international trade, making investments or conducting business overseas, or making speculations on currency price fluctuations, the members in this network purchase and sell currencies from various nations. The Islamic financial markets, in contrast to the conventional financial markets, emerged only in the 1990s as a result of the IFIs' successful mobilization of funds from expanding deposits, which they mostly invested in financial instruments related to trade financing or commodities (El-Hawary et al., 2007). IFIs had to concentrate on short-term financial instruments because of a lack of liquid assets and restricted investment prospects, but they soon learned that the growth of capital markets was essential to their long-term survival and growth. In order to discover solutions for liquidity and portfolio management, traditional financial institutions and IFIs worked closely together during the wave of capital deregulation and liberalization that occurred in the late 1990s. As a result, efforts were concentrated in two primary areas: a portfolio of Islamic securities, mostly in the form of equities shares and commodities, and debt-like security in the form of an asset-backed security.

Chapter 6

ISLAMIC PRACTICES IN BANKING AT SOUTHEAST ASIAN REGIONS

Contents

6.1. INTRODUCTION

Judaism and Christianity are the two major monotheistic faiths in the world and Islam is one of them. All three have similar historical beginnings and many shared beliefs, one of which being their regard for the prophets of the Old Testament. Islam prohibits eating pig and any other flesh that hasn't been ritually slaughtered, much like Judaism does (halah). Muslims acknowledge Jesus (Isa) as a prophet, but they do not hold the notion that he is god's son. They also reject the Christian idea of the Trinity and insist on the oneness of God (Allah), without acknowledging the existence of the holy spirit. They also reject the idea of original sin and the idea that there is a way for someone to stand in between a person and God. According to Islam, everyone must work toward their own salvation by faith, good deeds, and a sincere effort to uphold God's rule, which is outlined in the Quran. The Quran contains revelations from God that the prophet Muhammad received. The revelation was given in Arabic. All Muslims regard the recitation of the Quran with great reverence and attach great importance to it; in order to recite the Quran, one must perform ritual cleansing (wudu). The Arabic root Salema, which connotes purity, peace, obedience, and submission, is where the name Islam originates (Dobiyanski, 2018). Islam is a religion that emphasizes adherence to God's law and surrender to his will. It establishes personal and social systems of obligation by governing relationships between people; it also establishes ritual obligation by governing relationships between people and God.

6.2. ISLAMIC FOUNDATION

All stable constructions have strong foundations, and Islam is said to rest on five pillars that are mandated by God and upheld by all genuine Muslims. Obviously, the fundamental beliefs of Islam are that Muhammad is the prophet of Allah and that Allah is the one God. One of the most essential aspects of being a good Muslim is praying regularly. Muslims are obligated to pray five times a day: at dawn, noon, midday, after sunset, and night. Furthermore, Ramadan, the ninth month in the Islamic calendar, is a time when all Muslims are supposed to fast. Adult Muslims who are in excellent health at this time are not allowed to eat or drink during the day. A Muslim must also make the annual obligatory donation of zakat, or a certain percentage of their total wealth, to the underprivileged and needy. Every Muslim who has the means to do so ought to visit Mecca at least once in their lives. The Haj is a pilgrimage that can only be completed correctly on Eid Ul-Adha, which falls on the first day of the Muslim calendar each year. All Muslims adhere to these five pillars of Islam, which form the foundation of Islam as a religious organization. The main place of prayer in Islam is the communal mosque, or masjid. The Prophet Muhammad's Medina home served as the first mosque. The Prophet and his wives had quarters in this modest rectangular enclosure, and on the south side was a covered space where they could pray while facing Mecca, the site of the Prophet's and Islam's birthplace. Muhammad then constructed a minbar, from which he preached, and this fundamental design served as the model for all other mosques. The prayer hall, also known as the musalla, is essentially a sizable, empty space with a mihrab, in one wall that indicates which way Muslims should face Mecca during their prayers. Worshippers sit on mats laid on the floor, occupying the clear interior area save for the minbar. There are restrooms available outside since it is a prerequisite of Islam for believers to be emotionally and physically pure before praying. In addition to being a site of religious worship, the mosque also serves as a community center, a learning space, and occasionally a courthouse.

6.3. RELIGION

Muslims contend that Islam is the original religion of the ancient prophets, including Adam and Abraham, and that it was modified throughout time by the Jews and later the Christians, to the point where their sacred texts, the Torah and the Bible, no longer accurately represent the word of God. God therefore sent the last prophet, Muhammad, and the last revelation, the Quran, to give everyone one last chance to choose the right path. Muhammad was born in 570 A.D. in Mecca, Saudi Arabia. His family was the Quraysh, a well-known tribe in the region at the time. Muhammad is said to have occasionally retired to a solitary cave on Mount Hira. During the month of Ramadan, he was taken aback when he unexpectedly found himself in the company of the angel Gabriel, who gave him instructions to recite the verses stitched on a green brocade. He left the cave out of fear that he had been taken over and told his wife, Khadijah, about what had happened. She proceeded to see her wise Christian cousin Waraqah, who reassured her that the vision was real, and that Muhammad had been chosen by God to be a prophet to his people. The Prophet started to regularly see Gabriel, who would bring revelations that he had to recite out loud. He gradually drew a small group of followers around him, but the Quraysh did not take kindly to this new preacher who called on people to stop worshiping idols and turn to only one God. As a result, they persecuted Muhammad and everyone who followed him; the Meccan merchants were particularly adamant in their opposition to Muhammad because they disagreed with the Quran's implied criticism of their customs.

6.4. PROPHET MUHAMMED

Muhammad and his followers eventually left Mecca and moved to Medina, where they were welcomed by the locals, because the persecution had gotten so bad (Arjomand, 2009). This occurred in 622 A.D., and the first year of the Muslim calendar, denoted by the letters "AH," is the year of migration (Hijrah). Muhammad established himself in Medina during the subsequent years, but he and his ever-growing group of supporters had to engage in numerous conflicts before they could defeat the Quraysh and return to Mecca, where the idols in the Ka'bah were destroyed and Islam triumphed. The golden age of Islam in Southeast Asia occurred by trade rather than military conquest. Arab traders were trading Eastern commodities with India even before Islam arrived. Arab sailors were the first to take use of the Indian Ocean's seasonal monsoon winds. It was via business that Islam was first introduced to South-east Asia by Arab traders. Direct trade with the East offered a huge economic incentive. The majority of Oriental commodities had a lengthy and sometimes risky journey to the marketplace, and each time products were traded, there was a large markup in price. The benefits increased with one's proximity to the source.

Regarding Southeast Asia (Figure 6.1), Arab vessels began to navigate Malay and Indonesian seas in the sixth century. Their presence in China was partly due to trade with China, but it may have been fueled even more by the profitable trade in spices, mostly from Java, Sumatra, the Moluccas (Maluku) and Banda islands at the eastern end of the archipelago, which included pepper, cloves, and nutmeg. Without a doubt, the earliest Arab traders in the area were only transient, brave traders who packed their cargo with spices and other exotic goods before sailing back to India and the Arabian Peninsula with the arrival of the northeast monsoon. However, throughout time, Muslim traders set up permanent trading facilities at key spots inside the Malay and Indonesian Archipelago, as well as at numerous points along the trade route between India and China. Many of these trading centers, which had once been little more than a village at the mouth of a river, had developed into thriving enterprises by the 15th century, their prosperity based on transshipment between East and West and regional trade, mostly in spices. City-states such as Aceh in northern Sumatra, Malacca on the Malay Peninsula, and Banten, Cirebon, and Demak in Java became independent mini-superpowers that engaged in rivalry and warfare. In addition, they were internationally recognized hubs for the arts and sciences that drew scientists, writers, poets, and artists from as far afield as China, Persia, and the Arabian Peninsula. Despite their varied racial and religious composition, the ruling class of these empire nations was always Muslim by the middle of the 16th century, with a Sultan sitting on the throne.

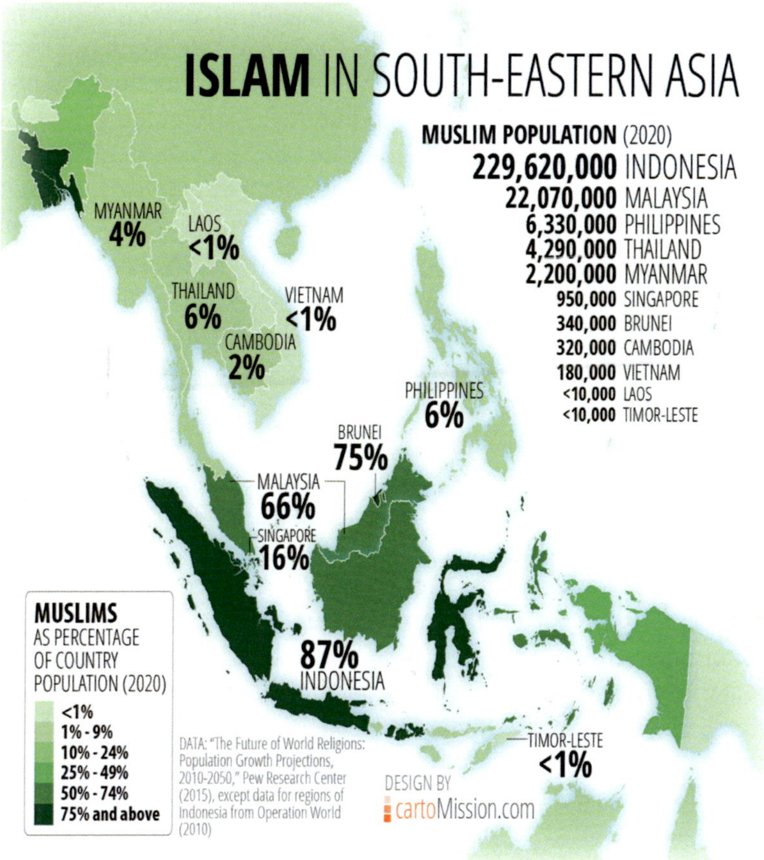

Figure 6.1. *Southeast Asia.*

Source: CartoMisson [cartographer], (2015). Islam in South-Eastern Asia [map]. Scale not given. Retrieved from: https://cartomission.com/2015/08/28/islam-in-south-eastern-asia/, Creative Commons License.

6.5. ISLAMIZATION

Islamization continued in eastern Indonesia during the 16th and 17th century (Wellfelt & Djonler, 2019). Muslim sultans ruled the island nations of Ternate and Tidore and Muslim merchants had established themselves in the Banda Islands in the 16th century. The monarch of Gowa, in southern Sulawesi, converted to Islam in 1605, and he later imposed the faith on the rulers of neighboring regions. Up to the late 17th century, Muslim missionaries were dispatched to Lombok, Sulawesi, and Kalimantan from the north shore of Java. The period of Islamic dominance in Southeast Asia spanned just a few centuries, and at the start of the 17th century, these maritime sultanates encountered significant disputes with Christian adversaries contending for authority over the profitable trade in spices such as pepper, cloves, and nutmeg. Early in the 16th century, the Portuguese were the first to appear on the scene; the Spanish, English, and Dutch soon followed. By the end of the 17th century, the great days of the Sultanates had passed, and the Muslim initiative in South-east Asia had been put on hold.

The deletion of Islam as a global political and military force and its reduction to the status of just another religion alongside others are results of European colonization of significant portions of SE Asia in the 18th to 19th centuries, as well as the subsequent subjugation of Muslim politics in the region to European rule. From a South-east Asian perspective, Islam itself had to contend with strong competition from Christianity, while the international order that had previously reinforced the authority of local monarchs in the region had collapsed. A new global order, new institutions, and new ideals were introduced by Western colonization. New political boundaries were drawn that ignored historical facts and were based on secular ideals. Modern bureaucracies were established, and western conceptions of justice, commerce, and governance were introduced. Large plantations were built in Java, Sumatra, and the Malay Peninsula, with the main products being coffee, sugar, tobacco, and eventually rubber. Immigrants from China and India were transported to the area to provide labor. The development of telecommunication connected South-east Asia to the outside world, while steam-based transportation and the Suez Canal increased Europe's proximity to the continent. Even though they continued to sit in their palaces, the sultans were marginalized both politically and economically. Muslims were mostly immobilized, resistance to change was strong, and religious education was prioritized. Additionally, even while Muslims in Southeast Asia still looked to the Middle East for guidance and inspiration, the region was also seriously threatened by the West at this time. As a result, the Ottoman Empire collapsed and was dismantled at the end of World War I (Faroqhi, 2004).

Islam at the turn of the last century provided the foundation for a new beginning. Islamic revivalism emerged as new perspectives on how Islam should respond to contemporary society replaced the traditional, dogmatic interpretation of Islam. Islam began to decline in the 16th century and was supplanted by Europe that was growing on all sides. The reconquest of Russia and Spain marked the start of the process. After circumnavigating Africa, Western Europeans started to assert their increasing dominance in Southeast, Southern, and finally South-West Asia. In a sense, Islam found itself in a firm position between the peoples of Western Europe in the south and Russia in the north. The intimidating military strength of the Ottoman, Persian, and

Mughal empires temporarily concealed or delayed these shifts, but eventually these too collapsed and were unable to withstand the European march. Western dominance persisted until the colonial empires of Britain, France, Holland, and Italy were destroyed and their former colonies gained independence following World War II. In South-east Asia, the war in the Pacific signaled the beginning of the end of colonialism, if only because it disproved the widespread belief that Caucasians were inherently superior to everyone else. In actuality, the Japanese, who arrived as liberators, proved to be even harsher rulers than the colonial administrations they had replaced, essentially converting their newly conquered lands into police states governed by mistrust and terror. The triumphant Allies received in the majority of their former colonial possessions, but they returned to a completely different world from the one they had fled in 1942. Even though they had defeated Japan, they were unable to ignore the truth that their chances of maintaining their imperial holdings in Southeast Asia were few.

6.6. PHILIPPINES

The Philippines (Figure 6.2) became independent in July 1946, ending over 50 years of American domination (Romulo, 1961). General MacArthur did, as he had promised, return to the Philippines, but only for a brief period of time. The Philippines was the first country to achieve independence. In the case of the Netherlands East Indies, nationalists from Indonesia held out until 1950 before giving up their claim to their former holdings in South-east Asia, even though the Dutch had unilaterally declared their independence following Japan's surrender. Malaya was given over by the British in a far more structured and transparent manner, even though the colonial government had to wage a bloody war against communist rebels in the years preceding the country's complete independence in 1957. Six years later, Singapore became independent and joined the newly formed Malaysia. However, in 1965, Singapore broke away from Malaysia to become a sovereign republic. While Brunei, a British protectorate since 1888, attained complete independence in 1984, British North Borneo and Sarawak, which had previously been governed by the British, joined Malaysia in 1963. Muslims in South-east Asia face significant challenges as a result of the emergence of new nation-states that demand new types of allegiance and are strongly impacted by western political culture after independence. They served as a symbol of the pre-colonial social order that had survived to some extent. In the case of the Malay sultans, in fact, the colonial experience had arguably strengthened their position in terms of consolidating their territorial control and power base. However, the realities of their time had changed so drastically, especially at the national, regional, and international levels, that they were forced to become marginalized. Muslim groups in the region most likely found it more difficult to adapt to the demands of the nation-state than did other religious communities. The transition to modern nationhood, which is based to varying degrees on the idea of a liberal democracy in the western tradition, has been challenging because they were unfamiliar with new political institutions essential to the formation of the nation-state, such as a secular constitution, an independent judiciary, citizenship, political parties, elections, and so on.

Figure 6.2. *Philippines.*

Source: https://en.wikivoyage.org/wiki/Philippines#/media/File:Map_of_Philippines_(en).png, Creative Commons License.

6.7. MALAYSIA

Malaysia and Brunei, both have Islam as their official religion. Although there are five recognized religions in Indonesia, Muslim, Protestant, Roman Catholic, Hindu, and Buddhist, Muslims make up 88% of the country's population. Though just about 5% of people in the southern Philippines are Muslims, the religion has a strong hold there. The Muslim population in Singapore is estimated to be 14%. The legal framework of Brunei is founded on English common law, with Islamic law exclusively applicable to Muslims. Malaysia's legal system is founded on English common law, with important legal contributions also coming from Islamic law (Shariah) and customary law (Adat), especially when it comes to issues of personal status. Due to the three legal systems that the independent state of Indonesia inherited, its legal system is incredibly complex: Dutch colonial law, Islamic law, which frequently governs disputes between Muslims, and Adat law, which has historically served as the foundation for resolving social disputes in the traditional village environment. The Spanish and American legal systems, such as those pertaining to family and property and taxes, trade, and government, have a significant influence on the Philippine legal system. The Majlis Ugama Islam Singapore (Singapore Islamic Council), which was established by the Muslim Law Act of 1966 to advise the President on topics pertaining to Islam, is the foundation of Singapore's legal system, which is based on English common law (Neo, 2020). Because of this, Islamic law is most prevalent in the legal arrangements of Indonesia and Malaysia where Shariah law has been incorporated. In contrast, laws in Singapore and Brunei permit less involvement with Islamic law, and in the Philippines, Islamic law is essentially absent from the legal framework. Islam, for instance, has long been associated with a philosophy of resistance in the Philippines, first against the Spanish-led spread of Christianity during colonial times and then, following independence, against the power of the Christian-majority Republic of the Philippines.

The Muslim Moro people in the south of the Philippines felt oppressed by the Christian majority in the north after World War II, and they were angry that their region was less developed politically and economically than the north. This was true even though the country was almost immediately granted independence from the US. They have successfully garnered the backing of Muslims worldwide, including Saudi Arabia, since the 1950s. These Muslims have collectively voiced their objection to what they believe to be the mistreatment, if not outright persecution, of their fellow Muslims in the southern Philippines. Islamic regimes have backed Muslim Filipino students studying in Saudi Arabia and given money they were making from the petroleum trade to Muslim

Filipinos. They have dispatched Islamic missionaries to teach Islam in the southern Philippines, and they still do. They have also invited Muslim leaders to conferences in the Middle East to discuss their issues. In Mindanao and the other smaller islands in the southern Philippines, Islam is still widely practiced today. More than 300 years ago, in the 16th century, Muslims in the southern Philippines fought against Spanish colonization and subsequently American imperialism for nearly 50 years, beginning the Bangsa Moro people's quest for statehood. Resistance to the Philippine government has existed throughout the modern era from the 1950s until the present.

The country of Malaysia has seen a very easy transition to independence and nationhood, notwithstanding certain difficulties encountered along the route. The Colony of the straits settlements was established in 1826 when the British settlements of Malacca, Penang, and Singapore were merged. The British established protectorates over the Malay sultanates on the peninsula in the late 19th century, based on these lands. The Federated Malay States were formed in 1895 when Pahang, Perak, Selangor, and Negri Sembilan were combined. Large-scale tin and rubber production was developed, public services were expanded, and a well-organized system of public administration was built while under British rule. The Japanese invasion and occupation of this area from 1942 to 1945 caused a break in this control. In an attempt to regain control after World War II, Britain created a plan in October 1945 to unify all of the Federated and Unfederated Malay States, as well as Penang and Melaka, under a single, centralized administration known as the Malayan Union. But due to its economics, racial composition, and strategic significance, Singapore was left out and was to stay a British colony. It was viewed as a distinct situation. But the Malays were furious when the Malayan Union proposal was released, particularly because it diminished the Sultans' authority and position and denied the Malays their rights collectively.

6.8. BRITISH

The British Government (Figure 6.3) decided to scrap the project completely due to the strong opposition in Malaya and criticism at home. A sort of temporary caretaker administration was erected in its place while the British established a working committee made up of Malays and, subsequently, a consultative committee to which representatives of the other Malayan races were invited to submit comments. The Federation of Malaya Agreement was drafted by the British Government based on the conclusions from the committees, and its contents were implemented in February 1948 (Fernando, 2016). Its borders were the same as those of the defunct Malayan Union. The Malay sultans had to approve the appointment of the British High Commissioner, who served as the

Federation's top official. The sultans belonged to the Conference of Rulers and there were two councils: the Executive Council and the Legislative Council. Compared to the Malayan Union, the Federation's citizenship requirements became far more stringent. In response to the combined forces of a communist uprising and the growth of a potent Malay nationalist movement, the British instituted municipal elections in 1951. The creation of the Alliance, which included UMNO, the Malayan Chinese Association or MCA, and the Malayan Indian Congress or MIC, fostered political collaboration among the three major ethnic groupings in the nation: Malays, Chinese, and Indians. On September 16, 1963, the British colonies of Singapore, Sarawak, and Sabah (formerly known as North Borneo) became a part of Malaysia by joining the Federation.

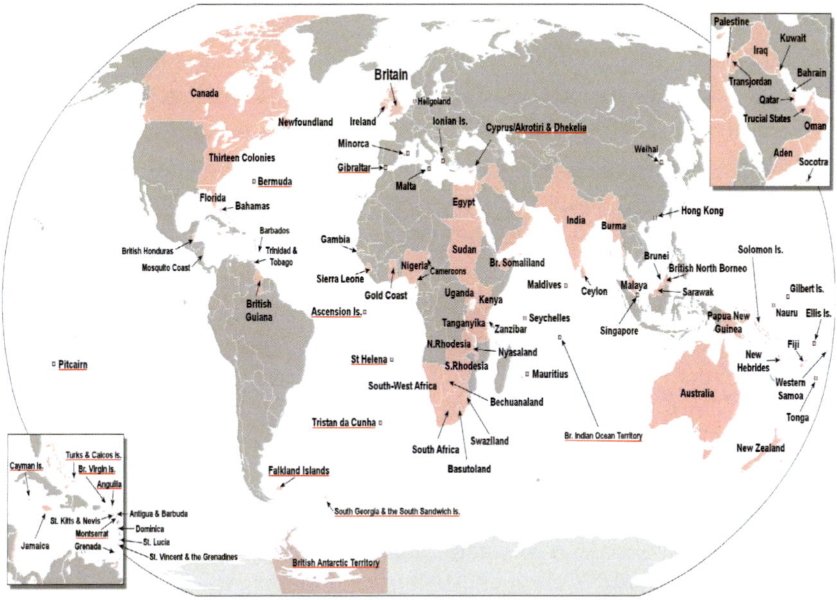

Figure 6.3. *British empire.*

Source: https://en.wikipedia.org/wiki/Territorial_evolution_of_the_British_Empire#/media/File:The_British_Empire.png, Creative Commons License.

Singapore became a self-governing republic on August 9, 1965, when it left the Federation. The creation of Malaysia was opposed by neighboring Indonesia, which launched an offensive of economic, political, diplomatic, and military confrontation against the new country that didn't conclude until 1966 with the overthrow of President Sukarno. A state of emergency was declared in 1948 as a result of a protracted, violent insurrection led by the local communists, almost all of whom were Chinese. Along the border with southern Thailand, small groups of guerrillas continued to hold bases and would periodically cross into northern Malaysia. In December 1989, these insurgents and the Malaysian government ultimately signed a peace treaty. In Sarawak, a smaller-scale communist insurgency that started in the middle of the 1960s came to an end in October 1990 with the signing of a peace agreement. Mahathir Mohamed, the previous prime minister of Malaysia, oversaw the country's fast development and modern infrastructure transformation. However, in a secular country with a majority of Muslims and affluent Chinese and Indian minority, race and religion continue to be contentious issues. In order to create a thriving, multiethnic country, Mahathir kept radical Islam at bay for 22 years without alienating the majority of Muslims. Malaysia, a democratic country of 25 million people, does not uphold strict Islamic rule or Shariah and has a sizable non-Muslim community (Weiss, 2004).

Brunei maintained its independence on the inside but came under British protectorate rule over its exterior affairs in 1888. A British resident was given executive authority in 1906, and this gave Brunei even more British influence. The resident advised the ruler on all issues except those pertaining to native customs and religion. Large oil fields were discovered in the 1920s, which led to Brunei's economic boom. The nation was taken over by the Japanese in 1941 and returned to Britain after the Australians freed it in 1945. Year 1950 saw the rise of Sir Omar Ali Saiffuddin Saadul Khairi Waddien (1916–1986), better known as Sir Omar, to the throne. A new constitution was drafted in 1959 designating Brunei as an independent nation, although the United Kingdom continued to oversee its security, defense, and foreign policy. A 1962 attempt to establish a legislature with limited authority that was partially elected was shelved when Partai Rakyat Brunei, the opposition political party, staged an armed insurgency that the government put down with the aid of British forces. The government also rejected calls to include Sarawak and Sabah, two neighboring states, in the newly established Malaysia in the late 1950s and early 1960s. Eventually, Omar, the sultan, declared that Brunei would stay a sovereign nation. A treaty of cooperation was signed on January 4, 1979, between Brunei and the United Kingdom. Brunei Darussalam gained complete independence on January 1, 1984. Though the constitution guarantees religious freedom, Islam is the official religion of Brunei, which is ruled by an Islamic monarchy. It is an affiliate of the Organization of the Islamic Conference or OIC, the Association of Southeast Asian Nations (ASEAN), the Asia Pacific Economic Cooperation (APEC) conference, and the United Nations. There is also strong support for enacting legislation based on Islamic law in several spheres of the government and society.

It may be argued that some scrutiny of Brunei's current British colonial legal system, which includes a large amount of English-language legislation, is an essential component of the country's decolonization process. It is important to keep in mind that Brunei did not achieve complete independence until the middle of the 1980s. The influence of religion from Malaysia, where there has been a strengthening of Islamic institutions since the 1970s, is another factor to take into account while attempting to explain the contemporary Islamic zeal in political, legal, and social domains. However, there are two problems with replacing the colonial-based legal system with one that is more influenced by Islam. Although being influenced by long-standing Muslim monarchy traditions, Brunei is more of a moderate Muslim state than a fundamentalist one. The government actively works to foster a strong sense of Islamic brotherhood and loyalty among the Malay people. The government of Brunei aims to establish itself as a significant player in the ASEAN, especially as a hub for trade in the East Asian growth region, which includes the southern Philippines, Malaysia's Labuan, Sarawak, and Sabah, and Indonesia's Sulawesi, Moluccas, and Kalimantan. It will be necessary to strike a compromise between the desire to portray Brunei as a growing economic enterprise that is particularly appealing and hospitable to the international business community, and the demands to impose a more strongly Islamic legal framework. The post-Second World War experiment with nationhood is still ongoing, as is the persistent issue of violent Muslim insurgency in Southeast Asia aimed at achieving secessionism. Liberal democracy has many obvious flaws. Following the more widespread global resurgence of Islam in the 1970s and 1980s, many Muslims felt compelled to reevaluate the entirety of Western institutions, ideas, and values because they seemed to have stoked conflict, discontent, and even discouragement among the populace. Desecularization and Islamization have been demanded. In Malaysia, the Philippines, and Indonesia, there is obviously an Islamic revival. The economic and religious future of the Muslims in South-east Asia appears to be brighter due to the region's abundant resources, which include labor, capital, raw materials, markets, entrepreneurial talents, and a likely revitalized and religiously inspired vigor to seek out alternatives.

6.9. SOUTHEAST ASIA

South-east Asian countries' political constitutions were significantly impacted by colonialism, which replaced the authoritarian rule of an absolute monarch and his court with concepts of parliamentary governance, an autonomous judiciary, and democracy in the western tradition (Tan, 2013). Naturally, this was more of a survival from the colonial past than an actuality at the time, but in the modern era, it can be argued that all of Southeast Asia's nations are indebted to the west, if only in the sense of the concept of a nation state with well-defined borders. The degree of this debt to the west varies from nation to nation, for example,

Brunei's Sultan still rules by decree and lacks political parties, while Myanmar's military junta controls the country, but everywhere there is evidence of western influence in the political system. Even Thailand, which was obviously never colonized, has an elected parliament in addition to a constitutional monarchy. The way Islamic law has been applied in contemporary Southeast Asia, and specifically how Shariah law interacts with secular state legal frameworks, has largely depended on state policy. For instance, in Myanmar (Burma), Islam served as both the personal law and the religion of an immigrant population that was founded under the cover of British colonialism. However, during Burma's 50 years of independence, all Burmese governments have clamped down on ethnic minorities' freedoms, viewing them as a threat to the effective execution of political-economic initiatives like the Burmese way to socialism. The outcome has been the nearly total eradication of Islam in Burma and a large flight of the immigrant commercial community. In contrast, Muslim law in Southern Thailand has remained mostly unaltered, despite the fact that ethnic Malay Muslims have long been a marginalized minority group limited to family law. Nevertheless, a number of Muslim freedom movements had emerged, and in 1977, a Muslim separatist group was blamed for an attempted assassination of King. Therefore, the focus of government policy has been on integrating the Muslim minority, possibly even forcing them to do so, especially through education. Because of this, even if Muslim law is recognized by Thai law, it is most likely applied informally. The Malay people in Peninsula Malaysia adhere to Islam as their official religion. The modern state administration of Islam originates from Britain's recognition during the colonial era of both the Islamic and indigenous elements of Malay sovereignty. Because of the religion's official recognition in the state and federal constitutions of Malaysia, it has gained direct relevance in modern Malaysian politics and has become a constitutional problem.

Malaysia (Figure 6.4) is a multiethnic nation with a secular constitution that was inherited from the British, along with a legal system and court (Ahmad, 2007). This is an unusual historical position in that Shariah law was shaped by the colonial experience, much as English common law was modified to suit the needs of ruling peoples of different religions and cultures in Malaya. Malaysia offers a fitting case study to highlight how non-Islamic influences, primarily western ones, it must be noted, have impacted Southeast Asian Sharia law. With the exception of those who lived in Malacca's near vicinity, the Portuguese conquest of Malacca in 1503 had little direct impact on the publics of the Malay Peninsula, despite its great significance in terms of regional geopolitics. Nor did the Dutch overthrow the Portuguese in 1641, and western ideas didn't start to seep into traditional Malay culture until the English East India Company bought the island of Penang (Pulau Pinang), off the northwest coast of Malaya, from the Rajah of Kedah in the late 18th century. This occurred in 1786, and Penang quickly developed into a thriving enterprise. However, it was not quite in the ideal location, as it was slightly too far north to fully benefit from the maritime trade between East and West. Before the building of the Suez Canal, the Sunda Straits, which separate Sumatra from Java, were the most popular route from Europe to China. Then, in the southernmost point of the Malay Peninsula, on the island of Singapore, Stamford Raffles opened a second trade post in 1819. With its advantageous location on the sea route connecting Europe and China, as well as its excellent natural harbor, Singapore quickly emerged as the main commercial hub of the region. Following Britain's purchase of Malacca from the Dutch in 1824, the three principal ports on the Strait of Malacca came to be referred to as the Straits Settlements (Thia-Eng et al., 2000). The Straits Settlements were governed by the Indian office following the British government's dissolution of the East India Company in 1858, and they were granted their independence as a crown colony in 1867.

Figure 6.4. *Malaysia.*

Source: https://en.wikipedia.org/wiki/Geography_of_Malaysia#/media/File:My-map.png, Creative Commons License.

At that time, Malay sultans, who were often at war with one another, ruled over the whole Malay Peninsula, with the exception of Malacca. This was mostly an agrarian culture, with rivers serving as the main channels and a largely undiscovered rainforest that was not even visited by the Malays. Chinese immigrants started to settle in considerable numbers on the west coast of the Malay Peninsula by the middle of the 19th century, driven away from the increasing poverty and instability of their native country. There, they worked along with the local Malay rulers to mine tin. As they forged agreements with rival Malay chiefs, the Chinese organized themselves into clan-based societies. This quickly resulted in an endemic state of petty conflict and disorder as various Chinese factions fought for control of mineral riches. The potential mineral wealth of Malaya also drew in British businessmen, but they were cautious of the chaotic political climate in the Malay Peninsula. The British Government resisted getting involved in the sultan's affairs for a long time, but in the end, they gave in to the pressures of the Straits Settlements' merchant community. On January 20, 1874, a treaty was signed between the British and Sultan Abdullah of Perak on the west coast island of Pangkor, formalizing British involvement in the state's political affairs through the appointment of a resident, who served as the British government's authority.

The British improved their act and appointed more capable representatives, and eventually other Malay states adopted the resident system. The initial British intervention into Malayan internal affairs was harsh and insensitive. Kuala Lumpur served as the capital of the Malay Federation, which included Perak, Selangor, Negeri Sembilan, and Pahang. Although the English common law was brought to the Malay Peninsula by the British, it was not exactly the same system that existed at the time back in England. The long-term effects of the English doctrine of precedent were one significant outcome. It was not required to consult the traditional Arabic sources in order to determine what Islamic law meant in British India or, later, British Malaya. Instead, one only needed to look at the model. Certain court findings that were in fact against Islamic law came to be considered authoritative in certain contexts. There are even cases from the highest courts that rejected traditional Arabic rulings since to uphold them would have required reversing long-standing local practice. There were other changes happening as well. For instance, Islamic standards of proof began to be marginalized and disregarded more and more. Simultaneously, access to the ideas of Islamic law was hampered by British court personnel's lack of adequate training in the subject. This resulted in the continued application of Roman law, English law, and other legal guidelines. The adoption of English as the official language of the Indian justice system and the creation of a hierarchical general court structure naturally tended to favor decisions made in conformity with English law above regional legal norms. The Malay States were sovereign states under the treaties and conventions, and unlike in the Straits Settlements, English law was not legally implemented. Rather, the laws that were in effect in any Malay State at the time they were brought under British protection remained so, barring any changes made by legislation. Naturally, a significant portion of English law was adopted through the adoption of Indian or Straits legislation. Judges also completed a thorough reception in an attempt to close any gaps in the laws of each state. There was a great deal of legal ambiguity during the early stages of the development of contemporary Muslim personal law in the Malay Peninsula, and state-to-state variations in practice prevailed. Nevertheless, Muslim law was generally recognized as a general law up until the Second World War. States were given jurisdiction over the application and legislation of Shariah starting in 1948. From 1952 to 1978, new laws known as the administration of Islamic/Muslim law enactments were promulgated in Muslim-majority states in Malaysia and Sabah (Shamsul, 2005).

6.10. ENGLISH COMMON LAW

The English Common Law does not consider the Shariah law found in the Quran or practices. Therefore, it does not serve Muslims' needs in directing their way of life along the Islamic path. There is potential for conflict between the Shariah and English legal systems due to their separate courts; in such cases, a determination of which system is superior must be made based on the specific circumstances. The Shariah Is emphasis on a direct interaction with Allah rather than through formalized religious institutions presents another issue. Islam's strength is in its ability to facilitate instantaneous communication and contact between humans and God, but it also has a flaw in that it lacks a well-developed legal theory that considers the role of governmental authority. Islam has particularly struggled to accept the concept of the "State" as it was introduced to the Muslim world from western Europe. As far as the current analysis is concerned, the fundamental point of contention has been the issue of whether English law, when applied in circumstances where it conflicts with Muslim law, is valid. This is the most essential part of disputes; it basically questions how one choose which law to apply when there is a disagreement between the principles of Islam and the rules of the state. The fundamental problem with trying to respond to this question is that neither Islam nor secular legal systems can fully address it. Since each is exclusive, each must insist on its own application, making the solution to the issue at least partially, if not entirely, a matter of policy. It is important to remember that policy decisions frequently take on legal forms, some of which are extremely intricate. This line of reasoning, which was criticized for being mechanical and unsuited to the needs of a multiethnic society like Singapore, where different racial and religious groups coexist, was based on an orthodox interpretation of the law in a situation where there was a serious conflict of legal principles. This has led to violent political confrontations between Muslims and the authorities of the state. Placing the social ramifications of a choice ahead of the technical limitations of laws which are not intended to handle the ramifications of internal conflicts regarding personal laws would have prevented this impasse. However, because it tends to disregard a fundamental tenet of common law conflicts of laws, namely, that domicile determines the power to decide how a personal law is applied, such a solution can be seen as a little too radical.

Although the newly independent Malaya chose to maintain the British legal system that was in place at the time, the country's Islamic legal system has been evolving recently to more closely and directly apply Islamic principles. In order to respect the religious sensibilities of the Malay peoples, the law administration throughout the colonial era focused mainly on enforcing those principles that were immediately necessary. This effectively restricted Islamic law to Muslim family law, which was further constrained by Adat, or local customary law, in some areas and for some issues. The establishment of the state religious departments, the legislature, and the religious courts have all played significant roles in this. There is still an intrinsic tension between state law and Muslim law in Malaysia today because of the English common law's enduring effect on the country's legal framework. Due to Malaysia's multiethnic populace and secular constitution, which work against the implementation of Shariah as state law, this situation is largely inevitable. Malaysia is one of the Asian nations striving to become a financial hub for the area, and it is working hard to develop its financial sector. The complete integration of Islamic banking and financial services within the nation's current financial system is a unique aspect of Malaysia's economy (Akram Laldin, 2008).

In response to ethnic Malay Muslim protests against ethnic Chinese dominance in the commercial sector in Malaysia in the late 1960s, the government launched a program to redistribute wealth and give Muslim Malays greater political blow. At the same time, Islamic traditionalists were demonstrating against what they perceived as western influences that had become entrenched in Malaysia and were tainting the country's moral and cultural life. The government started Islamic banking in parallel with regular banking on a trial basis, in part to appease these activists and to offer commercial opportunities targeted primarily at Muslim Malay people. After 10 years, it permanently integrated Islamic banking into the financial system and is becoming proud of its Islamic banking industry. The Islamic Banking Act (IBA) of 1983 and the concurrent creation of Bank Islam Malaysia brought Islamic banking to Malaysia (Ariff & Rosly, 2011). The introduction of a dual banking system made it possible for Islamic and traditional banking to coexist. There are Islamic securities and money markets, and nearly all financial institutions in Malaysia have established specialized Islamic sections. At the same time, there were two fully Islamic banks: Bank Islam Malaysia Berhad, which was previously mentioned, and Bank Muamalat Malaysia Berhad, which in 2003 had 40 branches and RM7.3 billion in total assets. In order to regulate the activities of Islamic banks in Malaysia, the IBA of 1983 was introduced. As with other licensed banks, it gave Malaysia's central bank, Bank Negara, the authority to oversee and control Islamic banks. At the same time, the Government Investment Act 1983 was passed, giving the Malaysian government the authority to issue Government Investment Certificates (GICs), which are government securities issued in accordance with Shariah. Islamic banks may use GIC investments to satisfy mandated liquidity requirements because they are considered liquid assets.

6.11. FINANCIAL INSTITUTIONS

With the backing and encouragement of the government, Malaysian financial institutions have chosen their own approach to interpreting Islamic law, which has allowed them to develop a wide range of Islamic financial instruments, in contrast to the Islamic banks that have been established in Arab countries since the end of the 1970s. Naturally, they still need to adhere to Sharia law in this regard. Shariah compliance is an essential part of the Islamic system of financial management, and it cannot be compromised. The National Supervisory Commission for Islamic Banking and Takaful (Islamic insurance) was created by the central bank of Malaysia in 1997 to oversee the uniform and consistent application of Islamic regulations (Berkem, 2014). The Shariah Supervisory Council was established by statute, as mandated by the IBA and the BAFIA. While the BAFIA requires Malaysia's central bank, Bank Negara, to set up a National Shariah Supervisory Council at the national level to advise the central bank on matters pertaining to Islamic banking, the IBA is imposed on a bank that wishes to conduct Islamic banking. Modifications were implemented specifically to acknowledge and tackle the necessity of harmonizing the distinctions between Islamic and traditional banking. The Real Property Gains Tax or RPGT of 1979 forbids double taxation, and the Stamp Duty Act of 1989 was modified to avoid double stamp duty. Any gain from the transaction that is realized within five years of the date of disposal shall be deemed chargeable gain and subject to taxation under the modified clause. The rate of interest would be 30% of the profit or gain from the transaction if the acquisition and disposal were completed in the same year. In Malaysia, Islamic financial goods were first made available to customers through an Islamic Window, which allowed established conventional banks to offer Islamic banking products to their clientele rather than opening new Islamic banks. The Malaysian government aimed to establish an Islamic banking system in tandem with the traditional system. The Malaysian central bank created an interest-free banking scheme in March 1993, putting the concept of an Islamic window into practice.

Chapter 7

EUROPEAN UNION AND ISLAMIC BANKING

Contents

7.1. INTRODUCTION

In order to maintain continuity with the holy principle that forbids interest of any type, Islamic banks have adopted an ethical and religious character that is part of a shared historical legacy. Early western banks both sprang from the same cultural infusion. These institutions only seem to have forgotten about the moral considerations surrounding lending and, by extension, the so-called irregular deposits in more recent times. Regarding Islam, the basic and unchanging conflict between ethics and the market had already become evident in pre-capitalist times. The historical setting in which the relationship between the Qur'anic ban on interest and the financial demands of medieval trade surfaces is that of Mecca, which appears to have been one of the most prosperous trade centers during the Prophet's lifetime and thus demonstrates an undeniable understanding of such demands (Ibrahim, 1981). It becomes clear that this specific dialectic is distinct from the other social situations in which the other monotheistic religions were established and developed. The first instance of divine intervention in the economic sphere is said to have happened during the genesis. These historical narratives are widely accepted by the monotheistic faiths. Rather than contradicting the logic of profit derived from daily labor, the logic of solidarity completes it. Consistent with the Old Testament, the Qur'an consistently pits greed (riba) against charity (Sadaqa); selfish pursuits against unity; and personal gain against the good of society. In order to establish the obligatory responsibility (zakat) of supporting orphans, widowed women, pilgrims, slaves, and all those who dedicate their lives to spreading and defending the faith, God urges the wealthy to share their prosperity with the weak in his community.

7.2. DEFINITION

Usury, or riba, has a consolidated legal definition in Islam, which includes any form of profit that is not justified by human labor as well as any imbalance brought about by power, abuse, or risk in commercial relationships. In this particular field, the discrepancy between theory and practice is evident in the historical experience of developing a number of fictions (Hiyal) that allowed one to circumvent the rigorous divine prohibition by adhering to the legal doctrine's guidelines. Simultaneously, however, a notable strengthening of associative relationships among traders emerged, primarily based on familial ties; these alliances functioned as appropriate mechanisms for the transfer of capital while evenly distributing the risks associated with current commercial operations. As the pre-capitalist idea of money as something different from a commodity and not tradeable like all other goods gradually fades in Europe, debt or interest owed to the creditor within a material relation of trade is acknowledged as a beneficial mechanism for economic growth and the advancement of commerce. In contrast, Islam did not theorize autonomous rules and regulations regarding religious jus commune prior to the 19th century, which was the period of codification and the birth of nation states. Instead, the autonomous nature of state law has primarily meant a slavish adaptation to the civil and commercial normative models of colonial western powers. Because of this, in the latter half of the 20th century, contemporary Muslim doctrine pursued the design of a new Islamic economy based on a more careful interpretation of the prohibition against usury (riba), envisioning the possibility of creating a valid alternative to the social projects based on socialist statalism and capitalist liberalism, one that would replace the monetary interest system with one based on profit and risk-sharing.

Whether intentionally or inadvertently, all merchants in the Mediterranean Sea region used this kind of agreement, which was operational and enforceable even before the Prophet Muhammad lived. These contractual agreements, like the mudaraba, which already demonstrated strong affinities with medieval lending activity in the fifth and sixth century, were taken up by the Prophet, a proficient merchant in his own right, and are still in use by Muslims today. The mudaraba and commenda are very similar, and this development continues in contemporary European corporate law; in this case, however, there is a progressive separation that culminates in the bank becoming completely neutral with regard to the risks associated with the transactions of its clients (Harris, 2009). However, the ideological framework that established the Islamic banking system purposefully incorporated and operationally reinforced the client-partner model. Based on this, the system has grown more competitive by developing specific financial products that adhere to Islamic values, principles, and ethical-juridical principles. This is where the real difficulty facing the conference seems to lie: piecing together the past and present by reading and critically evaluating a different experience with the banking system. For Europeans, the relevance of such a system goes beyond the recent announcements of the establishment of the Islamic Bank of Britain, the first Islamic institution within an EU member state, or the issuance of Islamic bonds (sukuk) in German Lands. Instead, it is an ethical conundrum that centers on the contemporary interpretation of the ban on riba, reinterpreted in the context of the core principles of justice and equity in the social and economic spheres, as well as solidarity and cooperation. Private and public financial and entrepreneurial endeavors ought to be founded on these ideals; this is a goal that is also being sought in the west by a number of bank initiatives, including ethical banks, microcredit, and a resurgence of cooperative credit.

7.3. BANK OPERATIONS

The first 'bank without interest' experiment took place in Egypt approximately 40 years ago. While it would be interesting to compare this experiment to the cooperative credit banks and rural banks of the European tradition, the Islamic bank system is based on the adoption of an associative relationship between the bank and the client, which is morally acceptable in place of the arithmetical calculus of interest in both giving and taking. Since the client provides the capital to the bank, they cannot be considered an outsider to the business; rather, they become a partner, accepting the risks associated with this role and gaining the right to potential profits from the bank's operations based on the standard profit-loss sharing pattern. This has necessitated both the rapid and intricate testing of novel operational instruments and the regulation of traditional tools. The core component of an Islamic bank is, at least in theory, the implementation of the partnership scheme of sharing between bank and client in the majority of transactions, both active and passive. This is not so much the lack of interest in giving and taking, though this is a clearly distinctive aspect when compared with the Western bank experience. Taking on financial risk validates the profits that both parties derive from the utilization of capital and permits human action to outweigh the profitable automatisms of capital. Theoretically, this guarantees the greatest degree of equality between the two contracting parties by relieving the contractual relationship of speculative aspects. The recovery of traditional forms of labor and capital associations, like mudaraba or qirad, or more commonly corporate forms, like musharaka, where the profit divided among the partners is always the outcome of the enterprise's activity, implemented with the participation of both parties, must be examined within this conceptual framework (Lewis, 2001). The profit-loss sharing model is used for unitization, savings management, and fund transactions. Takaful contracts, which translate to solidarity, are used to create a system akin to traditional mutual insurance in which the element of solidarity outweighs the speculative factor.

7.4. MUDARABA

The mudaraba, or qirad, is the model for business in the Muslim tradition. It is a money and labor exchange akin to limited partnerships and joint ventures. In the mudaraba, the capitalist (rabb al-mal) gives an agent (mudarib) control and use of his capital (Ra's Al-Mal) in generally established trading operations. At the conclusion of the deal, the agent consents to return the capital and any agreed-upon profit, keeping the remaining profit as payment for his services. The capitalist bears all financial risk, and in the event that the contract falls through for reasons beyond his control, the agent is not liable for any reimbursement. The main cause of this institution's historical success is the union of the elements of qard (loan), Wakala (mandate), and Sharikah contracts. The process of classifying bank deposits in Islamic banks involves taking into account the possibility of sharing administration of the same deposits through the use of a Mudarabah as a profit-loss sharing mechanism. The bank promises to reimburse the full amount of money at any given time and may use the deposit funds in accordance with a Wakala, or client mandate. Although there is no set amount of compensation, clients who open large accounts may receive rewards at the end of each financial year, at the discretion of the bank. These rewards may take the form of small cash donations (Hiba), in-kind payments (Hadiyya, Ikramiye), or special conditions on credit access that allow for the sponsorship of small projects or the installment purchase of durable or instrumental goods. With the exception of not having interest-based compensation, the structure of an Islamic bank account is the same as that of a non-Islamic one.

7.5. TRANSACTIONS

On the other hand, transactions pertaining to savings accounts are typically documented on a nominal passbook, or daftar, that is registered in the name of the beneficiary or depositor. Combining investing and savings accounts is an additional choice. These are essentially time deposits, the types of which can differ significantly; they can be intended for a particular investment project or repurposed by the bank for its regular financial operations, such as investing in bank-managed musharaka deposits. In this situation, the depositor might need to affix his signature to a mandate that details the uses of his money that the bank may carry out. In the absence of a specific mandate, the bank creates various, distinct investment funds or spends the money anyway it pleases. This specific requirement is meant to ensure higher levels of openness to the management, giving the customer and Shariah Control Councils or other control organizations within or outside the bank's strong authority over the moral and religious aspects of transactions (Haridan et al., 2018). The lack of a clear obligation to reimburse the public funds collected may be one of the primary causes of incompatibility with European bank discipline. Theoretically, the general implementation of the participatory principle and the ensuing idea of risk permeating the entire activity of the Islamic bank, result in the prohibition of any form of guarantee on the deposit. There is a difference to be made in this regard between the protection of cost-free deposits and that of participation deposits.

The distinction between deposit funds and bank capital, which is directly impacted by management costs and possible liabilities, is still present even with the implementation of profit-loss sharing. In accordance with this principle, Islamic banks follow the same organizational framework as non-Islamic lending organizations, repaying deposits with capital and reserves as needed. This structure is required because both Islamic and non-Islamic banks are subject to the general bank legislation in effect in the legal order to which they belong, especially the regulations pertaining to liquidity and reserves. This is true even with the elimination of the capital remuneration system based on interest and the introduction of the profit-sharing mechanism. Furthermore, diversification of assets and associated risks results in a protection of participation accounts, albeit a restricted one. It is also evident that only those who are willing to undertake the risks associated with the institution's operations may put such a model into practice. Liquidity management is one of the biggest issues facing Islamic banks, particularly in the long run. In this regard, it is important to highlight the differences between the two systems' deposits' functions. The primary functions of bank deposits in the majority of Islamic nations are capitalization and maintenance assurance. In contrast, bank deposits are, or were until very recently, a combination of short-term savings and investment instruments in Western nations. The primary challenge Islamic banks encounter, which is the ban on interest, becomes the inability of entering the interbank market and investing in conventional bonds with short maturities and low risk, such government bonds, which have stable profits and readily available cash. Certain types of Islamic bonds, or Islamic titles issued by governments and other public administrations through the securitization of public commodities, have been used in several Islamic countries to address this issue. The rise in Islamic mutual funds, which currently serve as the primary source of funding and investment vehicle for Islamic banks, has helped to alleviate the short-term liquidity management issue. These funds are a legal substitute for traditional obligations, which are prohibited by Shariah as debit and interest funds.

7.6. FUNDING

There is a wide range of Islamic funds available globally. Currently, there are about 150 Islamic funds operating on a national and/or global scale (Alam Choudhury & Hussain, 2005). Over 60% of all funds in this category follow the overall trend of investing in stocks on domestic, international, and regional markets. This is partly because conventional investment inclinations toward risk-sharing models and the preference for equity investments in light of the Qur'anic system of Riba contribute to this. Gradually, a number of standards for identifying businesses that adhere to Islamic principles were developed. These businesses are compiled in national and international directories on a regular basis. For instance, the Securities Commission's Shariah Council oversees audit activities in Malaysia and manages stock market operations. In India, private organizations have commissioned the use of a directory akin to this one (Parsoli

IBF-Net Equity). Unquestionably, the Islamic financial market's continued growth is related to its attraction to Muslim investors. This appeal stems from two factors: the possibility of supporting, reviving, and confirming Islamic principles in the modern economic environment, as well as the banking and financial practices' adherence to ethical and religious standards. The growth of the Islamic banking sector is still heavily reliant on capital and equity from Gulf Cooperation Council members, which has a significant impact on the operational and theoretical frameworks used.

Financial firms that follow the beliefs of Islamic banking have just lately begun to do business in the USA and Europe. The Islamic Bank of Britain was established in February 2004. In an effort to gain more credibility on a local and global scale, this presence in the west, while still not statistically significant, is generating management operational models that are separate and independent from the original models. It is hard to argue against the fact that the expansion of Islamic banking and finance in Europe is a positive development, as it effectively boosts the penetration of financial services and, in turn, promotes social inclusion. Members of the sizable Islamic population in Europe can now profit from the financial market without going against religious principles, as they were previously prohibited from receiving financial services benefits. Nonetheless, the new companies providing Islamic banking services are posing a threat to the oversight and regulatory organizations. The task that regulatory agencies have in overseeing and monitoring traditional financial institutions is very different from the task presented by the creation of these institutions. These institutions have a unique regulatory difficulty as a result of the strategies they utilize to raise money and use it to make money. The methods that Islamic banks can and do use to raise capital are all unconventional and, to some extent, novel to the authorities. Regulators who are tasked with overseeing and controlling Islamic banks have a number of concerns and queries. For example, some funding mobilization strategies may call for asset management. In the context of the traditional understanding of commercial banking, the involvement of commercial banks in asset management is a completely new phenomenon. It is understandable that regulatory bodies will be concerned about how to define firewalls that maintain the legal, administrative, and operational separation of commercial banking and asset management in order to guarantee adequate oversight and monitoring of the bank's operations.

Reliability and legal challenges arise when regulating authorities and Islamic bank lawyers have to decide which Shariah-compliant banking products and services to leave to institutions that may not qualify as banks, and what Shariah-compliant operating modes of Islamic banking an institution to be called a "bank" should provide within the European banking framework. Comparably, when it comes to using money, Islamic banks will employ contracts with clauses and provisions that don't work with Europe's traditional banking system. The utilization of non-traditional contracts to provide financial services products can give rise to various concerns regarding corporate governance norms, identification, and mitigation of novel risks, and enforcing market discipline on Islamic banks in line with those established for conventional banks. For instance, many financial products may have entirely different risk profiles, which may not have been covered by the Basel II accord, which primarily addressed traditional banking operations. Both the assets and the liabilities margins of the balance sheet of Islamic banks show the new dimensions of risk. Islamic banks will utilize contracts on the assets side of their balance sheet called Ijara, Murabaha, Istisna,' and Salam. These contracts have more intricate implications for risk management than do the products on the assets side of a conventional bank's balance sheet. Regarding liabilities, depositors will be able to access profit-sharing investment accounts through Islamic banks. These depositors are thought to partake in the bank's profits and losses, but they do not qualify as the bank's capital nor as its liabilities in the traditional sense of the accounting. This creates issues with various metrics and indicators as well as the capital adequacy4MV] formula. The challenge for the lawyers of Islamic banking intending to conduct business in Europe, as well as the challenge for the regulators who will be assessing the proposals for establishing Islamic banks in Europe, will be how to make the accounts of Islamic banks comply with European banking laws without breaking Shariah provisions.

7.7. REGULATORS

The regulators are not faced with any new challenges when it comes to accounts with Islamic banks. The alternative type of account is known as a profit-sharing investment account (PSIA), where depositors are expected to share the bank's profits rather than obtaining a fixed rate of return on their money (Baldwin & Alhalboni, 2020). There isn't a comparable account in traditional banking. These deposits are neither the bank's liabilities nor can they be regarded as a component of its capital. The risk of loss on the use of these deposits by the banks falls on the holders of these accounts, not the Islamic bank. In addition to concerns for risk management, this has consequences for corporate governance. Unlike in the case of commercial banking, regulators will need to consider PSIAs from the perspective of protecting investors as well as depositors. PSIAs are thought to have an impact on traditional banks' capital adequacy ratios and risk management strategies. Regulators may be wondering how to adjust the capital adequacy requirement to account for the unique risks and characteristics of

PSIAs. The bank gives the client permission to purchase products on the bank's behalf, which are then promptly resold to the client at a profit. The customer will either make periodic payments to the bank or pay in full at a later time. Collateral is acquired to guarantee timely repayment of debts. Other financing methods are predicated on the ideas of Salam, Istisna, and Ijara. Based on these ideas, contracts can be set up so that, when it comes to liquidity and riskiness, they are equivalent to receivables under Murabaha transactions and, consequently, to loans on a traditional bank's financial statement. The procedures to guarantee this can be readily worked out by Islamic bank regulators and attorneys. The issue stems from the requirement that Islamic banks adopt the position of a trader or a lesser one in order to implement the financing methods in accordance with Shariah regulations. The European banking laws might not allow for this.

On the asset side of the Islamic banks, another issue would be the receivables non-tradability or non-negotiability. By law, these receivables cannot be offered at a discount in the market. Because of this, the receivables on the financial statement of a traditional bank are not as liquid as the loans. It might also be helpful to remember that using Islamic financing methods necessitates that Islamic banks eventually take ownership of the underlying assets. Even though it might only be effective for a very short time in some situations, owning assets entails taking on the risks that come with ownership, regardless of how long it is believed to last. Of course, insurance is an option for these risks, but it will come with additional costs. In addition to the effectiveness of offering a substitute product, there is also the matter of who will bear the associated expenses. The rate of return on depositors' money will be affected if they bear the expense. Transparency regarding all charges and their effects on the bank's depositors' returns as well as the fees incurred by clients looking to borrow money from the bank would thus be a concern. Receivables, which account for more than 75% of the assets, have always been and continue to be the most dominant element. The risk profile of receivables and loans, as previously stated, is essentially the same. The restricted liquidity characteristic of receivables is the only risk factor. Regarding this element, the primary concern is enabling the banks to participate in the financing process by selling, buying, and renting assets. The issue of liquidity, while significant, is handled globally by Islamic banks.

Since these are riskier investments, this element is exclusive to Islamic banks and is not included on regular banks' balance sheets. This could involve making direct investments in the clients' equity as well as providing financing based on the mudaraba and musharaka modes, which entail the bank sharing in the profits and losses of its clients as a result of satisfying their financing needs. It is empirical to determine the significance of this element on the balance sheet.

According to Islamic banks' past experiences, neither banks nor clients appear particularly eager to conduct business in this way. But regardless of how much demand there is for these kinds of modes, the regulators must investigate ways to let the banks operate in accordance with national banking regulations. Because of the significant risk, the regulatory body is also concerned. However, Islamic banks have been successful in creating internal and external control mechanisms and contractual clauses that reduce the risks associated with musharakah-based financing, even to a very small degree for Islamic banks. Yet, mudaraba and equity participation continue to be high-risk professional items on the balance sheet; however, the balance sheets of the current Islamic banks show very little, if any, amount allocated to these matters. Islamic banks obtain their liabilities from two primary sources of funding: investment accounts, where the bank shares its profits with depositors, and current account deposits, on which the bank guarantees the deposits but does not give any return to the depositors. A significant percentage of current accounts at certain Islamic banks is liabilities.

7.8. AUTHORITY

Before it becomes a problem for the authorities, this is an issue for Islamic banks. Islamic banks will have a difficult time luring deposits that carry a risk of being lost in a setting where depositors are accustomed to getting a guarantee of their principal amount. Restricted account deposits are utilized in pre-specified projects using pre-specified mechanisms. Islamic banks have been successful in creating products for these types of accounts that guarantee depositors a return that fluctuates within a very small range and virtually eliminates the risk of loss. Depositors can therefore have their funds in Islamic banks with the same risk profile that customers of a traditional bank will receive on their savings accounts, even though these accounts are profit-loss sharing accounts. It remains to be shown empirically if Islamic banks will be able to offer their depositors a return comparable to that of regular banks. Therefore, there is no significant regulatory problem associated with these accounts in terms of depositor money protection. However, the way these accounts operate would force Islamic banks to take on risk, which entails investing activity on the bank's side, for which the nation's banking regulations have a provision. However, unrestricted profit-sharing investment accounts present the biggest regulatory problem. The depositors give the bank permission to use their funds for any kind of investment the bank deems appropriate, and they explicitly consent to splitting any profits or losses from these ventures. There is no guarantee on this account regarding the principal amount of deposits or any rate of return. This goes against the traditional definition of what a bank is. Guaranteeing a principal amount for such accounts is against Shariah law. On this matter, there are, nonetheless, a few feasible options. Such solutions can be found by the Islamic banks' lawyers and regulatory bodies.

The bank will use account holders' deposits to fund investments that it chooses; account holders won't have any influence over this decision. When depositor funds are utilized more for the bank's benefit than for the benefit of the depositors, moral threat may occur. While depositors and shareholders share the bank's profits, depositors are not represented on the board and no Islamic bank has been able to establish robust internal control mechanisms that would protect investment account holders' interests from those of shareholders and bank management. The authorities will face a significant struggle in the disciplined financial and investment environment of Europe with this matter. Laws alone might not be sufficient to address this corporate governance challenge. There are elements that, in this regard, also pertain to ethical concerns. For instance, holders of investment accounts deposit their funds with Islamic banks in accordance with their religious convictions. Perhaps the greatest way to protect PSIA interests without negatively impacting Islamic banks' performance is to strictly adhere to a properly crafted code of ethics that is typically provided to investment businesses, rather than prudential regulations that govern banking operations. Additionally, it would be the responsibility of Islamic banks to disclose all relevant information in a transparent manner so that customers may feel confident that their financial uncertainties are being taken into account when allocating their cash. This is complicated, though, because many religious perspectives exist regarding what constitutes an Islamic and non-Islamic lifestyle (Rassool, 2000). To make the proper pronouncements, a religious board would need to lay forth precise guidelines and moral principles. Reserves are another item in the sources of funds. The one variation in this element is that certain Islamic banks prefer to retain a portion of their profit as a reserve before disclosing it to depositors. The purpose of these reserves is to mitigate significant fluctuations in the profit on profit-sharing investment accounts. They are employed to make up for any anomalous drop in profits for the depositors in any given year. To guarantee that there are no moral risk situations on this account and that certain depositors are not reimbursed from what is truly owed for other depositors, certain prudential and ethical requirements are required.

7.9. RISK

A bank failure could have a cascading effect. Banks are liable to one another. A collapsing bank may force excessive withdrawal demands on other banks, and the failure of one bank may scare depositors of other banks, who may run on other banks out of fear that other banks would follow suit. Therefore, if the banks do not have enough capital to cover unforeseen withdrawal requests, the entire banking system could be in jeopardy. Regulatory bodies are constantly concerned about the adequacy of capital in banking institutions because they want to safeguard depositors and the banking system. The Basel I and Basel II documents are a set of guidelines developed by the Basel Committee on banking supervision, a division of the Bank of International Settlements, for determining capital adequacy (Sbârcea, 2014). The framework gives regulators instructions for evaluating the capital sufficiency of financial organizations, notwithstanding its complexity and contentious aspects. This framework becomes relevant for Islamic banks as well because the most recent version of it (Basel II, 2004) covers banking institutions that continue to conduct banking operations with securities operations and provides different capital adequacy criteria for categories of operation. The Basel II criteria for the securities operations of banking institutions can be used to evaluate the capital adequacy for non-banking activities like trading, mutual funds, as well as non-financial investments. The question of whether Islamic banks should be subject to the same strict capital adequacy regulations as conventional banks and whether they should be subject to the same capital adequacy necessities as such is still up for debate. Depositors in Islamic banks are not covered by capital sufficiency. With the knowledge that they can lose their deposits, they make their money. Adequate capital isn't what can keep depositors from suffering losses. In order to safeguard depositors in Islamic banking, strict regulations and corporate governance requirements must be in place. Only then can Islamic bank managers be prevented from using depositor funds to indulge their desire for risk. Rather than enforcing strict capital adequacy standards, sensible regulations and oversight of Islamic banks' investment plans would need to address the moral issue.Furthermore, since the bankruptcy of an Islamic bank is unlikely to endanger the stability of the banking system as a whole, there is no justification for strict capital adequacy rules based on fear. There is no justification for a strict capital adequacy requirement to lessen the likelihood of a bank collapsing. Imposing market discipline on banks while a deposit guarantee program is in place, which can encourage banks to take on greater risk than depositors are willing to accept, is another justification for capital adequacy. The market might not penalize banks for holding insufficient capital to absorb the risk by using depositors' money in dangerous ventures if there is a deposit guarantee program in place. Regarding PSIA deposits, the case does not support the imposition of a capital adequacy requirement. Because participating in a deposit guarantee program would violate Shariah, Islamic banks do not. Although Islamic law allows a third entity (central bank) to guarantee the deposits, the question of who will bear the bill for insurance will come up under Sharia. There's a chance that a central bank in some Muslim nations will offer free deposit guarantees to Islamic banks. At least for the time being, it is possible to rule out such a scenario in the European environment. Therefore, no additional attention to capital sufficiency is required due to deposit insurance plans. It may be argued that Islamic banks cannot be presumed to be immune from loss and a significant volume of panic withdrawals, even in spite of PSIAs' capacity to absorb shocks on the asset side. If an Islamic bank were to experience a significant liquidity problem, such a scenario might be possible.

Islamic banks that implement appropriate risk management techniques and instruments can mitigate a number of the risks associated with Islamic banking. Islamic banks receive ongoing assistance in this regard from financial engineers and specialists. The only task for supervisory authorities is to keep an eye on these efforts to prevent Islamic banks from failing on this account. In addition, prudential guidelines and moral principles can be established to control operations and guarantee depositor safety. While capital sufficiency will always be crucial, it must be considered holistically, together with other risk management strategies and sound corporate governance practices, rather than just as a formula applied to conventional banks' structures. This is crucial if Islamic banking is to be pushed as an essential but complementary component of a nation's financial system in the spirit of expanding social inclusion, rather than as an addition on the financial system's perimeter. Islamic banking needs to be included into the core of the financial system rather than being treated as a peripheral activity, both on its own merits and in light of how crucial it is to serving the requirements of Muslim communities in Europe. By imposing pointless extra costs on Islamic banks and adopting an adversarial stance when it comes to overseeing Islamic banking, capital adequacy regulation will be the only or primary means of denying the Islamic financial sector a level playing field, which will limit the sector's ability to integrate into the larger global financial market. The Islamic Financial Services Board (IFSB), which is overseen by the governors of the central banks of the countries where Islamic banking is practiced, was established to assist the regulators and supervising bodies in providing a level playing field for Islamic banks without sacrificing the efficiency and ethical standards already in demand in the national and international financial markets (Alam, 2021). In order to promote best practices for the industry on a national and international scale, the Board is currently creating prudential and monitoring standards in these areas.

7.10. MANAGEMENT

In addition to the creation of the Islamic Financial Services Board, important institutional advancements are also being made to help the Islamic banking sector. Liquidity management is one of the key components of risk management in Islamic institutions. The issue with liquidity management stems from the fact that Islamic banks are unable to use the majority of conventional instruments available for this purpose since they are interest-based. Therefore, a major obstacle to effective liquidity management is the lack of an Islamic money market and an Islamic interbank market. The emergence of the International Islamic Financial Market in Bahrain presents a favorable prospect for Islamic banks to handle their liquidity, since it will serve as a secondary market for Islamic securities. An important part in integrating and harmonizing the accounting and auditing practices is the Accounting and Auditing Organization for Islamic Financial Institutions (AAOIFI). Another new piece of infrastructure is the Islamic Rating Agency (IRA). Every kind of financial innovation compels regulators to retrace their boundaries and the suitability of the current regulations for financial institutions, tools, and cultures that differ from those for which the regulations were originally drafted. From this angle, the growing presence of Islamic banks in the western banking system poses an intriguing challenge to the Basel capital discipline's ability to balance the goal of preserving a level playing field through uniform and standardized regulations with a flexible and discretionary approach, which is required to deal with this kind of intermediation. Islamic banking is inconsistent with prudential capital requirements in several respects. On the one hand, it makes sense that its operations, which differ greatly from the traditional models that the regulatory bodies are accustomed to dealing with, would be seen as potentially riskier and hence be subject to more stringent capital requirements. However, the very nature of profit-sharing agreements appears to make this kind of intermediation more resilient to unforeseen losses than traditional banks, casting doubt on the same rationale for capital requirements.

It appears difficult, both practically and theoretically, to reconcile Islamic intermediation, which is based on profit-sharing, with the principles and goals of regulation, which is focused on minimum capital requirements. For the sake of stability, capital is more important the more the intermediary transforms risk. In addition to limiting the moral hazard associated with the coexistence of explicit and implicit deposit insurance and lending, the regulation will also lessen the conflict of interest between depositors and shareholders that is typical of banking, which is characterized by opaque assets and high leverage, if it places a financial burden on the shareholders that increases with the intermediation risk. The basis of Islamic banking is the profit-sharing agreement, or mudaraba. After this agreement, the owner of the funds provides the entrepreneur with the funding required to finance his or her business or a particular investment project. In exchange for their labor and managerial prowess, entrepreneurs are rewarded (mudarib); in the event of a loss, these rewards are nullified (Archer et al., 1998). If there are losses, they are solely the responsibility of the fund's owner, and the entrepreneur, if acting in good faith, is not required to repay the capital obtained. The profits are divided between the fund's owner and the entrepreneur in accordance with a predetermined formula.

In systems where financial exclusion and/or high inflation prevail, and mutual financial institutions serve as the primary or exclusive means of accessing banking services, profit-sharing contracts appear to be the investment of choice for. But when Islamic banks compete with conventional banks or operate in a more sophisticated market, their market power comes from their ability to provide investors with a product that not only complies with Sharia laws but also yields a competitive return. This is what gives Islamic banks their advantage over other financial institutions. Thus, in lieu of market rating, the return provided to holders of investment accounts serves as a kind of insurance against the bank's reputational risk, which if it deteriorates, could lead to hastened disintermediation processes that would be detrimental to the stability and performance of the credit system. Even though it isn't mentioned in the contracts, the necessity to safeguard the investment deposits' economic value manifests itself in practice and frequently serves as the foundation for a tacit understanding between the public, banks, and the monetary authorities. The Islamic Financial Services Board (IFSB) confirmed the possibility that the displaced commercial risks were borne by the shareholders in its recent proposal of capital regulation for Islamic banks.

7.11. LIMITATIONS

Islamic banks and conventional banks share managerial limitations related to maximizing financing stability and preventing bank runs (Hassan et al., 2009). In light of this, it is clear that market strategies which are supported by the same sensible regulation are designed to lessen the volatility of the return rate offered to investors' account holders, even when internal reserves of self-insurance are developed. Despite varied portfolio performance over time and among different banks, the empirical evidence confirms that return rates on investment deposits tend to be steady and reasonably uniform across the different banks. Hence, even Islamic banks are compelled to alter portfolio risk in favor of investor-depositors due to the implicit guarantee of deposits' economic worth. This suggests that the customary conflicts of interest between creditors and shareholders that characterize universal banks will reappear; additionally, it lessens the ability of profit-sharing funding to completely supplement owners' capital as a loss absorber. This result clearly modifies the function of Islamic banks' prudential capital regulations, especially with regard to how investment accounts are treated when determining the minimum Basel capital adequacy criteria. Because the holders of investment accounts in these circumstances have asymmetrical preferences with respect to the shareholders, their involvement in profits and losses does not negate the necessity for prudential supervision to protect bank solvency and the stability of the system. The hypothesis, which is valid empirically even for Islamic banks, holds that there are conflicts of interest between shareholders and other investors and that neither market discipline nor governance mechanisms are sufficient to create enough incentives to healthy and prudent management, which is necessary to protect society from systemic risk. The minimum capital requirement is one of the tools that the regulator has at their disposal, albeit not always the most effective.

Foreign investments in the Paris banking and financial center are welcomed by French banking regulators (Kapstein, 1992). The French banking industry is highly receptive to international investment; as of the end of 2007, there were more commercial banks controlled by foreigners than by French nationals. This foreign-owned bank dominance, however, does not translate into market shares because foreign-owned banks have embraced a niche strategy, concentrating on particular client categories and unique financing and market activities, rather than attempting to expand their retail and network banking operations. Furthermore, France is already home to a sizable number of banks from the Middle East, the Gulf, and Islamic nations; some of these banks have been there for 30 years. By the end of 2007, for example, six banks from Lebanon, four from Iran, two from Pakistan, two from Qatar, one from Egypt, one from Abu Dhabi, one from Kuwait, and one from Jordan had established themselves in France. None of these organizations have formally requested that the French government look into the idea of offering Islamic goods in France up to this point. Furthermore, CECEI has not received any notifications of requests made by other European banking authorities in favor of so-called Islamic banks that they would have authorized regarding the right of establishment and the freedom to provide services within the framework of the European mutual recognition procedures. The fundamental concerns are about how much real demand there is in France for these kinds of goods. There appears to be a disconnect between the amount of money that can be invested in so-called Islamic projects which is evidently significant on a global scale and the emergence of tangible projects in the banking industry, particularly in retail banking. This money is primarily from Gulf countries.

Banks, financial services organizations, and insurance companies are increasingly more likely to create cross-sectoral groups for which it is simpler to introduce wide product lines into the market. In the past, banks and insurance companies had only sporadic relationships, but in the present, strong financial conglomerates with a global presence have arisen in Germany. It is anticipated that the trend toward integrated bank-assurance groupings will continue. The German regulator can effectively oversee the market due to its extensive powers and comprehensive understanding of it, which helps to maintain Germany's stability as a financial hub. This aids in preventing competitive imbalances, which are easily brought about by regulatory variations in a fragmented supervisory framework. Sector-specific differences are taken into consideration in the organizational structure, which saw the creation of distinct organizational units for asset management, insurance, and securities trading oversight. Many cross-sectoral departments that are organizationally distinct from the traditional supervisory roles handle the cross-sectoral activities made necessary by the developments in the financial markets. These departments' responsibilities include overseeing financial conglomerates, coordinating efforts in global supervisory forums, and fighting money laundering in all its forms. Furthermore, this framework of German supervision has strengthened Germany's position as a financial hub and its capacity to compete globally since May 2002 (Hüfner, 2010).

In essence, the supervisory directorates that made up the BaFin now carry out the supervisory responsibilities of the independent supervisory offices. The BaFin has a wide range of measures and sanctions at its disposal that it can implement in cases of inadequacies in business organization, inadequate liquidity, or equity capital, and in cases of a risk to the security of bank deposits. However, not all of these are applicable to the banking industry in practice. A board member may be subject to a demand for removal if their dependability is questioned, if they are found to be unsuitable for their position due to substantial misconduct, or if they persist in their unlawful behavior after warnings. A board member has the right to object if they disagree with a warning or a demand for their dismissal. The objection must be decided by the law section. He or she may proceed to the administration court if this doesn't work out. Although BaFin typically prevails in court, different rulings may occur. In addition to these steps, fines may be imposed by the Federal Financial Supervisory Authority if there is a risk to the security of bank deposits. It can forbid making loans, give management directives to the institution, or temporarily forbid the institution from taking in bank deposits and from issuing loans, so temporarily closing the bank. It can also designate supervisory staff to the bank or impose prohibitions on operations. The bank's license being revoked is the most drastic action.

Chapter 8

RISKS IN ISLAMIC FINANCE: BANKING AND FINANCE

Contents

8.1. INTRODUCTION

Developing nations closely monitored financial liberalization, a component of globalization, during the 1990s (Wyplosz, 2002). Financial institutions now have easy access after a number of limitations were loosened. One crucial component of this liberalization was thought to be loosening the regulations. The driving force was thought to be self-control. A number of malpractice cases, financial frauds, and failures were reported. Governing bodies began examining the current standards and strategies for resolving the conflict between control and liberty. It was determined that the current requirements were insufficient, and that additional guidelines and revisions were therefore required to implement solid financial risk-management methods. Over the past few years, risk management practice has completely changed, moving from basic capital provisions for hazardous assets to a comprehensive framework. Regularly, new special regulatory rules are developed to guard against the failure of financial systems. Every nation has its unique laws that are determined by a number of factors. The most prevalent one is the need to maintain a minimum amount of capital that is based on the bank's operations.

8.2. CAPITAL

Capital adequacy laws are a crucial component of the regulatory provisions because the bank's capital provides the majority of its safety. The more the capital, the stronger the protection against insolvency. However, as capital is an expensive choice, possessing a lot of capital increases costs. Overcapitalized banks have low capital returns and are unable to provide their shareholders with respectable rewards on investment. In addition, undercapitalized banks may have delayed expansion and are more vulnerable to the risk of going bankrupt. Therefore, it is in the best interests of banks and shareholders to determine an optimal level of capital. By establishing the required amounts of capital, or regulatory capital, regulators aim to keep an eye on the amount of capital kept by the banks. The foundation of central banks' global supervisory operations is capital adequacy. It serves as a crucial measure for the financial institution's stability. When it comes to controlling lending, capital adequacy is thought to be a more effective instrument than deposit reserve requirements. The Basel I accord's suggested minimum safe level of 8% of risk-weighted capital was adopted by a number of Central Banks in the 1980s.

The earliest international financial institution was founded on May 17, 1930, and is known as the Bank for International Settlements (BIS). It functions as the central banks' bank. It gives the central banks a forum for cooperative consultation. BIS's function has evolved to meet the demands of the global financial industry. These days, BIS also serves as a clearinghouse for the aggregation, and distribution of financial and economic data. It actively supports the stability of the world economy. Additionally, it handles gold and foreign exchange transactions for the central bank community, fulfilling its conventional banking role. Its committees focus on various facets of global financial stability. The Governors of the G-10 countries established the Basel Committee for Banking Supervision at the close of 1974 (Drach, 2022). Starting in 1975, the Committee published a number of papers on banking supervision. With an emphasis on credit risk, the original accord was the first significant international capital adequacy standard published by BIS. The Committee mandated a minimum capital of 8% of risk-weighted assets. A rudimentary risk-weighting framework was provided. The original agreement aimed to put capital adequacy at the forefront of banking oversight. However, because of the quick developments in the banking and financial industries, it quickly proved inadequate and out of date. A number of shortcomings in the current agreement were discovered, leading to the introduction of revisions in 1996 that placed more emphasis on market risk. Operational risk was increasingly common in technology-driven banks, and this kind of risk was not considered in the modified pact. Furthermore, there were significant global changes in the financial sector.

With liberalization and globalization, banking now faces additional risks. The risk exposures changed as a result of evolving supervisory procedures. It was discovered that the current standards had several shortcomings. Initially, it established a single capital adequacy`,R rate regardless of the level of risk within the category. There was no incentive for high-quality credit, therefore there was no way to differentiate between poor and excellent credit when it came to capital provision. It did not recognize operational risk sufficiently. There was no discussion of risk associated with more recent financial tools like derivatives and asset securitization. At BIS, there were multiple rounds of consultations with academics, researchers, bankers, central banks, and industry specialists. Thus, a thorough version of the Basel II revised framework was documented in 2006 following numerous changes and consideration of all these elements. The Committee has made a significant contribution to the advancement of improved oversight. In addition to changing how risk was viewed, persistent work has compelled banks to adopt best practices, improving the financial stability of banks and other financial institutions. Over 100 countries have voluntarily ratified the agreement. Financial risk management is measured in the new Basel II agreement. Enhancing the risk management procedures of globally operating banks is one of Basel II's goals, which will help to advance global financial stability. When it comes to risk recognition, Basel II has significantly improved upon the initial agreement. The revised agreement offers a clearer understanding of market and credit risks in addition to acknowledging the significance of operational risk. Basel II represents a change in supervision from transaction-based to risk-based. It offers a large selection of risk weights that can be used to determine the necessary capital. Additionally, it offers a variety of menu options for the risk measuring methodology. Many risks that were not previously addressed by the original agreement have been covered by Basel II, including reputational, legal, liquidity, and nation risk. Effective capital management has received a lot of attention. It has been acknowledged how important it is to build internal capacity for risk assessment, and Basel II emphasizes creating an organizational culture of risk management as opposed to just providing a framework. Basel II has enhanced risk management. First, by utilizing the most recent advancements in financial engineering, it offers enhanced risk assessment techniques.

Second, by offering a variety of indicators that regulators can utilize, it improves risk monitoring. Third, by incorporating market disclosure as the third Pillar, it makes an effort to highlight the significance of reporting. Ultimately, it closes the gap in risk management by placing Pillar 2's responsibility of supervision at its center. The three carefully calibrated Basel II Pillars support one another and offer the necessary foundation for creating a solid, steady, and adaptable risk-management framework. Being a component of the global financial sector, the Islamic finance industry cannot continue to be unaffected and indifferent. Whether a bank is conventional or Islamic, the fundamental problem for risk management will always be capital adequacy. The financial market as a whole will be impacted by the failure of a conventional bank or an Islamic bank, therefore risk management must be integrated. In Islamic banking, the notion of having enough capital is universal and cannot be disputed. As a result, Basel II application involves adapting the standard to the requirements of the Islamic financial sector. The Basel II agreement rests upon three interdependent pillars. The introduction of market discipline and supervisory review, in addition to the basic minimum capital requirement, forms the three pillars of the initiative. The mutual support that each of the three pillars provides is what makes Basel II so strong. The committee has introduced supervisors, who were previously not directly involved in risk management, to the field of risk management by including the supervisory review. It also gave supervisors the upper hand in deciding whether the minimum capital calculation is valid, reinforcing their importance in overall risk management. A key factor in highlighting the value of transparency throughout the spectrum of risk management activities was market discipline. Together, the three pillars offer a flexible, risk-sensitive framework for capital management that has the power to alter how financial institutions view risk.

In the Islamic financial sector, the minimum capital requirement plays a crucial role, even if the capital charge computation may vary based on the risk exposures (Ariss & Sarieddine, 2007). Because of the way the Islamic financial sector is changing, supervisors play a more important role. The Islamic banking sector needs strong regulatory support in the form of oversight and help. In Islamic finance, social responsibility holds paramount significance. When an Islamic financial institution makes a profit, it should pay Zakat and refrain from engaging in haram activities. Additionally, transparency is given more weight, making Basel II's third pillar more applicable to the Islamic banking sector. Financial institutions can compute two forms of capital when evaluating the minimum capital requirements: regulatory capital and economic capital.

The amount of capital required to cover and safeguard shareholders against possible economic losses is known as economic capital, as determined by the bank's management. The amount of capital that regulators mandate institutions maintain as protection against hazards is known as regulatory capital. While regulatory capital primarily aims to evaluate the bank's financial capacity to manage its inherent risks, economic capital serves as a tool for transaction-level decision making. Economic capital is the internal estimate of required capital, as contrasting to regulatory capital, which is determined by the regulators. A bank should utilize the regulatory capital, if any, and the economic capital, if any, for its evaluation if it is subject to regulatory capital constraints.

8.3. BASEL

In an effort to lessen the potential for regulatory arbitrage, Basel II aims to more closely link economic and regulatory capital (Beltratti & Paladino, 2016). An increase in the economic capital ceiling gives lenders more room. A comprehensive framework for risk management that may link regulatory and economic capital is emphasized by Basel II. The problem of reconciling statutory capital and economic capital is especially challenging for Islamic financial organizations. The lack of a secondary market, an interbank money market for Islamic banks, and liquidity support from the money market all contributed to increased pressure on the capital requirements of Islamic financial institutions. This increases the capital requirements for Islamic financial institutions, in addition to the commitment for holders of current and investment accounts. Credit risk arises when counterparties fail to fulfill their contractual obligations to a financial institution and the institution is anticipating payment and the counterparties are unable to do so. When the counterparty's rating is altered or underestimated, credit risk is also created. Due to the emphasis on loan in the Murabaha, leasing in the Ijūrah, guaranteeing to provide or buy in the Istisnë and Salam, and investing on company success in the Mushūrakah and Mudūrabah contracts, financial institutions that offer Islamic financial products are also susceptible to credit risk. One or more of the obligors' default causes could be financial issues pertaining to the individual counterparties or to broader economic conditions. Islamic contracts are primarily motivated by agreements with distinct and personal features. Compared to more traditional contracts, these qualities are more qualitative in nature and are not usually well defined and documented. For example, there may be situations when it is not clear whether or how the exposure to credit risk is covered by guarantees and collaterals during the term of Islamic contracts.

It's also vital to keep in mind that because Islamic financial contracts have just recently been implemented, little is known about the quantitative and qualitative standards that were used to determine the contracts. The aforementioned institutions also have difficulties when it comes to adding new or altered contract and portfolio structures.

8.4. RISK MANAGEMENT

Credit risk management is becoming more difficult due to factors like the globalization of financial markets, the country's economic situation, and unique cultural traits in various markets and areas (Tchankova, 2002). Most credit risk assessments for Islamic financial products are based on subjective analysis, as opposed to conventional contracts. Banks operating in Islamic nations or offering Islamic contracts are frequently driven by data from many obligors, and the decision to approve (or disapprove) a contract, such as a Murōbaha contract, may be made subjectively and based on the opinions of experts. Financial institutions used to place a lot of importance on their relationships with their clients, but in the modern day, they also need to be able to forecast and take into account how their clients will behave when it comes to their payment commitments. Financial institutions must use techniques and methodologies for implementing sophisticated models in order to upgrade their credit risk management systems and objectively approve or reject applications for Islamic contracts because they have a large number of borrowers from a variety of market sectors and financial statuses. The risk analysts should give careful thought to the definition and application of the credit risk modeling methodology.

Financial institutions use qualitative approaches to evaluate a borrower's creditworthiness before agreeing to Islamic financial transactions. These techniques provide frameworks that rely on the opinions of specialists engaged in the credit-approval procedure. The resulting expert systems incorporate observations and practical experience from the professionals applying the analysis, along with a study of the debtor's creditworthiness. As such, the degree to which empirical models of expert systems faithfully capture the expert's subjective experience is a critical determinant of their quality. The majority of the time, empirical methods are used to identify the criteria that are taken into account during the creditworthiness examination of the debtor; additionally, the weight and effect of these factors in the final assessments are derived from subjective experiences. Rules that synthesize the standards applied to the expert's judgments inform the building of the expert systems. The objcctive of these systems is to create expert rules by considering past experiences that are connected to the client's behavior. Furthermore, any information pertaining to the nature of the contracts, the state of the market, and any other elements that may affect the client's behavior must be taken into account by the regulations. More analytically, the usual approach is for the experts to predefine a number of creditworthiness traits that are crucial to the obligor's future behavior based on their experiences. The degree of creditworthiness is graded according to a predetermined rating scale. Every grade is based on the unique qualitative traits of the obligee that relate to his or her anticipated behavior. For example, qualitative factors pertaining to family, education, and work history may be used to assess and record the degree of rating in accordance with the experts' subjective assessment of the particular obligee. The actual contracts that the client has committed to, the terms pertaining to future market conditions (economic recession), and market risk considerations are some additional elements that may influence the aforementioned ratings. Keep in mind that ratings are given by credit officers using data, financial ratios, and their opinions on quality control. Islamic financial markets are where the concept of market risk management has just emerged.

8.5. PRINCIPLES

These guiding principles of risk management for institutions offering Islamic financial services are provided by the Islamic Financial Services Board (Alhammadi et al., 2020). The market value of Ijūrah agreements, the market value of Murabaha assets acquired to be delivered over a particular term, the market value of foreign currency rates, and the current and future volatility of market values from specific assets are examples of hazards associated with market risks. Moreover, trading positions in Sukuk items exhibit market risk. Due to the intrinsic existence of market risk in Islamic financial markets during the duration of Islamic contracts, its rising severity has drawn market participants to participate in its identification, modeling, and control. In westernized conventional financial products, interest rates are an important component that are used to evaluate, align, and harmonize the products' current and future market pricing with the related market movements. However, the form of an Islamic financial product prohibits the use of interest rates. However, there are certain risks associated with the earnings of Islamic financial institutions due to changes in the market interest rate. Therefore, financial institutions use a separate rate termed the rate of return, which is based on distinct benchmarks, when constructing Islamic contracts in order to account for the risk arising from market fluctuations. The rate of return that is taken into account in Murabaha financial contracts should be in line with the repayment installments, which comprise both the institution's profit and the commodity price. There can be a loss in the benefits that should result from this contract if the rate of return, which is set in the Murabaha contract, seems to deviate from the real market rate. Furthermore, the rate of return payments specified by the institution's benchmarks in the Ijūrah leasing financial contract must also match the real market pricing. In the event of a failure, the institution will forfeit the ability to benefit from the lease of the Ijūrah. Financial institutions should specify the commodity price with regard to the future delivery date using the expected benchmark rates by offering Salam contracts. The institution may find it difficult to resell and reinvest the given commodity and earn the anticipated profit from the Salam agreements if the real market price is different from the rate of return value.

Islamic financial contracts are non-adjustable with respect to changes in benchmark market rates because their fixed income assets are based on rates of return. Financial institutions that provide these contracts must therefore consider the risks associated with changes in inflation and market interest rates. Keep in mind that financial institutions use benchmark rates, which are often based on the London Interbank Offered Rate or LIBOR, in the absence of an Islamic index. A common benchmark for short-term interest rates is this one. This index is meant to match changes in LIBOR rates to the market risk related to Islamic financial products (Alaoui et al., 2015). These days, index polls are the primary basis for defining new benchmark rates in all markets. Conversely, the forecast market rates are mostly modeled using various forms of market yield curves. The market yield curve is a graphical representation of the yields for a range of terms to maturity that gives information about the market's expectations. For example, a yield curve can show yields for maturities ranging from one day to 30 years periods. The yield curves are thought to be able to forecast future economic activity and may even indicate impending shifts in the underlying economic data. But there isn't a single yield curve that fits all scenarios and can accurately forecast future shifts in the economy. The currency that a yield curve is designated in is one of the most crucial aspects in defining it. Furthermore, one of the main factors that should be taken into account when evaluating the yield curve is the economic status of the countries and businesses that use each currency. Therefore, by taking into account the anticipated economic and market conditions, financial institutions and investors who deal with Islamic financial contracts and agreements may mix several forms of yield curves. For example, Islamic financial contracts could use the inverted yield curve to map the factors associated with market risks during recessionary times. The steep yield curve should be used to represent the market prices for built assets, such as buildings, that the financial contracts are investing in because they are rising quickly in these extreme market conditions.

Market participants analyze and keep a close eye on the yield curve's shape and direction. As lenders and investors demand longer lending terms and higher rates from borrowers, yield curves, or those found in Islamic financial contracts such as Murabaha, typically slope upward asymptotically with a positive slope. The longer the maturity, the higher the yield, with fading marginal growth. There are not many reasons to explain this phenomenon. It's possible that the market is expecting the risk-free rate to climb; if investors wait to invest, they might get a better rate later on since there is a greater likelihood that the borrower would default when the loan matures, and lenders will demand payment appropriately. The anticipated rate of inflation has an impact on the yield curves. In contracts such as Murabaha, the profit added to the repayments takes the predicted rate of inflation into account. Investors therefore seek higher premiums for longer terms to offset this uncertainty in the case that the future predicted inflation rate tends to be higher. As a result, the upward-sloping yield curve's profit margin increases with term length. But take note that there is currently a significant increase in the demand for shorter-term contracts, which causes long-term yields to decline relative to short-term yields. This curve slopes downward and is essentially an inversion of the yield curve. Due to this unusual and contradictory situation, the high cost of short-term contracts diverts from profits that would otherwise be obtained through investments and business expansions; nonetheless, in the long run, the bank may accept lower yields if it has strong indications that the economy will slow or even decline in the future. As a result, the economy becomes more susceptible to shocks and slows down, eventually entering a recession. Physical assets having special qualities are called commodities. The risk related to changes in commodity prices is known as commodity risk. One major cause of market risk is the volatility of commodities prices. Contracts in Islamic finance that deal with the production or purchase of commodities are subject to commodity price risk.

8.6. COMMODITY RISK

Commodity risk arises from the possibility of price fluctuations in a commodity that is intended to be bought or sold, as in Islamic financial contracts known as Murabaha (Siddiqui, 2008). In Murabaha contracts, the buyer and seller agree that the seller will supply a certain good. The contract is being financed by the bank based on an additional profit over the initial commodity price. The actual exposure of the associated risk that banks take is the difference between the agreed-upon and the future market price of the commodity. Moreover, banks are subject to commodity risk while offering Islamic financial contracts such as Salam. The financial institution, acting as the buyer under the Salam contract, pays in advance for a commodity at the agreed-upon price. The product will, however, be delivered at a certain point in the future, and its price may vary from the predetermined amount. The Islamic Financial Services Board (IFSB) standards state that when losses arise from breaches in internal controls involving people, procedures, and technology, financial institutions are subject to operational risks. Institutions should also take into account potential reasons for losses arising from failure to uphold Shariah and from fiduciary obligations. The close relationship between the institution and the parties is a unique feature when implementing Islamic financial contracts. Moreover, both parties may split gains and losses while implementing partnership agreements. As a result, the source of the operational risk involves all parties.

8.7. OPERATIONAL RISK

Operational risk analysis can be grounded on both actual operational risk losses and risk variables that impact the institution's business performances and objectives. The process of identifying and quantifying real risks and the losses they cause necessitates a unique structure and labor from the organization. Maximizing wealth has been a key objective of financial institutions for many years. Better revenue generation is a continuous goal. For a number of years, traditional financial institutions have served as financial intermediaries. The specifics of this function have, however, undergone significant modification. From modest lending and borrowing establishments, they have developed into enormous companies offering a vast array of financial services, and their size has increased to the point that the stability of these companies affects the stability of the whole financial system. Several elements are essential for the organization to provide effective financial intermediation. First, there must be a fundamental infrastructure in place, such as local money markets, payment networks, a broad and deep financial market, and a suitable regulatory framework. Second, it needs systems, processes, people, and goods. Third, from a risk standpoint, an organization needs to integrate all of its activities. And lastly, it requires a stable economy under close control. Effective risk management in financial institutions can have a major impact on how well the economy functions as a whole. In the past 30 years, Islamic financial institutions have made a comeback. Throughout history, they existed informally. With the establishment of IDB and DIB, the structured Islamic financial sector got underway. Islamic finance is based on the values of protecting the poor, distributing wealth, and protecting them.

BIBLIOGRAPHY

1. Abdelhak, M., (2016). The Muslim society during the life of the prophet Mohammed and after his death. In: Tiliouine, H., & Estes, R. J., (eds.), *The State of Social Progress of Islamic Societies: Social, Economic, Political, and Ideological Challenges* (pp. 3–23). Springer International Publishing. https://doi.org/10.1007/978-3-319-24774-8_1.
2. Abu-Munshar, M. Y., (2007). *Islamic Jerusalem and its Christians*, 1–256. https://www.torrossa.com/it/resources/an/5209166 (accessed on 02 April 2024).
3. Ahmad, A. U. F., Muneeza, A., Farooq, M. O., & Hasan, R., (2018). Post-default sukuk restructuring: An appraisal of Shari'ah issues. In: Kabir, H. M., & Rashid, M., (eds.), *Management of Islamic Finance: Principle, Practice, and Performance* (Vol. 19, pp. 113–128). Emerald Publishing Limited. https://doi.org/10.1108/S1569-376720180000019006.
4. Ahmad, Z., (2007). Multiculturalism and religio-ethnic plurality. *Culture andReligion*, *8*(2), 139–153. https://doi.org/10.1080/14755610701424008.
5. Ahmed, E. R., Islam, M. A., Alabdullah, T. T. Y., & Bin, A. A., (2018). Proposed the pricing model as an alternative Islamic benchmark. *Benchmarking: An International Journal*, *25*(8), 2892–2912. https://doi.org/10.1108/BIJ-04-2017-0077.
6. Akram, L. M., (2008). Islamic financial system: The Malaysian experience and the way forward. *Humanomics*, *24*(3), 217–238. https://doi.org/10.1108/08288660810899377.
7. Alam, C. M., & Hussain, M., (2005). A paradigm of Islamic money and banking. *International Journal of Social Economics*, *32*(3), 203–217. https://doi.org/10.1108/03068290510580760.

8. Alam, Md. K., (2021). A proposed centralized Shariah governance framework for Islamic banks in Bangladesh. *Journal of Islamic Accounting and Business Research*, *13*(2), 364–389. https://doi.org/10.1108/JIABR-03-2021-0106.
9. Alam, N., Gupta, L., & Zameni, A., (2019). Emergence of shariah-tech and its landscape. In: Alam, N., Gupta, L., & Zameni, A., (eds.), *Fintech and Islamic Finance: Digitalization, Development and Disruption* (pp. 63–79). Springer International Publishing. https://doi.org/10.1007/978-3-030-24666-2_4.
10. Alamad, S., Hidayah, N. N., & Lowe, A., (2021). A shared boundary object: Financial innovation and engineering in Islamic financial institutions. *The British Accounting Review*, *53*(3), 100958. https://doi.org/10.1016/j.bar.2020.100958.
11. Al-Bawwab, R. A., (2023). Zakat: Changing the framework of giving. *Islamic Economic Studies*, *30*(2), 86–103. https://doi.org/10.1108/IES-08-2021-0026.
12. Alexakis, C., & Tsikouras, A., (2009). Islamic finance: Regulatory framework – challenges lying ahead. *International Journal of Islamic and Middle Eastern Finance and Management*, *2*(2), 90–104. https://doi.org/10.1108/17538390910965121.
13. Alhammadi, S., Archer, S., & Asutay, M., (2020). Risk management and corporate governance failures in Islamic banks: A case study. *Journal of Islamic Accounting and Business Research*, *11*(9), 1921–1939. https://doi.org/10.1108/JIABR-03-2020-0064.
14. Alqahtani, F. A. A., (2016). *Islamic Banking and the Global Financial Crisis: Evidence from the Gulf Cooperation Council.* Thesis, ResearchSpace@Auckland]. https://researchspace.auckland.ac.nz/handle/2292/29212 (accessed on 02 April 2024).
15. Alshater, M. M., Saba, I., Supriani, I., & Rabbani, M. R., (2022). Fintech in Islamic finance literature: A review. *Heliyon*, *8*(9), e10385. https://doi.org/10.1016/j.heliyon.2022.e10385.
16. Altine, Z., (2023). An appraisal of the contribution of imam Al-Tabari to the Islamic historiography. *Al-Risalah: Jurnal Studi Agama Dan Pemikiran Islam*, *14*(2), Article 2. https://doi.org/10.34005/alrisalah.v14i2.2702.
17. Al-Zumai, F., & Al-Wasmi, M., (2016). 2008 financial crisis and Islamic finance: An unrealized opportunity. *International Journal for the Semiotics of Law – Revue Internationale de Sémiotique Juridique*, *29*(2), 455–472. https://doi.org/10.1007/s11196-016-9469-6.
18. Archer, S., Abdel, K. R. A., & Al-Deehani, T., (1998). Financial contracting,

governance structures and the accounting regulation of Islamic banks: An analysis in terms of agency theory and transaction cost economics. *Journal of Management and Governance*, *2*(2), 149–170. https://doi.org/10.1023/A:1009985419353.

19. Ariff, M., & Rosly, S. A., (2011). Islamic banking in Malaysia: Unchartered waters. *Asian Economic Policy Review*, *6*(2), 301–319. https://doi.org/10.1111/j.1748-3131.2011.01208.x.
20. Ariss, R. T., & Sarieddine, Y., (2007). Challenges in implementing capital adequacy guidelines to Islamic banks. *Journal of Banking Regulation*, *9*(1), 46–59. https://doi.org/10.1057/palgrave.jbr.2350059.
21. Arjomand, S. A., (2009). The constitution of medina: A sociolegal interpretation of Muhammad's acts of foundation of the umma. *International Journal of Middle East Studies*, *41*(4), 555–575. https://doi.org/10.1017/S0020743809990067.
22. Asare, M. O., & Afriyie, J. O., (2021). Ancient mining and metallurgy as the origin of Cu, Ag, Pb, Hg, and Zn contamination in soils: A Review. *Water, Air, & Soil Pollution*, *232*(6), 240. https://doi.org/10.1007/s11270-021-05166-4.
23. Ashrafkashani, S., (2015). The role and responsibilities of shariah boards in the context of Islamic finance and their position in law. Doctoral, University of London. In: *Institute of Advanced Legal Studies*. https://sas-space.sas.ac.uk/9512/.
24. Askari, H., Iqbal, Z., & Mirakhor, A., (2014). Economic and social justice: The policy objective in Islam. In: Askari, H., Iqbal, Z., & Mirakhor, A., (eds.), *Challenges in Economic and Financial Policy Formulation: An Islamic Perspective* (pp. 31–46). Palgrave Macmillan US. https://doi.org/10.1057/9781137381996_3.
25. Ayub, M., (2020). Making Islamic finance a vehicle for social inclusion: A case for revisiting the liquidity management practices by Islamic banks. In: Elzahi, S. A. A., Ali, K. M., & Khaleequzzaman, M., (eds.), *Enhancing Financial Inclusion Through Islamic Finance* (Vol. I, pp. 109–136). Springer International Publishing. https://doi.org/10.1007/978-3-030-39935-1_7.
26. Bakar, N. B. A., (2008). Zakat and taxation: A conceptual comparison. *TAFHIM: IKIM Journal of Islam and the Contemporary World*, *2*(3). https://tafhim.ikim.gov.my/index.php/tafhim/article/view/66 (accessed on 02 April 2024).
27. Baker, C. R., & Hayes, R., (2004). Reflecting form over substance: The case of Enron corp. *Critical Perspectives on Accounting*, *15*(6), 767–785.

https://doi.org/10.1016/j.cpa.2002.08.001.

28. Baldwin, K., & Alhalboni, M., (2020). The impact of profit-sharing investment accounts on shareholders' wealth. *Journal of International Financial Markets, Institutions and Money*, *69*, 101253. https://doi.org/10.1016/j.intfin.2020.101253.
29. Beltratti, A., & Paladino, G., (2016). Basel II and regulatory arbitrage. Evidence from financial crises. *Journal of Empirical Finance*, *39*, 180–196. https://doi.org/10.1016/j.jempfin.2016.02.006.
30. Berkem, Z., (2014). Effective supervision of Islamic insurance according to Malaysian experience (1984-2012). *International Journal of Social Economics*, *41*(12), 1220–1242. https://doi.org/10.1108/IJSE-08-2013-0182.
31. Bonne, K., & Verbeke, W., (2008). Religious values informing halal meat production and the control and delivery of halal credence quality. *Agriculture and Human Values*, *25*(1), 35–47. https://doi.org/10.1007/s10460-007-9076-y.
32. Bordo, M. D., (2014). Tales from the Bretton woods. *Open Economies Review*, *25*(5), 981–991. https://doi.org/10.1007/s11079-014-9326-8.
33. Box, R. C., Marshall, G. S., Reed, B. J., & Reed, C. M., (2001). New public management and substantive democracy. *Public Administration Review*, *61*(5), 608–619. https://doi.org/10.1111/0033-3352.00131.
34. Bradbury, D., (2013). The problem with Bitcoin. *Computer Fraud & Security*, *2013*(11), 5–8. https://doi.org/10.1016/S1361-3723(13)70101-5.
35. Burr, E. G., (2005). Learning to teach Islam as a non-Muslim in the twin cities. *Teaching Theology & Religion*, *8*(3), 155–163. https://doi.org/10.1111/j.1467-9647.2005.00239.x.
36. Chad, L. T., (2011). Islamic banking and finance: Perseverance and success in the modern-day financial crisis, current issues, and long-term future. *Journal of Islamic Law and Culture*, *13*(2, 3), 183–192. https://doi.org/10.1080/1528817X.2012.733133.
37. Chapra, M. U., (2008). The nature of Riba in Islam. *Millah: Journal of Religious Studies*. https://journal.uii.ac.id/Millah/article/view/431 (accessed on 02 April 2024).
38. Daly, S., & Frikha, M., (2016). Islamic finance: Basic principles and contributions in financing economic. *Journal of the Knowledge Economy*, *7*(2), 496–512. https://doi.org/10.1007/s13132-014-0222-7.
39. Delle, F. A., & Keshminder, J. S., (2022). Challenges and opportunities of SRI sukuk toward financial system sustainability: A bibliometric and

systematic literature review. *International Journal of Emerging Markets*, (ahead-of-print). https://doi.org/10.1108/IJOEM-04-2022-0601.

40. Dobiyanski, C., (2018). A qualitative analysis of key concepts in Islam from the perspective of imams. *Electronic Theses and Dissertations*. https://stars.library.ucf.edu/etd/6186 (accessed on 02 April 2024).
41. Dodge, T., (2021). 'The failure of peacebuilding in Iraq: The role of consociationalism and political settlements.' *Journal of Intervention and Statebuilding*, *15*(4), 459–475. https://doi.org/10.1080/17502977.2020.1850036.
42. Donald, D. C., (2005). Shareholder voice and its opponents. *Journal of Corporate Law Studies*, *5*(2), 305–361. https://doi.org/10.1080/14735970.2005.11419937.
43. Drach, A., (2022). A globalization laboratory: European banking regulation and global capitalism in the 1970s and early 1980s. In: *Rethinking European Integration History in Light of Capitalism*. Routledge.
44. Drennan, D., (2012). *An Introduction to Islam*. https://opus.lib.uts.edu.au/handle/10453/115075 (accessed on 02 April 2024).
45. El Alaoui, A. O., Dewandaru, G., Azhar, R. S., & Masih, M., (2015). Linkages and co-movement between international stock market returns: Case of Dow jones Islamic Dubai financial market index. *Journal of International Financial Markets, Institutions and Money*, *36*, 53–70. https://doi.org/10.1016/j.intfin.2014.12.004.
46. El-Gamal, M. A., (1999). Involving Islamic banks in central bank open market operations. *Thunderbird International Business Review*, *41*(4, 5), 501–521. https://doi.org/10.1002/tie.4270410412.
47. El-Hawary, D., Grais, W., & Iqbal, Z., (2007). Diversity in the regulation of Islamic Financial Institutions. *The Quarterly Review of Economics and Finance*, *46*(5), 778–800. https://doi.org/10.1016/j.qref.2006.08.010.
48. Ending, S. E. S., (2018). The system zakat reform of management and the Zakat in Indonesia. *International Journal of Financial Management (IJFM)*, *7*(1), Article 1. https://papers.ssrn.com/sol3/papers.cfm?abstract_id=3116720 (accessed on 02 April 2024).
49. Engku, A. E. R. A., & Oseni, U. A., (2017). Towards an effective legal and regulatory framework for Islamic financial transactions: Major initiatives of the Central Bank of Malaysia. *International Journal of Law and Management*, *59*(5), 652–672. https://doi.org/10.1108/IJLMA-04-2016-0038.
50. Faroqhi, S., (2004). *The Ottoman Empire and the World Around It*, 1–304.

https://www.torrossa.com/it/resources/an/5215256 (accessed on 02 April 2024).

51. Fernando, J. M., (2016). Constitutionalism and the politics of constitution-making in Malaya, 1956–1957. In: *Constitution-Making in Asia*. Routledge.
52. Fernando, M. L., (2010). Reconfiguring freedom: Muslim piety and the limits of secular law and public discourse in France. *American Ethnologist*, *37*(1), 19–35. https://doi.org/10.1111/j.1548-1425.2010.01239.x.
53. Ghafar, B. I. A., & Tohirin, A., (2010). Islamic law and finance. *Humanomics*, *26*(3), 178–199. https://doi.org/10.1108/08288661011074954.
54. Goodhart, C., (2001). What weight should be given to asset prices in the measurement of inflation? *The Economic Journal*, *111*(472), 335–356. https://doi.org/10.1111/1468-0297.00634.
55. Gunn, T. J., & Sabil, O., (2023). Sharī'a in the Qur'an: A word meaning "law" or a metaphor evoking "path"? In: Possamai, A., Richardson, J. T., & Turner, B. S., (eds.), *The Sociology of Shari'a: Case Studies from Around the World* (pp. 23–54). Springer International Publishing. https://doi.org/10.1007/978-3-031-27188-5_2.
56. Haji, M. M. T. S., (2015). Theoretical and trustees' perspectives on the establishment of an Islamic social (Waqf) bank. *Humanomics*, *31*(1), 37–73. https://doi.org/10.1108/H-05-2013-0032.
57. Haneef, M. A., & Furqani, H., (2009). Developing the ethical foundations of Islamic economics: Benefitting from Toshihiko Izutsu. *Intellectual Discourse*, *17*(2), Article 2. https://journals.iium.edu.my/intdiscourse/index.php/id/article/view/77 (accessed on 02 April 2024).
58. Haqqi, A. R. A., (2017). Islamic law in state life of Brunei Darussalam. *Journal of Malay Islamic Studies*, *1*(2), Article 2. https://doi.org/10.19109/jmis.v1i2.2540.
59. Haridan, N. M., Hassan, A. F. S., & Karbhari, Y., (2018). Governance, religious assurance, and Islamic banks: Do Shariah boards effectively serve? *Journal of Management and Governance*, *22*(4), 1015–1043. https://doi.org/10.1007/s10997-018-9418-8.
60. Harris, R., (2009). The institutional dynamics of early modern Eurasian trade: The commenda and the corporation. *Journal of Economic Behavior & Organization*, *71*(3), 606–622. https://doi.org/10.1016/j.jebo.2009.04.016.
61. Hashmi, S., (2003). The Qur'an and tolerance: An interpretive essay on verse 5:48. *Journal of Human Rights*, *2*(1), 81–103. https://doi.org/10.10

80/1475483032000054978.

62. Hassan, D. M. A. U., Rehmani, A. I., Fareed, G., Khursheed, D. M., Hussain, D. T., & Keifatullah, H. M., (2023). The historical and critical thinking of Usul-Ul-Fiqh and its evolution in contemporary era. *Central European Management Journal, 31*(2), Article 2. https://doi.org/10.57030/23364890.cemj.31.2.88.
63. Hassan, M. K., Aliyu, S., Huda, M., & Rashid, M., (2019). A survey on Islamic finance and accounting standards. *Borsa Istanbul Review, 19*, S1–S13. https://doi.org/10.1016/j.bir.2019.07.006.
64. Hassan, T., Mohamad, S., & Khaled, I. B. M., (2009). Efficiency of conventional versus Islamic banks: Evidence from the Middle East. *International Journal of Islamic and Middle Eastern Finance and Management*, *2*(1), 46–65. https://doi.org/10.1108/17538390910946267.
65. Hawting, G. R., (2005). The rise of Islam. In: *A Companion to the History of the Middle East* (pp. 9–27). John Wiley & Sons, Ltd. https://doi.org/10.1002/9780470996423.ch2.
66. Headley, N., (1924). Pilgrimage to mecca. *Journal of The Royal Central Asian Society*, *11*(1), 20–35. https://doi.org/10.1080/03068372408724857.
67. Henderson, J. C., (2011). Religious tourism and its management: The hajj in Saudi Arabia. *International Journal of Tourism Research*, *13*(6), 541–552. https://doi.org/10.1002/jtr.825.
68. Hüfner, F., (2010). *The German Banking System: Lessons from the Financial Crisis*. OECD. https://doi.org/10.1787/5kmbm80pjkd6-en.
69. Hussain, M., Shahmoradi, A., & Turk, R., (2016). An overview of Islamic finance. *Journal of International Commerce, Economics and Policy*, *7*(1), 1650003. https://doi.org/10.1142/S1793993316500034.
70. Hussain, S., & Hassan, H., (2014). United Arab Emirates: The native land of Islamic banking. In: *The Islamic Finance Handbook* (pp. 521–532). John Wiley & Sons, Ltd. https://doi.org/10.1002/9781118936863.ch31.
71. Ibrahim, M., (1981). Conceptualizing the medieval period (A.D. 600-1500). *Trends in History*, *2*(3), 1–13. https://doi.org/10.1300/J265v02n03_01.
72. Ilieva, J., Ristovska, N., & Kozuharov, S., (2017). Banking without interest. *UTMS Journal of Economics*, *8*(2), 131–139. https://www.econstor.eu/handle/10419/195301 (accessed on 02 April 2024).
73. Joseph, N., (2015). Islamic finance in shipping: Dawn of a new reality. In: Schinas, O., Grau, C., & Johns, M., (eds.), *HSBA Handbook on Ship Finance* (pp. 323–341). Springer. https://doi.org/10.1007/978-3-662-43410-9_18.

74. Kamla, R., & Rammal, H. G., (2013). Social reporting by Islamic banks: Does social justice matter? *Accounting, Auditing & Accountability Journal*, *26*(6), 911–945. https://doi.org/10.1108/AAAJ-03-2013-1268.

75. Kapstein, E. B., (1992). Between power and purpose: Central bankers and the politics of regulatory convergence. *International Organization*, *46*(1), 265–287. https://doi.org/10.1017/S0020818300001508.

76. Karmali, A., (2009). The influence of sharia norms of dispute settlement and international law: The international court of justice, room for accommodation? *Arbitration: The International Journal of Arbitration, Mediation and Dispute Management*, *75*(3). https://kluwerlawonline.com/api/Product/CitationPDFURL?file=Journals\AMDM\AMDM2009055.pdf (accessed on 02 April 2024).

77. Kayed, R. N., & Hassan, M. K., (2011). The global financial crisis and Islamic finance. *Thunderbird International Business Review*, *53*(5), 551–564. https://doi.org/10.1002/tie.20434.

78. Kayed, R. N., (2012). The entrepreneurial role of profit and loss sharing modes of finance: Theory and practice. *International Journal of Islamic and Middle Eastern Finance and Management*, *5*(3), 203–228. https://doi.org/10.1108/17538391211255205.

79. Khan, B., Farooq, A., & Hussain, Z., (2010). Human resource management: An Islamic perspective. *Asia-Pacific Journal of Business Administration*, *2*(1), 17–34. https://doi.org/10.1108/17574321011037558.

80. Lewis, M. K., & Kaleem, A., (2019). Attitudes of Judaism, Christianity, and Islam to usury. In: *Religion and Finance* (pp. 40–74). Edward Elgar Publishing. https://www.elgaronline.com/display/9780857939029/chapter03.xhtml (accessed on 02 April 2024).

81. Lewis, M. K., (2001). Islam and accounting. *Accounting Forum*, *25*(2), 103–127. https://doi.org/10.1111/1467-6303.00058.

82. Maali, B. M., & Atmeh, M. A., (2015). Using social welfare concepts to guarantee Islamic banks' deposits. *International Journal of Islamic and Middle Eastern Finance and Management*, *8*(2), 134–149. https://doi.org/10.1108/IMEFM-12-2013-0125.

83. Maali, B., Casson, P., & Napier, C., (2006). Social reporting by Islamic banks. *Abacus*, *42*(2), 266–289. https://doi.org/10.1111/j.1467-6281.2006.00200.x.

84. Marmura, M. E., (1994). Ghazali's chapter on divine power in the Iqti ād. *Arabic Sciences and Philosophy*, *4*(2), 279–315. https://doi.org/10.1017/S0957423900001259.

85. Marzban, S., & Asutay, M., (2012). *The Impact of Asset-Based Versus Market Capitalization-Based Shari'ah Screening on US and Japanese Equities: An Empirical Analysis, 11*(2), 151–165. https://doi.org/10.14956/asafas.11.151.

86. Mirakhor, A., (2009). *Islamic Economics and Finance: An Institutional Perspective* [MPRA Paper]. https://mpra.ub.uni-muenchen.de/56017/ (accessed on 02 April 2024).

87. Mnif, Y., & Tahari, M., (2020). Corporate governance and compliance with AAOIFI governance standards by Islamic banks. *International Journal of Islamic and Middle Eastern Finance and Management*, *13*(5), 891–918. https://doi.org/10.1108/IMEFM-03-2019-0123.

88. Mohamad, M., (2020). Ring-fencing constituents. In: Mohamad, M., (ed.), *The Divine Bureaucracy and Disenchantment of Social Life: A Study of Bureaucratic Islam in Malaysia* (pp. 159–188). Springer. https://doi.org/10.1007/978-981-15-2093-8_5.

89. Mohammed, M. O., El Amri, M. C., & Shabani, R. M., (2021). Zakat on wealth and asset: Lessons for SDGs. In: Billah, M. M., (ed.), *Islamic Wealth and the SDGs: Global Strategies for Socio-economic Impact* (pp. 375–392). Springer International Publishing. https://doi.org/10.1007/978-3-030-65313-2_19.

90. Mohd, N. N. S., Mohd, S. M. H., & Ismail, A. G., (2019). The derivation of Shariah risk in Islamic finance: A theoretical approach. *Journal of Islamic Accounting and Business Research*, *10*(5), 663–678. https://doi.org/10.1108/JIABR-08-2017-0112.

91. Moon, C. H. S., (1987). Culture in the Bible and the culture of the minjung. *The Ecumenical Review*, *39*(2), 180–186. https://doi.org/10.1111/j.1758-6623.1987.tb01401.x.

92. Muhammad Al, A. M. A. B., (2016). Islamic finance: Principles and global growth. In: Muhammad Al, A. M. A. B., (ed.), *Islamic Finance and Africa's Economic Resurgence: Promoting Diverse and Localized Investment* (pp. 27–51). Springer International Publishing. https://doi.org/10.1007/978-3-319-28835-2_2.

93. Mülbert, P. O., (2011). Corporate governance of banks. In: *Risk Management and Corporate Governance*. Routledge.

94. Muneeza, A., Fauzi, M. F., Bin, M. N. M. F., Abideen, M., & Ajroudi, M. M., (2020). House financing: Contracts used by Islamic banks for finished properties in Malaysia. *Journal of Islamic Accounting and Business Research*, *11*(1), 168–178. https://doi.org/10.1108/JIABR-04-2017-0057.

95. Naughton, S., & Naughton, T., (2000). Religion, ethics, and stock trading:

The case of an Islamic equities market. *Journal of Business Ethics*, *23*(2), 145–159. https://doi.org/10.1023/A:1006161616855.

96. Neo, J. L., (2020). Legal pluralism in centralist Singapore. In: Tusseau, G., (ed.), *Debating Legal Pluralism and Constitutionalism* (pp. 251–271). Springer International Publishing. https://doi.org/10.1007/978-3-030-34432-0_8.
97. Omar, F. M., (2012). Exploitation, profit, and the riba interest reductionism. *International Journal of Islamic and Middle Eastern Finance and Management*, *5*(4), 292–320. https://doi.org/10.1108/17538391211282818.
98. Platteau, J. P., (2008). Religion, politics, and development: Lessons from the lands of Islam. *Journal of Economic Behavior & Organization*, *68*(2), 329–351. https://doi.org/10.1016/j.jebo.2008.06.003.
99. Radzi, R. M., & Lewis, M. K., (2015). Religion and the clash of "ideals" and "realities" in business: The case of Islamic bonds (sukuk). *Thunderbird International Business Review*, *57*(4), 295–310. https://doi.org/10.1002/tie.21706.
100. Rahman, A. A., (2013). The impact of reporting suspicious transactions regime on banks: Malaysian experience. *Journal of Money Laundering Control*, *16*(2), 159–170. https://doi.org/10.1108/13685201311318502.
101. Rahman, F. K., Tareq, M. A., Yunanda, R. A., & Mahdzir, A., (2017). Maqashid Al-Shari'ah-based performance measurement for the halal industry. *Humanomics*, *33*(3), 357–370. https://doi.org/10.1108/H-03-2017-0054.
102. Rassool, G. H., (2000). The crescent and Islam: Healing, nursing, and the spiritual dimension. Some considerations towards an understanding of the Islamic perspectives on caring. *Journal of Advanced Nursing*, *32*(6), 1476–1484. https://doi.org/10.1046/j.1365-2648.2000.01614.x.
103. Romulo, C. P., (1961). The Philippines since independence. *Current History*, *40*(235), 139–146. https://doi.org/10.1525/curh.1961.40.235.139.
104. Rosca, E., Arnold, M., & Bendul, J. C., (2017). Business models for sustainable innovation – an empirical analysis of frugal products and services. *Journal of Cleaner Production*, *162*, S133–S145. https://doi.org/10.1016/j.jclepro.2016.02.050.
105. Saad, J., & Rabiu, A. A., (2019). Assessing Goldziher's claim of fabrication of hadith by the companions of the prophet. *AL-BURHĀN: Journal of Qur ān and Sunnah Studies*, *3*(2), Article 2. https://journals.iium.edu.my/al-burhan/index.php/al-burhan/article/view/137 (accessed on 02 April 2024).

106. Saiti, B., (2019). *Islamic Finance in Southeast Asia*. http://openaccess.izu.edu.tr/xmlui/handle/20.500.12436/1699 (accessed on 02 April 2024).

107. Samadi, M., (2021). Foundations of Islamic law. In: *Advancing the Legal Status of Women in Islamic Law* (pp. 24–62). Brill Nijhoff. https://doi.org/10.1163/9789004446953_003.

108. Saniotis, A., (2012). Muslims and ecology: Fostering Islamic environmental ethics. *Contemporary Islam*, *6*(2), 155–171. https://doi.org/10.1007/s11562-011-0173-8.

109. Saud, P. M. A. F. A., (2013). The well of influence. In: *Global Leaders in Islamic Finance* (pp. 47–80). John Wiley & Sons, Ltd. https://doi.org/10.1002/9781118638804.ch3.

110. Sbârcea, I. R., (2014). International concerns for evaluating and preventing the bank risks – Basel I versus Basel II versus Basel III. *Procedia Economics and Finance*, *16*, 336–341. https://doi.org/10.1016/S2212-5671(14)00811-9.

111. Schüller, M., & Wogart, J. P., (2017). The emergence of post-crisis regional financial institutions in Asia—With a little help from Europe. *Asia Europe Journal*, *15*(4), 483–501. https://doi.org/10.1007/s10308-017-0491-4.

112. Schwartz, A., (2012). US housing policy in the age of Obama: From crisis to stasis. *International Journal of Housing Policy*, *12*(2), 227–240. https://doi.org/10.1080/14616718.2012.681549.

113. Shalim, K. M. Z. H., (2016). Revisiting life insurance in Islamic law. *Turkish Journal of Islamic Economics*, *3*(2), Article 2. https://dergipark.org.tr/en/pub/beuntujise/issue/24342/258017 (accessed on 02 April 2024).

114. Shamsul, A. B., (2005). Islam embedded: Religion and plurality in Southeast Asia as a mirror for Europe. *Asia Europe Journal*, *3*(2), 159–178. https://doi.org/10.1007/s10308-004-0114-8.

115. Siddiqui, A., (2008). Financial contracts, risk, and performance of Islamic banking. *Managerial Finance*, *34*(10), 680–694. https://doi.org/10.1108/03074350810891001.

116. Sovacool, B. K., (2010). The political economy of oil and gas in Southeast Asia: Heading towards the natural resource curse? *The Pacific Review*, *23*(2), 225–259. https://doi.org/10.1080/09512741003624484.

117. Tan, K. Y., (2013). The making and remaking of constitutions in Southeast Asia: An overview. In: *Public Law in East Asia*. Routledge.

118. Tchankova, L., (2002). Risk identification – basic stage in risk management. *Environmental Management and Health*, *13*(3), 290–297. https://doi.org/10.1108/09566160210431088.

119. Thani, N. N. T. N. H., & Hussain, M., (2010). Legal and regulatory issues concerning Islamic finance's development in Malaysia. In: *Current Issues in Islamic Banking and Finance* (pp. 81–98). World Scientific. https://doi.org/10.1142/9789812833938_0005.

120. Thia-Eng, C., Gorre, I. R. L., Adrian, R. S., Bernad, S. R., Gervacio, B., & Corazon, E. M., (2000). The Malacca Straits. *Marine Pollution Bulletin, 41*(1), 160–178. https://doi.org/10.1016/S0025-326X(00)00108-9.

121. Uddin, S. J., (2003). Understanding the framework of business in Islam in an era of globalization: A review. *Business Ethics: A European Review, 12*(1), 23–32. https://doi.org/10.1111/1467-8608.00302.

122. Uthman, Y. O. O. O., (2022). The approach of Al-Zarkashi to the roles of Mutlaq and Muqayyad in understanding the divine revelation. *Al-Mada: Jurnal Agama, Sosial, Dan Budaya*, *5*(1), Article 1. https://doi.org/10.31538/almada.v5i1.1839.

123. Vázquez-Fariñas, M., (2023). Major economic recessions in the last quarter of the 20th century: The oil crisis (1973–1980). In: *The Age of Global Economic Crises*. Routledge.

124. Wajdi, D. A., (2008). Understanding the objectives of Islamic banking: A survey of stakeholders' perspectives. *International Journal of Islamic and Middle Eastern Finance and Management*, *1*(2), 132–148. https://doi.org/10.1108/17538390810880982.

125. Weiss, M. L., (2004). The changing shape of Islamic politics in Malaysia. *Journal of East Asian Studies*, *4*(1), 139–173. https://doi.org/10.1017/S1598240800004410.

126. Wellfelt, E., & Djonler, S. A., (2019). Islam in Aru, Indonesia. *Indonesia and the Malay World*, *47*(138), 160–183. https://doi.org/10.1080/13639811.2019.1582895.

127. Wray, L. R., & Tymoigne, E., (2009). Macroeconomics meets Hyman P. Minsky: The financial theory of investment. In: Fontana, G., & Setterfield, M., (eds.), *Macroeconomic Theory and Macroeconomic Pedagogy* (pp. 234–251). Palgrave Macmillan UK. https://doi.org/10.1007/978-0-230-29166-9_13.

128. Wyplosz, C., (2002). How risky is financial liberalization in the developing countries? *Comparative Economic Studies*, *44*(2), 1–26. https://doi.org/10.1057/ces.2002.7.

129. Zaher, T. S., & Kabir, H. M., (2001). A comparative literature survey of Islamic finance and banking. *Financial Markets, Institutions & Instruments*, *10*(4), 155–199. https://doi.org/10.1111/1468-0416.00044.

130. Zaman, A., (2019). Islam's gift: An economy of spiritual development. *The American Journal of Economics and Sociology*, *78*(2), 443–491. https://doi.org/10.1111/ajes.12272.

INDEX

D

E

F

O

P

Q

R

S

FSC
www.fsc.org
MIX
Papier | Fördert gute Waldnutzung
FSC® C083411

Kolibri 360 GmbH
Ferdinand-Jühlke-Straße 7
99095 Erfurt, Deutschland
produktsicherheit@kolibri360.de